Symptoms of an Unruly Age

Symptoms of an Unruly Age

LI ZHI AND CULTURES
OF EARLY MODERNITY

Rivi Handler-Spitz

UNIVERSITY OF WASHINGTON PRESS *Seattle and London*

THIS BOOK IS MADE POSSIBLE BY A COLLABORATIVE GRANT
FROM THE ANDREW W. MELLON FOUNDATION.

Symptoms of an Unruly Age was also supported by grants from the Wallace Scholarly Activities Program at Macalester College, the Association for Asian Studies First Book Subvention Program, and the James P. Geiss Foundation, a private, nonprofit operating foundation that sponsors research on China's Ming dynasty (1368–1644).

Illuminating the Ming

COVER ILLUSTRATION: Detail from *Colorful Lanterns at Shangyuan* (Shangyuan dengcai[tu]). Image courtesy of the University of Oregon. Original: Anonymous, ca. 16th–17th cent. Hand scroll, ink and color on silk; 25.5 x 266.6 cm. Collection of Jeff Hsu.

© 2017 by the University of Washington Press

Printed and bound in the United States of America

21 20 19 18 17   5 4 3 2 1

All rights reserved. No part of this publication may be reproduced or transmitted in any form or by any means, electronic or mechanical, including photocopy, recording, or any information storage or retrieval system, without permission in writing from the publisher.

University of Washington Press

www.washington.edu/uwpress

Cataloging information is on file with the Library of Congress.

ISBN (hardcover): 978-0-295-74150-5
ISBN (ebook): 978-0-295-74197-0

The paper used in this publication is acid-free and meets the minimum requirements of American National Standard for Information Sciences—Permanence of Paper for Printed Library Materials, ANSI Z39.48–1984. ∞

CONTENTS

Acknowledgments	vii
Note on Names and Translations	xiii
Introduction	3
1. Transparent Language: Origin Myths and Early Modern Aspirations of Recovery	19
2. The Rhetoric of Bluff: Paradox, Irony, and Self-Contradiction	44
3. Sartorial Signs and Li Zhi's Paradoxical Appearance	69
4. Money and Li Zhi's Economies of Rhetoric	88
5. Dubious Books and Definitive Editions	107
6. Provoking or Persuading Readers? Li Zhi and the Incitement of Critical Judgment	127
Notes	153
Glossary of Chinese Characters	197
Bibliography	203
Index	233

ACKNOWLEDGMENTS

For a long time, I was unsure how to write this book. I wanted it to be as broadly and boldly comparative as works by Anthony Grafton, Zhang Longxi, David Porter, Timothy Brook, Richard Vinograd, and Kenneth Pomeranz. Yet my material seemed so vast and disparate—so utterly unruly—that I despaired of ever being able to contain or organize it. "Why not just write a tidy little monograph on Li Zhi, and leave Europe out of it?" I thought. But a casual comment by Timothy Brook decisively tipped the scales in favor of comparison.

My comparative studies have benefited enormously from the guidance of my teachers, especially the late Anthony C. Yu. Judith T. Zeitlin shared with me her deep knowledge of Chinese literature and at times also her well-founded reservations about comparative projects. He Yuming and Jacob Eyferth provided sinological guidance, and many years earlier Angela Zito introduced me to the serious study of Chinese texts. Philippe Desan generously lent his encyclopedic mastery of all things Montaigne-related. And Sherri Wolf laid the foundation by introducing me to Montaigne in her Lit Hum class. Richard Strier, Kathy Eden, Hannah Gray, Joshua Scodel, and Jean Howard each contributed to my understanding of Renaissance literature, history, and philosophy. And Joshua Scodel earned my enduring gratitude by rescuing this project at a critical juncture. Lee Behnke, Shadi Bartsch, and Lisa Mignone, each in very different ways, furthered my ongoing study of Latin. And Jonathan Lear and James Conant taught a course on Kierkegaard that contributed to this book in subtle, methodological ways that they will probably never know. Most important, Woody Howard fortified me with the tenacity to just keep going.

The book has benefited tremendously from opportunities to test out my developing ideas at conferences and invited lectures. Early drafts of several chapters were presented at the following conferences and venues: Coin of the Realm (Harvard, 2014), The Book in East Asia, (Oberlin, 2013), Reading, Textual Production, and Literati Culture in Late Imperial China (Pennsylvania State University, 2013), Writings, Virtue, and the Social World: Li Zhi and 16th-Century China (University of Chicago, 2013), the International Comparative Literature Association (Paris, 2013), the Association for Asian Studies (Chicago, 2009), the American Comparative Literature Association (Long Beach, 2008), and the Harvard Humanities Seminar (2011). I extend thanks to all those who included me in these scholarly exchanges, challenged my ideas, and provided suggestions and bibliographical leads. I also thank the two anonymous reviewers for the University of Washington Press, along with the many librarians who assisted me at the University of Chicago, Harvard and Brown universities, Academia Sinica, the Library of Congress, Middlebury College, and Macalester College. Especially deserving of credit are Connie Karlen and Katy Witzig of Macalester College, who worked tirelessly to secure hard-to-find resources for me. Colleen Mullarkey of the University of Chicago, too, contributed to this project in countless meticulous ways that only the best librarians can. Her cheerful face always brought a smile to mine. I am particularly indebted to David Porter, who provided unflagging support throughout this book's (seemingly endless) process of composition and revision, and to Haun Saussy, who likewise nurtured the development of this book. A version of chapter six appeared in *Chinese Literature: Essays, Articles, Reviews* (2013), where it benefited greatly from his broad cultural knowledge and editorial expertise.

Grants from the Dolores Zohrab Leibmann Foundation, the China Times Foundation, the Blakemore Foundation, the Mellon Foundation, and the Cogut Center for the Humanities at Brown University all helped fund the research for this book. Most significantly, a grant from Academia Sinica enabled me to spend a year in Taiwan, where I found a welcoming community of scholars, including Li Sher-hsiueh, Lü Miaw-fen, Yang Chin-lung, Wang Ayling, Liao Chiao-hung, Peng Hsiao-yen, Chiang Chiu-hua, and Wang Fansen. Perhaps the scholar at Sinica whose work has most deeply influenced my own is Wu Jen-shu. I am especially grateful for his generously discussing with me the ideas in chapter four and providing me with essential bibliographical materials. During that research year, Liu Chiung-yun, Aiwen Wang, Harrison Huang, Richard Jean So, and Anatoly Detwyler were my constant companions, with whom I shared copious quantities of mango *bing*, expat hamburgers, and many long, intense conversations.

This book would not have been possible in its current form had it not been for the experience of coediting and cotranslating selections from Li Zhi's writings for the volume *A Book to Burn and a Book to Keep (Hidden)*. For five years, Haun Saussy, Pauline C. Lee, and I lived intimately with Li Zhi's texts, exchanging hundreds of draft translations and working closely with dedicated contributors Timothy Brook, Timothy Billings, Chen Huiying, Drew Dixon, Jennifer Eichman, Martin Huang, Thomas Kelly, David Lebovitz, and Yan Zinan. This experience introduced me to portions of Li Zhi's corpus unknown to me at the time and enabled me to comprehend the author's style in new ways. In improving the quality of my own translations for that volume, I am especially grateful to Haun Saussy, Xu Peng, Zhang Ying, and Liu Chiung-yun, as well as to my teachers in Taiwan, Chen Yizhen, Zhu Jinghua, Yang Ningyuan, Chen Liyuan, and most especially Chou Chang-chen. My very first Chinese teacher, Meng Yuann-yuann, holds a special place in my heart, for it was she who set me on the path of studying Chinese. Her uncompromisingly high standards continue to inspire me.

As coeditor of the forthcoming volume of collected essays tentatively titled *The Objectionable Li Zhi*, I have also benefited tremendously by reading the work of Wai-yee Li, Maram Epstein, Kai-wing Chow, Robert Hegel, Zhang Ying, Martin Huang, Timothy Brook, Robert Batchelor, Tai Ching-hsien, Lü Miaw-fen, and Pauline C. Lee. Their scholarship has allowed me to see aspects of Li's literary corpus and its significance that had previously eluded me. It has been a privilege to work with Haun Saussy and Pauline C. Lee on editing that volume and organizing the conference that generated it.

The present volume also grows out of experiences in the classroom. Preparing for and coteaching the course The Confusions of Pleasure at Middlebury College with Stephen Whiteman opened up a world of interdisciplinary insights and brought me into contact with art historical scholarship I would not have found on my own. Stephen's depth of knowledge, questing mind, and cheerful, can-do attitude made our collaboration invaluable. Conversations that began in that class have seeped subtly into these pages. Discussions with students in other classes too, especially Ancient Poetics: China and the Greco-Roman World as well as Opulence and Decadence: China, Europe, and the Early Modern World have shaped the contours of this book.

Macalester College and the Twin Cities have provided me with the supportive environment and intellectual freedom I've needed to complete this book. For these I want especially to thank Satoko Suzuki, Yang Xin, Arthur Mitchell, Patricia Anderson, Jin Stone, Wang Fang, Lan Sijia, and Katie Scott, as well as Jim Laine and Chuen-Fung Wong of Macalester College. The University of Minnesota's Classical Chinese Reading Group, directed by the intrepid Ann Waltner, has devoted hours to checking many of the translations that appear in this book. Its members include Lars Christensen, Gao Ruchen, Jiang Yuanxin, Jin Hui-han, Li Kan, Katie Ryor, Zhu Tianxiao, and Karil Kucera. Li Yuhang also provided valuable help with translation.

The title for this book, as well as its guiding metaphor, was inspired by a remark by Catherine Vance Yeh, for which I am immensely grateful. Robert Hegel and Joseph Allen also deserve credit for persistently encouraging me to complete the manuscript and for graciously introducing me to my editor, Lorri Hagman. Her expert editorial guidance, along with that of Tim Roberts and Judith Hoover, enhanced the book's clarity and accuracy.

Karin Vélez and Alexis Peri took time during hectic semesters and hot summers to read and meticulously comment on the entire manuscript, providing equal measures of constructive criticism and praise. Zhang Ying and Suyoung Son were my most demanding readers. When drafts passed muster with them, I felt certain I was on the right track. Cynthia Brokaw kindly read an early draft of the manuscript and offered extremely incisive and helpful criticism, and Ann Waltner and Nathan Vedal supplied comments on more polished drafts. Oded Rabinovitch, living up to his name, could always be counted on for much-needed encouragement as well as pointed critique.

Throughout the long process of writing and revising this manuscript, friends near and far have lifted my spirits. They include many of the people mentioned above, as well as Suzanne Jung Angell, Anya Bernstein, Jeannie Britton, Marcella F. Ellis, Rachel Freeman, James Grimmelmann, Jeehee Hong, Irene Hsiao, Einor Keinan-Segev, Emma Kipley-Ogman, Julia Orell, Willard Kasoff, Margaret Litvin, Andrea Mühlebach, Louisa Stein, George Streeter, Rochelle Pereira, Brigid Vance, and Xu Dongfeng. Robert Schine patiently tolerated my stubborn refusal to take a break—ever—not even on the most beautiful summer days. He uncannily knew when to provide a nudge of encouragement, when to insist on a much-needed walk or swim, and when simply to leave me to my work. For his steadfast support in this and countless other endeavors I am enormously grateful.

Finally, my family has nourished me from the earliest age, instilling in me a deep and abiding love of Western literature and the arts, while at the same time fostering my increasingly intense explorations of Chinese culture. Their lives combine bold originality with the disciplined, principled, and relentless pursuit of excellence. They have consistently buoyed my confidence, encouraged my creativity, and simply *expected* me to finish this book.

NOTE ON NAMES AND TRANSLATIONS

Throughout the text, I have referred to late Ming figures by their given names (*ming*). However, in his letters Li Zhi frequently refers to his contemporaries by alternative appellations, such as style names and sobriquets (*zi* and *hao*). In most cases, these alternative names are recorded in the titles of Li's letters. However, where they are not evident in the titles, I have supplied this information in the notes. Readers seeking additional information should consult the extremely detailed footnotes to Zhang Jianye's *Li Zhi quanji zhu* (LZQJZ).

All translations are mine unless otherwise noted.

Symptoms of an Unruly Age

Introduction

Writing from his château in Dordogne before 1580, the French essayist Michel de Montaigne (1533–1592) characterized the era in which he lived as an "unruly age."[1] His words were truer than even he suspected. Thousands of miles away, the Chinese prose writer Zhang Dai (1597–1679) looked back on the same period and likewise remembered it as a time when everything was "chaotic," "topsy-turvy," and "jumbled" in the years preceding the collapse of the Ming dynasty.[2] The writings of the maverick thinker and intellectual provocateur Li Zhi (1527–1602) exemplify many of the contradictions of the period. A trenchant social critic, he relentlessly exposed the hypocrisy and deception he found rife among his contemporaries. Yet his opinions, which he disseminated in voluminous publications, paradoxically also contributed to the unruliness of the era. In essays and letters, occasional poetry, and commentaries on texts spanning the Confucian classics, Buddhist and Daoist religious and philosophical works, histories, and popular fiction and drama, he promulgated his iconoclastic and unorthodox views, publishing them in volumes with deliberately provocative titles like *A Book to Burn* (Fenshu) and *A Book to Keep (Hidden)* (Cangshu).[3] These writings, coupled with the author's flamboyant personality and eccentric behavior, earned him a reputation as one of the most controversial and incisive thinkers of his day.

In 1602, the imperial censor Zhang Wenda (fl. 1600) submitted a memorial to the throne denouncing Li Zhi for disseminating works that contained "outrageous and transgressive judgments" that "violated the norms of propriety" and "threw men's minds into confusion."⁴ Zhang's words came on the heels of a popular outcry against Li Zhi. In 1600, protesting his unorthodox writings and the potentially deleterious effect they might have on public morality, his detractors set fire to the monastery where he was living and desecrated the gravesite he had prepared for himself. Two years later, the Wanli emperor issued a proclamation calling for Li's arrest and ordering the destruction of all his writings along with the wooden blocks for printing them. Li Zhi was apprehended in Tongzhou and clapped in prison, where, at the age of seventy-five, he committed suicide by slitting his own throat. But the death of the author could not halt the spread of his writings or restrain his fame. News of his dramatic death and incendiary ideas boosted book sales, and contemporary accounts attest that his writings, although banned, continued to circulate widely throughout the empire, both in accurate editions and in a great many spurious and pirated copies. Reports of this remarkable author's writings and his sudden death even traveled to Europe.⁵

Li's texts captivated his contemporaries' imagination. Numerous readers averred that his writings dazzled them and "opened eyes that had been shut since antiquity."⁶ The boldness and originality with which he dared to buck interpretative conventions astounded them. He defended historical figures who had been reviled for centuries by orthodox Confucians, and condemned those the tradition had revered. Moreover, his own writings emboldened readers to question time-honored judgments rooted in tradition and authoritative precedent and to reinterpret both past and present in light of their own knowledge and experience.

Strong-willed and opinionated, Li embraced contradiction and reveled in self-dramatization. An outspoken opponent of the corruption and duplicity he deemed rampant in the contemporary Confucian, or Ru,⁷ civil bureaucracy, he nonetheless viewed himself as an avid defender of the core principles of Confucian philosophy as exemplified by the sage himself. He spent the better part of his adult life employed in the civil bureaucracy and, in addition to serving as prefect of Yao'an in the southwestern province of Yunnan, held reputable positions in both of the Ming capitals, Nanjing and Beijing. His years in official service, however, were fraught with difficulties;⁸ he found fault in and quarreled with his superiors and at the age of fifty-four, when he would have been eligible for a promotion, abruptly abandoned his position.⁹ In 1588, he retired to an unlicensed Buddhist monastery on Dragon Lake (Longhu), some thirty *li* from the closest city of Macheng in Huguang, modern-day Hubei province.[10] There he devoted his days to study; shaved off his hair, seemingly in conformity with Buddhist practice, but grew a long and incongruous beard; and strictly observed the morning and evening monastic rituals but profaned the premises by consorting with widows and refusing to abstain from eating meat.[11] It was from this mountain retreat that Li authored his most notorious works, including his most scathing attacks on the contemporary culture of officialdom, which he deemed hypocritical and corrupt to the core.

Li's writings attracted a wide readership not only because of his eccentric and unconventional behavior and the directness, incisiveness, and startling originality of his critiques but also because of the literary character of his writings. Composed in a sparkling style, his texts positively teem with self-contradiction, irony, and paradox, techniques to which I refer collectively as bluff.[12] Throughout his works, he disconcertingly juxtaposes earthy analogies with erudite allusions to antiquity and exhibits his virtuosic inventiveness and sardonic wit. By cultivating a rhetorical style that invites readers to question the veracity, authority, and reliability of his own texts, Li matches his prose style to the content of his writings—his critique of the prevalent social ills of deception and hypocrisy. Thus the very process of reading his works prompts readers to experience in textual form some of the uncertainties accessory to life in the early modern world in which they lived.

Li never voyaged beyond the borders of the Ming Empire, yet the rhetorical strategies prevalent in his works, along with the axial role of judgment and discrimination in his writings, link him to a world of ideas and aesthetic conventions far wider than the boundaries of the Ming state. Adjudicating between authenticity and falsity was a core concern common to far-flung regions of the early modern world. Culturally specific manifestations of this problem as well as a variety of responses to it cropped up concurrently and with equal force on opposite ends of the Eurasian landmass. In diverse forms, they pervade Chinese literature, philosophy, and visual arts of this period no less thoroughly than they suffuse cultural products of the European Renaissance. Motivating this sustained engagement with themes of judgment and discernment was the shared perception in both China and Europe that appearances and reality had become radically out of joint and the lurking suspicion that signs, both lexical and graphic, had lost their ability to transmit meaning in a stable, reliable manner.

These fears were grounded in practical realities. In China and Europe alike, counterfeit coins passed frequently for legal tender, and prices rose and fell unpredictably. In China, membership in the civil bureaucracy, which had once been strictly regulated by the examination system, widened to permit the purchase of official titles, and in Europe, noble titles and ecclesiastical offices also came up for sale. Commoners masqueraded as gentlemen, and the boundaries demarcating social classes grew increasingly permeable.[13] On coastal shores from Lisbon to Xiamen and Li's natal Quanzhou, foreign traders hawked exotic wares, while in China Catholic missionaries, including Li's acquaintance Matteo Ricci (1552–1610), preached doctrines never before heard. In Europe and China increasing numbers of printed books, many of dubious credibility, disseminated a tangle of facts, opinions, rumors, and beliefs. In daily life and in books, individuals of the period were assaulted by unreliable appearances, conflicting truth-claims, deception, pretense, and fraud. These circumstances challenged contemporaries to distinguish between surface appearances and the often discrepant realities below and to discriminate fact from fanciful exaggeration and outright lies.

Comparative early modern historians have identified a host of large-scale social and economic phenomena equally characteristic of China and Europe in this period.[14] These independent though interrelated phenomena, which have been called "horizontal continuities," included urbanization, rapid commercialization, improved technologies of navigation and printing, higher rates of book production, and increased social mobility.[15] Together these factors contributed to creating a situation in which monetary counterfeiting, impersonation, and book piracy flourished, and signs became increasingly difficult to decipher: the garments a person wore no longer necessarily denoted his social class, nor did an author's name printed on a book cover ensure that the contents of that book were composed by him. For Li, the most distressing of these phenomena was the tendency of contemporary government officials to dissemble virtue.

Independently, scholars of China and Europe have argued that in the regions they study concern over instabilities in the social and economic spheres seeped into general anxiety about deception, both literal and metaphorical.[16] Contemporaries worried not only about the fluctuating value of money and the unsteady meaning of clothing; the truth of words and statements also came to be seen in economic terms. Just as the value of a coin rises and falls depending on the degree of people's confidence in it, so too did it seem to some contemporaries that the values and meanings of words inflated and deflated as people gained or lost confidence in them. Li's writings exhibit many of these concerns. They demonstrate his disturbing recognition that an idea—even a lie—can *become* true if enough people believe it, and likewise, a proven fact, once popularly discredited, can *become* false. Taking Li Zhi's life and writings as its focal point, this book explores early modern Chinese and European fascination with the mutability and malleability of truth and the growing sense that individuals must judge and appraise emerging situations for themselves. Li's struggles with questions of authenticity and falsification find parallels in contemporary works of literature, philosophy, and art, both Chinese and European. And as such, they signal Li's writings' participation in an early modern cultural ethos characterized by pervasive doubt.

Undertaking to compare works from China and Europe in this period is a risky proposition. Ming China covered a wide expanse of territory, and not all regions were equally affected by the social and economic conditions of early modernity. Nor certainly did all countries in Europe exhibit similar characteristics or respond to social and economic pressures in identical ways. Throughout this book, I aim to acknowledge these differences and the cultural particularities they exemplify, while at the same time not losing sight of the epochal character of the early modern.[17]

The periodization "early modern" has been subjected to sharp and impassioned critique, and the term itself is admittedly marred by its own implicit teleology.[18] For the purposes of this book, I am concerned neither with the *earliness* of the early modern nor with its claim to incipient *modernity*. I might just as well have adopted the term "historical cosmopolitanism,"[19] since for me the heuristic utility of the term "early modern" lies primarily in its ability to provide a ground on which contemporaneous Asian and European phenomena may stand with equally firm footing.[20] The term "early modern*ities*" is also helpful, as it honors the plurality of manifestations of temporally synchronous though geographically disparate phenomena. More important for my ends, the concept of early modernities challenges entrenched habits of mind that comprehend cultural phenomena as exclusively significant—or at least primarily significant—within the confines of the nations in which they took form. Central to this book's method are questions of whether and to what extent global or transnational processes may affect, resonate with, or illuminate the study of culturally particular works.

In taking seriously issues of synchronicity and commensurability, I neither deny nor diminish the value of national histories. On the contrary, I draw heavily on the work of historians and literary scholars of China and Europe and hope to supplement and complement the regional narratives they have produced. The arguments developed in this book rely upon research focused on Li's roles in various local Chinese contexts, his engagement with late Ming syncretism, Confucian official culture, historiography, drama and fiction commentary, and more.[21] Yet my goal as a comparatist is, as David Porter writes in the introduction to *Comparative Early Modernities*, "to read creatively between and across . . . boundaries [and in so doing] to lessen [the exclusivity of] their hold on our categorical mappings, and to invite a more fluid and capacious conception of a range of cultural trajectories past and present."[22]

In an essay advocating the importance of transcultural comparisons as a corrective for exclusively national-based narratives of literary and intellectual history, Walter Cohen calls for the study of Eurasian literatures, including those of India, Southeast Asia, Russia, Europe, and the Far East. He even goes so far as to argue that privileging national literary histories may obscure or distort vital transregional connections.[23] From this perspective, the focus in the present volume merely on China and Europe may seem narrow. Before making claims about cultural early modernity one might wish to inquire whether themes and rhetorical patterns similar to those I have observed in China and Europe appear with equal frequency and resonate as strongly in Japanese, Southeast Asian, Ottoman, Safavid, or Mughal culture of the same period. Such inquiries are admirable and worthwhile; however, the present study is limited by my knowledge and linguistic abilities to works of literature, art, and philosophy from the major sites of origin and destination on the maritime trade routes that were gaining ascendancy at the turn of the seventeenth century. Comparison of these nodal points will, I hope, provide the basis on which other scholars may conduct further, more wider-ranging studies.

If the geographical scope of texts examined in this volume raises methodological questions, so may the wide range of genres studied here. Li Zhi himself experimented with a great many genres, both philosophical and literary. An incomplete list of these includes essays, letters, prefaces, colophons, obituaries, treatises, poetry, and commentaries on fiction, drama, history, and classical and religious texts. To these we must add the even greater number of works *about* which

Li wrote and the fact that throughout this volume I have on many occasions taken the liberty of comparing Li's writings to works of which he had no knowledge. I have undertaken such comparisons in the hope and with the conviction that by examining and comparing diverse cultural products, we in the twenty-first century may gain insight into features of the early modern world that may have eluded the comprehension or cognizance of contemporaries in the sixteenth century.

In recent years, historical arguments in favor of early modernities have begun to percolate into the disciplines of literary and art history. Studies have been conducted on the importation of Asian objects and their use in European societies and on Chinese artists' adaptation of Western techniques including chiaroscuro, perspective, and trompe l'oeil.[24] Timothy Brook's study of Vermeer, for example, highlights ways in which, through that artist's oeuvre, viewers glimpse facets of the emerging world economy: the mass production in China of porcelain for export and its connoisseurship and enthusiastic reinscription in paintings produced at the opposite end of the Eurasian continent.[25] Yet the majority of these studies have centered on what have been called "interconnections" or *rapports de fait,* material links between the production and consumption of objects from geographically disparate corners of the early modern world.

My work on Li Zhi differs methodologically from those efforts, for the correspondences I aim to unveil between the form and content of this author's texts and the form and content of contemporary works of art and literature both within and beyond China entail few if any direct, transregional material connections. While the writings I analyze each address and respond to local material conditions, which in turn echo local conditions elsewhere in the Indra's web of early modernity,[26] I am chiefly concerned with what historian Joseph Fletcher would call "parallel developments" or what literary theorists Alfred Aldridge and Zhang Longxi might classify as "affinities," that is, "resemblances in style, structure, mood, or idea" among works produced contemporaneously.[27] The balanced emphasis on matters of form ("style" and "structure") and content ("idea") highlights the interdependence of these features and constitutes a linchpin of my analysis. For despite the many differences both within and among Chinese and European artistic and literary styles in this period, I perceive a common set of salient *formal* elements that correspond to the shared thematic content and socioeconomic contexts described earlier. These formal features include a predilection for verbal self-contradiction, paradox, and irony;[28] the adoption of an array of incompatible perspectives; an obsession with the processes and pitfalls of representation; and a tendency to create "doubled," storied, or "second-order representations."[29] This constellation of intertwined forms and ideas was inextricably connected to the shared nexus of challenges—economic, social, philosophical, and psychological—facing developing early modern societies and their constituents.

Although in many cases Li Zhi was not aware of the transcultural ramifications of what and how he was writing, his texts nonetheless evince his efforts to grapple with the local manifestations of global problems. In form as much as in content, his texts and others of their ilk both reenact and respond to the crises of their day. In this respect, they corroborate a central tenet of classical Confucian poetics, namely that texts arise organically in response to specific historical conditions. This theory posits that an author's environment elicits from him emotions that find synecdochic expression in literature.[30] My reading of Li Zhi's texts grows out of this mode of interpretation: Li's works, I argue, display his own psychic state and simultaneously, like microcosms, enable readers to imagine—or even experience—how it may have felt to inhabit the unstable social world of the late Ming.

The metaphor of art and literature as *symptomatic* of society's ills has transcultural currency and appears frequently in writings of the period. In the preface to *A Book to Burn*, Li declares his intention to point out the intractable illnesses of his contemporaries. And elsewhere he refers to society as in need of healing.[31] This notion of the arts as symptomatic of problems facing the social milieus in which they were created meshes with indigenous Chinese interpretations that cast literature as an organic outgrowth of historical circumstance. Moreover, just as diverse individuals or populations infected with strands of the same disease may exhibit different symptoms, the works of literature and art analyzed here display a range of instantiations of and responses to the challenges of early modernity. My project is not to impose identity upon the symptoms I discover but rather to recognize the family resemblances they may share.[32] For I hope to show that whereas previous scholarship diagnosed the artistic "symptoms" arising in China and Europe in this period as evidence of *different* diseases, they may in fact have shared an etiology—a consanguinity—that renders their comparison instructive. Moreover,

Introduction

just as an epidemiologist learns most about a disease by assembling and comparing a wide array of case studies, so too do I hope that comparative analysis of the many aesthetic dimensions of cultural early modernity will yield a more nuanced understanding than would a tightly focused investigation of Li Zhi alone.

But how can I be sure, in analyzing the many and varied symptoms I have identified, that they are, as I claim, variants of a common illness and not in fact expressions of discrete diseases? Infected as I necessarily am by my own cultural background, education, and assumptions, might I not be guilty of imposing my own Western categories upon the Chinese material, and in so doing might I too fail to respect "the otherness of the other"?[33] These concerns acquire a certain urgency when we observe that the core issues of this study—anxieties produced by the perception that signs were losing their ability to represent the world adequately and reliably—have for decades been considered emblematic, defining features of the *European* Renaissance. In attempting to demonstrate that the preoccupation with representation and misrepresentation is characteristic of more than the European Renaissance alone, am I not guilty of foisting Western analytical categories on Chinese texts? And is there not arrogance and even cultural chauvinism in assuming that these terms and concepts can meaningfully be applied to works of Chinese literature, philosophy, and art?

To be sure, applying to Chinese texts terms and concepts originally developed to analyze Western literature or history has rightfully garnered criticism. The historian Lynn Struve scoffs at what she calls "we-too-ism," the habit widespread among Chinese and Western scholars alike of zeroing in on features characteristic of a certain period of Western history or literature and then systematically seeking (and uncannily always finding!) corollaries in Chinese history of a corresponding or earlier period.[34] This type of scholarship frequently gives rise to a tedious matching game in which isolated features of individual texts are lined up and tallied, irrespective of their discrepant meanings in dissimilar cultural contexts.[35] We-tooist arguments are often driven by the desire to solve problems like the Needham question, to wit: Why did the scientific revolution not happen in China?[36] Yet framing discussions in terms of China's *lack*, its *failure* to meet predetermined benchmarks of European modernity, tends to frustrate efforts to arrive at nuanced conclusions. It is not difficult, then, to fault the we-too-ists for ignoring indigenous categories and attempting bullishly to make alien cultures conform to their own procrustean bed of preset epistemological categories.

But is there any alternative? How can we avoid committing the offense of reducing "other" to "self"?[37] Is such an aspiration even feasible? And should our answers to this question differ depending on what sort of "others" we are considering? In an essay on the writing of history, R. G. Collingwood idealistically argues that the task of the historian is to "rethink for himself" the thoughts that occurred in the minds of individuals from the past. Indeed, he maintains, our only access to historical knowledge occurs through this kind of mental redoubling, the possibility of which he never seriously doubts. Rather, it seems evident to him that the moderns can, with minimal difficulty, reproduce the mind-sets of individuals from antiquity. He writes, "If the discovery of Pythagoras concerning the square of the hypotenuse is a thought which we to-day can think for ourselves, a thought that constitutes a permanent addition to mathematical knowledge, [then] the discovery of Augustus that a monarchy could be grafted upon the Republican constitution of Rome . . . is equally a thought which the student of Roman history can think for himself, a permanent addition to political ideas."[38] A bold conclusion! But Collingwood's imaginary student of Roman history is presumably of Western descent and familiar with the concepts of monarchy and republican democracy. What if one were to envision a student from a culture in which these institutions either do not exist at all or carry radically different associations? Would he or she too be able to conjure an identical thought?

Collingwood acknowledges the problem: "So far as the historian brings to bear on the [subject of his investigation] all the powers of his own mind and all his knowledge . . . , [his endeavor] is not a passive surrender to the spell of another's mind; it is a labour of active and therefore critical thinking. The historian not only reenacts past thought, he reenacts it *in the context of his own knowledge* and therefore, in reenacting it, *criticizes* it, *forms his own judgment* of its value, corrects . . . it."[39] But on what grounds does he form his own judgment? On what basis dare he try to "correct" it? The anthropologist Claude Lévi-Strauss argues that we have no criteria for judging foreign cultures because taking our own culture as a standard entails breaching the rules of objectivity, whereas adopting an outsider's viewpoint requires abandoning our own cultural norms.[40] Lévi-Strauss's statement applies equally to historical studies such as those Collingwood's hypothetical student may have undertaken—studies confined to a single geographical area or intellectual tradition—and to intercultural comparisons. The philosophical implications of this statement even extend to contemporary interactions. For one might well ask on what basis we presume to be able to grasp the meaning of words spoken to us by our contemporary interlocutors. They too contain seeds of difference. If identity between speaker or author and listener or reader is a prerequisite for communication or interpretation, we may as well fall silent. For this reason, perhaps, comparative literature has been declared an impossible, utopian discipline.[41]

Yet if we are to engage in scholarship at all, or even in conversation with other human beings, we must find strategies for releasing ourselves from such nihilistic arguments, which lead us ultimately to lonely solipsism. We must, as Confucius urges in a rather different context, "recognize the impossibility of the endeavor, yet undertake it anyway."[42] But how? Hans-Georg Gadamer avers that "alienness *and its overcoming*" are at the crux of the hermeneutic endeavor.[43] Taking Gadamer's "overcoming" as inspiration, we must find ways to acknowledge difference while at the same time attempting to bridge it through empathy and creativity. As Zhang Longxi writes, "East-West comparative studies cannot simply be a matter of application of Western theory or critical methodology to Eastern texts but must be based on theoretical issues that are common and shared by Chinese and Western traditions in different but comparable manifestations."[44] Criticism of this sort necessitates balancing categories of native and foreign, ancient and modern, self and other.

In undertaking scholarship of this nature, it is necessary to acknowledge one's own subjectivity as a critic, as well as the historical contingency of any argument one makes. One must additionally relinquish the utopian desire to "restore" philologically or reconstruct accurately the lost "original" meaning(s) of a text.[45] As Stanley Fish writes, the job of the critic is to *make* sense, to construct meaning actively from inert texts.[46] While Fish's polemical stance has been criticized for its presentist orientation and the activist role it accords to readers, his idea remains compelling because it acknowledges the unavoidable fact that all readers necessarily enter into this meaning-making activity; there is simply no pulling meaning *out* of a text without simultaneously reading meaning *into* it. The two stand counterpoised in ineluctable, irresolvable tension. For this reason no interpretation in any humanist field is ever conclusive. The process of semiosis yields only more signs, each one of which will in turn give rise to further signs in a process of endless proliferation.[47]

With these arguments in mind, I unapologetically embrace the subjectivity and contingency of the interpretations I propose in this book. It is not my contention that Li Zhi viewed himself as an early modern figure. He didn't. And he certainly had no knowledge of any of the European authors to whom I compare him (Ricci excepted). Yet our historical distance of more than four hundred years enables us to perceive and illuminate connections that contemporaries would not have been able to recognize.

The notion that readers may discover in texts meanings that lie beyond those the authors consciously intended was by no means alien to Li Zhi, the late Ming, or European early modernity. As He Yuming has recently argued, in China "hucksterish" (*baifan*), "generative" reading flourished in this period, as readers of miscellanies, joke books, and other popular genres were encouraged to draw on their knowledge of a wide range of texts, both highbrow and low-, and to recombine or juxtapose elements of them in novel ways, often for comic effect.[48] Li Zhi was at the vanguard of this trend in experimenting with "appropriative" reading practices. Along with his predecessor He Xinyin (1517–1579) and others, he was responsible for pioneering many such strategies of reading: quoting out of context, deliberately misreading, and insisting upon literal interpretations of passages traditionally taken figuratively. His hermeneutic methods privilege the subjectivity and creativity of readers over the quest for elusive authorial intentions. Thus although I have endeavored not to subject his writings to interpretations that intentionally distort or to read his writings in the deliberatively manipulative manner in which, as we shall see, he habitually read the works of other authors, I do see a certain affinity between the methodology of comparison I propose here and the practices that He Yuming posits as characteristic of reading in the late Ming. At that time, reading often entailed resourcefully "finding or establishing previously unexpected connections among far-flung sources."[49]

TEXTUAL COMPOSITION, ORGANIZATION, AND PUBLICATION HISTORY

A Book to Burn is an *assemblage* formed of disparate texts composed over many years and republished at intervals in different states

Introduction

of (in)completion. The book, like most Chinese collectanea of the period, has a miscellaneous quality. The entries are arranged loosely by genre, with letters occupying the first two fascicles (*juan*), essays and other short prose pieces the third, writings on history the fourth, and poetry the fifth and sixth. However within these large groupings, the entries exhibit no discernible organization and may be browsed or read in any order.[50]

The process by which Li published and republished his writings is not fully known.[51] However, we can say that he added to his literary creations repeatedly throughout his life and did not consider publication a culminating act. Neither the original manuscript of *A Book to Burn* nor the first printed edition is extant, and scholars are still debating what these documents may have contained, in what year the first edition may have been published, and from what years the several extant Ming editions may date.[52] What is clear, however, is that the book was in circulation before 1592 and that it was reprinted in several different forms during the late Ming.[53] We also know that whether or not Li succeeded in having the book reprinted before his death, he unquestionably strove to attain this goal.[54] Moreover, as statements scattered through the text attest, he added to his work over the course of many years. Following his death, his friend Wang Benke (fl. 1594) gathered his unpublished additions, organized them according to the same principles that governed the early editions, and in 1618 published them as *Another Book to Burn* (Xu fenshu). Like *A Book to Burn*, this collection contains a motley assortment of short pieces in several genres.

If *A Book to Burn* took shape gradually through a complex and multipartite process, so did Li's other major opus, *A Book to Keep (Hidden)*, the title of which puns on the meaning of the word *cang*, which calls to mind both storing away valuables for safekeeping and sequestering indiscreet or shameful materials so as to keep them from the public eye. *A Book to Keep (Hidden)* is a work of history modeled on the writings of the Ming literatus Tang Shunzhi (1507–1560), which in turn draws liberally on the ultracanonical historical biographies of the Han historian Sima Qian (145?–86 BCE).[55] Throughout the text, Li presents the biographies of historical figures and offers adversarial commentary that opposes the canonical, Confucian interpretations. Although he completed a draft of the book by 1588–1589, he continued to revise and amend it for over a decade until its first publication in 1599.[56] However, editing did not end upon the book's publication. After his death, his friends gathered together the many additions he had made subsequent to the book's initial publication and republished the volume under the title *Another Book to Keep (Hidden)* (Xu cangshu) in 1609. Like *A Book to Keep (Hidden)*, *Another Book to Keep (Hidden)* contains biographies of historical personages thematically arranged.

The practice of revising and republishing one's work was by no means unique to Li or late Ming China. Scores of Renaissance writers, including Erasmus (d. 1536), Bodin (1530–1596), Ronsard (1524–1585), Montaigne, and Bacon (1561–1626) came out with updated second and sometimes third editions of their writings. These subsequent publications, encouraged in part by the proliferation of printing houses and the increase in commerce, were often expansions of the original texts, and their covers advertised their status as such. Thus in this period publication was not viewed as the conclusive act we often consider it today; rather it was deemed a provisional step in the long and complex history of a text.[57] And revision did not necessarily mean smoothing out inconsistencies or eliminating errors; it often entailed the insertion of fresher material that would coexist side by side with earlier, sometimes contradictory statements.

Similar attitudes prevailed in late Ming China, where it was common practice for literati to revise, expand, comment on, and reprint their own writings and those of others.[58] This process took place both during an author's life and, as we have seen, often beyond it. Thus, whatever form the initial publication of *A Book to Burn* may have taken, we can safely infer that Li Zhi probably viewed the first edition merely as one instantiation of the text, not as a definitive version. And as his writings grew and changed over many years, they came to embody more and more richly anomalous inconsistencies and discrepancies.

CHAPTER OVERVIEW

Chapter one, "Transparent Language: Origin Myths and Early Modern Aspirations of Recovery," focuses on Li's endorsement of the conservative view that when a language operates smoothly it should clearly manifest the author's state of mind. A keen observer of the linguistic and behavioral habits of his peers, Li was distressed to discover among them the pervasive practice of hypocrisy and the widespread misuse of words. Alluding to early Confucian myths about the origin of language and European Renaissance beliefs in a primordial, pure, transparent semiotic system, the chapter demonstrates that like many of his European contemporaries, Li criticized the semiotic instability surrounding him and yearned for the restitution of a more reliable mode of communication.

Chapter two, "Rhetorical Bluff: Paradox, Irony, and Self-Contradiction," traces an opposing current in Li's thought: his open-armed embrace of linguistic inconsistencies such as paradoxes, irony, and self-contradictions puzzles and disconcerts readers. Although the widespread use of these sleights of hand has been deemed a quintessential feature of European Renaissance literature, I argue that such techniques were also widely in use in the visual and literary arts in China and therefore ought to be considered paradigmatic of the early modern period more generally. More importantly, paradoxical language itself may paradoxically be considered the truest or most accurate mode of expression in cultures in which the meanings of signs are constantly fluctuating.

The next three chapters examine particular instances of Li's behavior and use of language as they relate to core spheres of material life and semiotic activity in the early modern period: dress codes, economic conditions, and publishing. Chapter three, "Sartorial Signs and Li Zhi's Paradoxical Appearance," scrutinizes Li's peculiar personal self-presentation. Having resigned from the Confucian bureaucracy, Li took up residence in a Buddhist monastery and shaved his head. However, he continued to wear Confucian robes of office. The incongruous figure he cut, as well as the contradictory verbal explanations he provided for choosing to adopt this look baffled his contemporaries and challenged their ingrained habits of interpretation. Studying the sartorial conventions of the late Ming, their ideological implications, and their parallels to vestimentary norms in early modern Europe provides insight into the stakes of Li's decision to present himself in this incongruous manner. Here, as in chapter two, I argue that Li's embrace of bluff and his deviation from the expected dress code functioned ironically as a bid for authenticity.

Chapter four, "Money and Li Zhi's Economies of Rhetoric," situates Li's writings in the complex economic and monetary contexts of the late Ming, in which financial transactions were conducted through such diverse monetary instruments as barter, unminted lumps of silver, and a wide array of coins: foreign, domestic, ancient, contemporary, legitimate, and counterfeited. My claim here is that when the value of commodities—and even money itself—is considered unreliable and subject to unpredictable change, these conditions may affect literary style. A great deal has been written about the economic metaphors that suffuse monumental works of early modern European literature. This chapter extends those arguments to examine analogies between Li's idiosyncratic use of language and his advocacy of contradictory positions on the one hand, and on the other, the daily economic uncertainties facing him and his contemporaries.

Chapter five, "Dubious Books and Definitive Editions," pivots away from Li to address the flourishing print culture of the early modern period. Just as societies in this era were home to diverse currencies whose values fluctuated in time and space and whose authenticity was always in question, this period also witnessed the proliferation of real and forged books on all manner of subjects. Here I compare readers' concerns about the reliability of book editions in early modern China and Europe and chart the rhetorical strategies through which the editors and preface writers of two posthumously published volumes, Li's *Another Book to Burn* and Montaigne's *Essays*, strove to position their editions as valid and authentic. The several prefaces to these texts, printed within twenty-five years of one another in China and France, evince their editors' strenuous attempts to combat readers' fears of fraudulence and to convince them of the unassailable accuracy of these editions.

The final chapter, "Provoking or Persuading Readers? Li Zhi and the Incitement of Critical Judgment," tackles the question of how contemporary readers interpreted Li's bluff-laden texts. Focusing on Li's incendiary judgments of historical figures, I interrogate whether late Ming readers were inclined to take Li's assertions at face value and place their trust in them or whether contemporary readers were inspired by Li's provocative assertions to cultivate their own critical sensibilities and arrive at their own conclusions. Examining Li's contradictory statements on the role of the reader, the interpretive strategies with which he approached his own reading matter, and numerous accounts of late Ming and early Qing readers' responses to his texts reveals that although Li may not have consciously intended to spark readers to develop their powers of critical judgment, his texts did indeed serve this purpose. As such, they participated in an early modern trend toward weaning readers from their habitual dependence on ancient sources of authority and fostering readers' confidence in their ability to judge shifting situations for themselves. This skill would serve them well under conditions of both material and verbal indeterminacy.

CHAPTER I

Transparent Language

Origin Myths and Early Modern Aspirations of Recovery

At the end of the sixteenth century, in an era in which things were not always what they seemed and words often proved unreliable or deceptive, individuals in China and Europe expressed the sentiment that language had somehow strayed from its source, that meaning was increasingly difficult to convey precisely, and that ambiguity was infecting communication. Correspondingly, the relationship between language and the objects and ideas it signified came under intense scrutiny. Examining Li Zhi's views on the associations among language, authenticity, and ethics, and comparing his opinions to the attitudes of several prominent contemporaries in Europe and China reveals the existence of parallel yet distinct conservative currents in language theory: on opposite ends of the Eurasian continent, intellectuals strove to rediscover and restore a mythic, transparent language. The perception that this language had been lost would color their own diction and behavior, and it would heighten their awareness of the increasingly challenging task of interpreting the more opaque and unreliable forms of communication surrounding them.

In China, the project of seeking to rediscover this primordial language was closely associated with imitation of classical texts, a longstanding practice in both China and Europe. Whereas the Chinese literary establishment heralded imitation of ancient texts as a means to enhance scholars' literary style and to facilitate their ethical maturation, Li and several of his Chinese compatriots opposed imitation. Slavish imitation, they maintained, actually hampered individual self-expression and inhibited moral growth. Moreover, Li added, mimicking often led to acts of imposture and hypocrisy, which he decried. In an era of social pretense and increasing class mobility, Li particularly criticized contemporary Confucian officials who verbally portrayed themselves as paragons of virtue. But, Li claimed, unlike the sage authors of classical texts, whom they claimed to resemble, the imitators cultivated only a veneer of virtue. They simulated only enough virtue to promote their reputation and advance their career, and for this reason Li, who often touted his own keen powers of discernment, judged that their imitations lacked substance.

Li's hard-hitting critique of these self-styled Confucians attacked the problem of deceptive language on two levels simultaneously: it pointed out the gulf between what they *said* about themselves and what they actually *did*. That is, it highlighted the discrepancy between their moralizing words and their self-interested *actions*, and it also illustrated the divide between their words and the *objects* or ideas to which these words referred. In both cases, regardless of whether the discrepancies Li noticed arose deliberately or inadvertently, he condemned all gaps between words and their referents. Indeed his writings depict him as the antithesis of these hypocritical, superficial scholars. Unlike them, he claims, he clearly and honestly manifests his genuine feelings.

Several of Li's arguments against literary imitation correlate closely to opinions expressed by contemporary Europeans, even though the reasons prompting sixteenth-century Europeans to engage in literary imitation, their definitions of what it entailed, and the ethical values they attached to it all differed from Chinese attitudes toward the same issues. For Li, the desire to restore the seamless correspondence between language and its referents may be traced to myths concerning the natural origins of the Chinese writing system. It also contains an ethical imperative stemming from the Confucian doctrine of the rectification of names (*zhengming*). A different, biblically inspired theory of the origins of language animated sixteenth- and early seventeenth-century European intellectuals' impulse to purify their languages or return to a primordial ur-tongue. Nonetheless, spurred by aspirations similar to their Chinese contemporaries, Blaise de Vigenère (1523–1596), Francis Bacon, John Webb (1611–1672), and other Europeans struck out in quest of a perfect idiom, a pure, transparent means of communication freed from the ambiguity and deceit so prevalent in the early modern period. Ironically, their search led them to the Chinese language, whose ideographic script seemed to them to ensure its incontrovertible authenticity.

Unfortunately, the Chinese language could offer no solution to Europe's linguistic tribulations. As Li was well aware, the meanings of Chinese characters could alter over time and be deliberately manipulated. And Chinese words, like European words, could take on a variety of different meanings concurrently and could be deployed strategically for rhetorical effect. Thus, had the European language theorists of the turn of the seventeenth century had access to and been able to decipher Li's writings, they might have been astounded to discover that, far from exemplifying the clear signification they erroneously attributed to the Chinese language, Li's texts and those of some of his Chinese contemporaries registered distress over the slipperiness of signification and the unreliability of words in early modern China—problems uncannily akin to those troubling European thinkers of the same era. Studying the concurrent perceptions in Europe and China that language had been uprooted from its solid foundation in the real-world objects to which it referred provides a basis from which to understand the culture of bluff pervasive in the early modern period.

AN AGE OF IMITATION

By the end of the sixteenth century in China, and even earlier in Europe, imitation of classical texts had become so rigid and formulaic that it garnered open ridicule. Li Zhi displayed nothing but scorn for the "dimwitted disciples" who blindly copied out the transmitted words of the sages, and he exhibited contempt for the phony Confucian scholars who peppered their discourses with phrases culled from orthodox texts they scarcely understood.[1] Similarly in Europe, Erasmus and Gianfrancesco Pico della Mirandola (ca. 1469–1533), among others, mocked self-styled "Ciceronians," who imitated the diction of the great Roman orator by patching together speeches that were technically perfect but devoid of originality or genuine feeling.

In China, the vogue for imitating classical texts was associated with the Return to Antiquity Movement (Fugu pai), which dominated literary circles in the mid-sixteenth century and promoted the full adoption of ancient literary genres and archaic diction. Adherents to this conservative movement maintained that by imitating archaic literary style students would internalize the ethical principles that suffused the core texts of the Confucian tradition.[2] Even supporters of Wang Yangming's more progressive School of the Mind (Xinxue pai) agreed that studying and imitating ancient texts helped students to develop the rudiments of literary style and, more importantly, ethical character.³ Since, according to Wang, every person had the potential to become a sage, studies of this nature were particularly valuable for they provided the means by which individuals could cultivate and exhibit their innate ethical sensibility.

As early as the first third of the sixteenth century, however, even many proponents of the Return to Antiquity Movement came to recognize that the movement's heavy emphasis on technical proficiency in literary imitation was producing sterile writing, devoid of either ethical clout or emotional candor. One of the leaders of the movement, Li Mengyang (1475–1531), cautioned that in his day "poetry grounded in emotions had become rare, but that which was artfully phrased was plentiful."⁴ Others complained that what passed as poetry in their era was nothing more than words strung together.

Over time, criticisms of this kind multiplied, and by Li's generation many scholars and artists had come to revile the Return to Antiquity Movement as a program that advocated only restrictive, servile imitation. The painter and playwright Xu Wei (1521–1593), for example, acerbically analogized the popular writers of his day to "birds mimicking human speech" and accused them of manufacturing false emotions.⁵ Li's close friend Jiao Hong (1541–1620) equally scoffed, "I don't recognize contemporary writing. What are [authors] even talking about? Is it the Dao? Is it virtue? Is it accomplishments? They disdain the substance of literature, but preposterously write for the sake of writing. Those who live in enclosed spaces point to images of vast territories and oceans, while those who have no roof over their heads brag about entertaining lavishly. Not only do [such texts] fail to disguise their lack of substance, but what they do express is just smoke and mirrors."⁶ Jiao Hong's comments register his disapproval of contemporary writings, which he feels have forfeited their grounding in the author's personal experience. They thus suffer from a lack of authenticity. Li's acquaintance Yuan Zongdao (1560–1600) expressed similar views:

> Today, most writers are superficial. They have never engaged in serious study, nor do they harbor in their hearts any [original] ideas. But when they discover that among the ancients there were those who "established an everlasting reputation," and those who became famous on account of their literary talents, they too conceive the desire to pick up a brush, spread out a piece of paper, and enter the

business of trafficking in words so as to garner praise. Since they want to write great works but have no ideas of their own, what recourse do they have but to borrow phrases from Zuo Qiuming and Sima Qian[7]—like begging and stealing piss and shit? If one were to rub out all the archaisms and clichéd expressions in their writings, one would end up with nothing more than a blank sheet of paper![8]

These condemnations of imitative writings seem to blend aesthetic and ethical concerns. Highlighting the latter, Jiao Hong declared, "What in ancient times would have been considered pillaging is now the rule."[9] Even Wang Shizhen (1526–1590), one of the Second Seven Masters of the Return to Antiquity Movement, concurred: "Plagiarizing and imitation," he opined, "are a great defect in poetry."[10] These authors held that stitching together pastiches of older works was not only unoriginal but actually immoral since it constituted an act of usurpation. By passing off someone else's work as one's own, they implied, a writer falsified his talents and laid claim to aesthetic abilities—and more importantly, ethical virtues—he did not necessarily possess. Perhaps the most scathing attack on such behavior came from Jiang Yingke (1553–1605), who quipped, "Any poet who cannot come up with his own approach, and who obsequiously limits himself to the poem titles and themes established in the past, calling this 'returning to antiquity' is truly a louse living in somebody else's pants!"[11] The vast majority of these late Ming critiques of literary imitation—and indeed a great many others—find analogues in Pico della Mirandola's epistolary correspondence with the most famous Ciceronian of the age, Pietro Bembo (1470–1547).[12] Similar instances may be cited in Erasmus's extremely popular satirical dialogue *The Ciceronian*, published in 1528. This text pokes fun at a pretentious fictitious scholar named Nosoponus, who adheres so closely to Ciceronian style in his composition of Latin speeches that he dares not even deploy a single conjugated verb form that does not appear in Cicero's *opera omnia*. Throughout the dialogue, Bulephorus, the *porte-parole* for Erasmus, compares Nosoponus's imitation of Cicero to that of an ape, a "lying mirror," and a person hiding behind a mask.[13] Bulephorus asks how anyone can "acquire the name of Ciceronian, that is, of a man who speaks in the best possible way, if he talks about subjects he does not thoroughly understand [and] in which his feelings are not involved?" "Such a person," Bulephorus admonishes, "makes no secret of his determination to reproduce his model, and so who will believe he speaks with sincerity? And what kind of approbation will he get in the end? Only the sort acquired by those people who write patchwork poems—who possibly give pleasure, but only for a short while and only if one has nothing better to do; and they neither impart information, nor stir the emotions, nor rouse to action." Bulephorus further castigates "ignorant pupils and bad sons"—a phrase reminiscent of Li's "dimwitted disciples"—for putting on airs, trying to impress others by their borrowed erudition, and attempting to earn a reputation they do not deserve. Such imitation, he charges, amounts to "a form of imposture," a "conjuring trick" in which one does not express oneself but appears in the guise of somebody else.[14]

The similarities among these near-contemporaneous Chinese and European denunciations of excessive imitation are plain to see, yet these examples obscure substantive differences between the cultures of literary imitation in Europe and China during Li's lifetime. In China the primary mode of written communication remained the classical language (literary Sinitic or classical Chinese), whereas in Europe vernacular languages were on the rise.[15] To be sure, in China lowbrow genres such as novels and drama often featured vernacular language, but these texts did not usually imitate classical models. Rather, it was the more reputable Chinese genres such as poetry and examination essays (*bagu wen*), composed in the classical language, that could and did repeat verbatim the words of the model texts on which they were based. In Europe, by contrast, although Latin scholarship persisted well into the eighteenth century, the strong position of vernacular languages meant that imitation more often involved considerable adaptation. Indeed, a major component of Renaissance European literary imitation consisted in recasting in national vernaculars works originally composed in Latin and Greek. For example, in the *Défense et illustration de la langue française*, a programmatic treatise outlining techniques for "enriching" the French language, Joachim Du Bellay (ca. 1522–1560) explicitly recommends this technique of adaptation, which had no direct corollary in early modern China.[16]

A second major difference between the cultures of literary imitation in China and Europe was ideological. Ever since its establishment as the state ideology in the Han dynasty, Confucianism had maintained its central position in Chinese thought, despite variations in ritual practice and textual interpretation over successive dynasties. This situation enabled early modern Chinese intellectuals to experience a sense of continuity with their past, which in turn inspired confidence that by imitating ancient texts they could plausibly cultivate in themselves the same ethical values embodied by the sages of their tradition. In Europe, where Christianity had supplanted the pagan religions of ancient Greece and Rome, the situation was rather different and required scholars to contend with the problem of reconciling their Christian faith—be it Protestant or Catholic—with their desire to immerse themselves in the cultures and literatures of classical antiquity.[17] In illustration of this, Erasmus's Bulephorus repeatedly addresses the thorny issue of how to read classical texts correctly so as to benefit from their literary style without becoming contaminated by unchristian thoughts.

Li's writings highlight yet a third salient difference between early modern Chinese and European cultures of literary imitation, namely, the existence in China of the imperial examination system.[18] The scale and scope of this vast, nationally centralized institution, which defined the lives and careers of the upper echelons of Chinese male society, had no parallel anywhere in Europe. To prepare for these examinations, young men memorized the Confucian classics and the full corpus of orthodox commentaries by the Song scholar Zhu Xi (1130–1200). Additionally, they strove to master the literary form of the eight-legged examination essay, a structure of paired antithetical arguments so rigid that one modern scholar has referred to it as more of a "grid" than a true literary genre.[19] Students writing such essays were discouraged from developing their own critical views and instead encouraged to "speak on behalf of the [ancient] sages" (*wei shengren li yan*), a practice that often meant regurgitating memorized texts.

In preparing for these examinations, scholars of Li's day were assisted by the flourishing print industry of the late Ming, which made available abundant affordable volumes of model examination essays. These texts gained such popularity by the late sixteenth and early seventeenth century that some scholars feared students were abandoning the classics entirely and only poring over the study guides.[20] These concerns seem to have had some merit. In 1595 and again in 1616 scandals erupted when reports leaked out that scholars had passed the exams on the strength of essays they had copied verbatim from commercially printed study manuals.[21] Li joked about engaging in such behavior himself. Although the depth of erudition evident throughout his corpus makes clear that he took no scholarly shortcuts, an autobiographical essay he wrote around 1578 describes his state of mind prior to sitting for the examinations: "This [exam] is just play-acting, for which plagiarizing and superficial reading constitute adequate preparation. How could even the examiners be thoroughly conversant with every facet of the sage Confucius' teachings?"[22] Li's sarcastic statement attests to the prevalence of rote imitation and to his conviction that even the examiners themselves possessed imperfect mastery of the classics.

But Li reserves his most scathing attacks on the culture of imitation fostered by the examination system for his frequently cited essay "On the Childlike Mind." Here he mocks contemporaries who study ancient Confucian texts merely in the hope of *appearing* scholarly, knowledgeable, and even virtuous. But because their learning is not rooted in any deep understanding or authentic feeling, they produce nothing but "artificial words" and "artificial deeds," which their everyday actions betray rather than reinforce. Li denounces such behavior, arguing that words and deeds must mutually reflect and strengthen one another.[23] Anyone who fails to recognize this and instead seeks to cram his head full of borrowed opinions risks actually damaging his innate faculty of aesthetic and ethical judgment, which Li terms the "childlike mind" (*tongxin*).[24] He writes, "Impressions and sensations, crowding in through the ears and eyes, come to dominate the inner life and suppress the childlike mind. Then words and ideas learned from without come to dominate, and suppress the childlike mind.... Once the childlike mind has been vanquished, its expression in language can only be indirect and superficial; its action in governing will be without deep roots, its writing style will be weak."[25] Criticisms of this kind were far from unusual among late Ming adherents to Wang Yangming's School of the Mind, the most radical branch of which, the Taizhou school (Taizhou pai), Li was affiliated with. Such critiques were not infrequently paired with threats that students who failed to preserve their creativity would never amount to much, even if they did manage to pass the imperial examinations.[26]

Although European contemporaries were spared the grueling experience of having to conform to the rules incumbent upon imperial examinees, Erasmus's Bulephorus would likely have understood and agreed with all of the above arguments. Like Li, this character extolled the value of speaking "from the heart" and, whenever necessary, adapting the words of the ancients to fit one's individual temperament and contemporary circumstances.[27] "Minds differ," he instructs the dullard Nosoponus, and "the mirror [of imitation] will lie unless it reflects the true born image of the mind."[28] Bulephorus therefore encourages Nosoponus—and by extension all would-be imitators—not to be limited by the texts they copy but rather to seek to "surpass" them by applying them to new circumstances.[29] As I argue in chapter six, Li fully embraced this attitude toward reading, and even imparted it to some of his more astute late Ming readers.

If rote imitation risked robbing students of their creativity, it also raised the threat of social imposture, which in China was exacerbated not only by the frequent violations of sumptuary laws but also by changes to the imperial examination system. In theory at least, the examination system ensured that only the most learned and capable men could enter the government. The years of rigorous study required for passing these exams were designed to mold young men's character and instill in them the righteousness requisite for engaging in government service. In 1451, however, admission to the Imperial Academy came up for sale. And this "back door" entry into officialdom expanded so rapidly that by the mid-sixteenth century over 40 percent of students enrolled at the Imperial Academy had bought their way in.[30] Needless to say, the notion that individuals could now accede to office simply on the basis of wealth—not virtue—greatly discomfited many contemporaries.[31] Li Zhi, who had passed the prefectural and provincial examinations purely by dint of his own industry, was a particularly harsh critic of such upstart colleagues. Repeatedly throughout his writings, he rebuked any official who placed career and reputation ahead of ethical and orderly administration of the state.

Li unstintingly voiced his repugnance for individuals who, in his words, "[desire] riches, but put on an affected appearance, use cunning words, and pretend to be unwilling [to accept office]." "They deploy this method because they think it is the ladder that will lead them to honor. And they select virtuous, benevolent, and righteous deeds with which to cover up their true motives."[32] Li observed, "People of [this] generation lack sincere aspirations; they have sunk into dejection and filth. That's why they say yes when they mean no; their words may be pure, but their actions are tainted." He continued, "I have yet to encounter a single person who actually exemplifies [through his actions] fondness for loftiness or cleanliness."[33] In another text, Li exposed the duplicity of the "countless people who . . . night and day, without a pause, in great halls and before large audiences, . . . sycophantically wait upon the wealthy and powerful, in order to garner a moment's attention. In dark rooms they perform servile deeds, hoping to enjoy an instant of glory. Everybody," this letter grandiosely concludes, "[behaves this way] all the time."[34] Li's remarks indiscriminately blend attacks on the gulf between contemporary officials' virtuous veneers and their venal motivations with critiques of their imprecise and misleading use of language.

Similar conflations occurred in Europe in this period and were abetted, at least in part, by the sale of noble and ecclesiastical titles, the weakening of the nobility, and the concomitant rise of the urban bourgeoisie. For instance, in a treatise on literary imitation, the Italian humanist Celio Calcagnini (1479–1541) confessed to being "amazed" that "the more corruptly a person speaks, the more advancement and praise he receives from the public and the higher the salary he is thought to deserve."[35] However, what distinguishes these European accounts from Li's attacks on careerist Confucian officials is that Li, more so than his European contemporaries, regards the bumbling imitations of "dimwitted disciples," the calculated verbal deceptions of self-promoting bureaucrats, and the hypocritical actions of the latter group as interconnected.

To Li engaging in hollow discourses on subjects foreign to one's own experience is just as deplorable as rushing about intent on securing a vacuous reputation for virtue, lying about one's moral accomplishments, or posturing as a Confucian official. He therefore condemns all of these behaviors equally. And in his writings he portrays himself as the antithesis of the posers who perpetrate these transgressions. Unlike them, he avers, he pays no heed to his material well-being, writes only when truly moved, and expresses only authentic sentiments.

CHINESE SOURCES OF AUTHENTIC LITERATURE

Li believed that, unlike contemporary writings, which he deemed pretentious and unoriginal, true literature must flow freely from the heart and reveal the author's sincere emotions and genuine ethical convictions. To Li, what mattered was less a work's topic or content, be it factual or fanciful, than its groundedness in authentic sentiment. Like his friend Jiao Hong, who insisted that "elegant wording is not the most crucial aspect of literature," Li based his assessment of all genres—and indeed his definition of good writing—on the single criterion of emotional authenticity.[36] Fiction, philosophy, or history—Li approved of any work that he judged sprang directly from the author's heart. In evidence of this, he states in an essay on literary criticism that "those who are truly able to write" do not begin with the conscious *intention* to create literature, much less to reap material benefit from their writing. Rather,

> their bosoms are filled with . . . indescribable and wondrous events. In their throats are . . . things that they desire to spit out but dare not. On the tip of their tongues . . . they have countless things they wish to say but no one to whom to express them. They store up these feelings to the bursting point until, after a long time, *their propensity [to be expressed] cannot be stopped*. [Then], as soon as such writers see a scene that arouses their feelings or encounter something that catches their eye and sets them sighing, they snatch a winecup and drown their accumulated burdens. They pour out the grievances in their heart, and for thousands of years after, people are moved by their ill fortune.[37]

The phrase Li uses to sum up this outpouring of emotion is "They are unable to stop themselves." Loss of control is axiomatic to his conception of artistic creation, for it testifies to the work's emotional authenticity. Elsewhere, for example, he affirms, "An author is one who, when his emotions stir within him, cannot refrain from pursuing his aspirations, or when his feelings animate him, cannot slow the flow of words rushing out of him."[38] Thus unlike those whom Li derides as imitators, who craft and polish the *form* of their writings, giving little thought to ethical content or emotional clout, Li elevates emotional authenticity over formal perfection.

For Li, the defining characteristic of outstanding literature is its ability to convey sincere emotion. His preface to the contemporary vernacular novel *Outlaws of the Marsh* (Shuihu zhuan) cites several examples of this type of superior writing, beginning with the *Historical Records* (Shiji) of the Han imperial historian Sima Qian and culminating with contemporary Ming fiction. Drawing implicitly on the Confucian idea that individuals vent their righteous indignation through poetry, Li writes, "The Imperial Historian [Sima Qian] said: *The Difficulties of Persuasion* and *Solitary Resentment* were written because a virtuous sage [Han Feizi, the author of these texts] was angry. From this perspective, the virtuous sages of antiquity *did not write unless they were [morally] outraged*. To write when one is not angry is like shivering when one is not cold or like groaning when one is not sick. Even if people *do* write [when they are not angry], why would anyone want to read their works? *Outlaws of the Marsh* was written because the author was outraged."[39] The visceral language of this passage palpably conveys the intimate relationship Li posits between signifier and signified: a freezing body shivers just as a tortured soul groans. These expressions of heartfelt indignation, like the untutored outpourings of the childlike mind, arise involuntarily. Subject neither to cognition nor to aesthetic molding, they simply manifest emotion.

The belief that artistic expression arises—or ought to arise—directly from emotional experience has deep roots in the history of Chinese literary thought and found numerous advocates among Li's contemporaries. The "Great Preface" to the *Classic of Poetry* (Shijing)—arguably the most authoritative surviving piece of ancient Chinese literary criticism—states, "The affections are stirred within and take on form in words."[40] Here poetic self-expression is depicted as what literary scholar Stephen Owen calls a process of "entelechy": emotions once contained inside the recesses of the poet's mind become outwardly *manifested* in poetically patterned language. Borrowing the terminology of the nineteenth-century semiotician Charles Sanders Peirce, we might characterize the relationship between such emotions and the signs that manifest them as indexical, since this bond is governed by contiguity or causality. Thus, according to this theory of self-expression, language—especially poetic language—is understood as the externalized residue (or record) of internal emotions.[41]

As Owen and Pauline Yu have each argued, this ancient Chinese understanding of the origins of literary creation differs sharply from the Western concept of poetry.[42] Etymologically, the very word "poetry," which derives from the Greek *poiein*, meaning "to make," posits a conscious effort on the part of the author or artist—an act of deliberate shaping, often in imitation of either life or previously existing art. Thus whereas the Chinese theory sketched out above casts literature as an involuntary outgrowth of nature and therefore potentially free of contamination by any type of imitation at all, the Western understanding yokes poetry ineluctably to the process of imitation, mimesis.[43]

The authors and artists of the late Ming placed a high premium on this involuntary self-expression—or at least on the myth of this involuntary self-expression.[44] Channeling the Song dynasty poet Su Xun (1009–1066), Li praised "writing so effortless it moves like wind over water."[45] And paintings by Li's contemporary Xu Wei, whose anti-imitative literary criticism was mentioned earlier, often exhibit a blotchy, spattered quality, which seems to testify to the painter's inebriation or incomplete self-control: the loose, erratic brushwork suggests that these works may have been executed in moments of creative fury.[46] Perhaps inspired by such works of visual art, the playwright Tang Xianzu (1550–1616) compared human creativity to winds and waters that cannot be reined in: "They burst in through locked doors and overtake riverbanks."[47] They "come when one is in a trance and involve no [conscious] deliberation."[48] In a similar vein, the poet Yuan Hongdao (1568–1610) admired his younger brother Yuan Zhongdao, remarking, "When his emotion encountered the right environment, he could write a thousand words in a moment, like water pouring eastward [into the sea]."[49] And Li's "intellectual heir," the prolific fiction, poetry, and drama commentator Jin Shengtan (1608–1661), compared poetry to the "sudden outcry from the human heart."[50] These comments evince a shared conception of the artist as a conduit for artistic expression rather than as a conscious or deliberate craftsman.[51]

For his part, Li Zhi not only affirms that good writing must flow naturally from raw emotion; he actually denies that it could originate from any other source. He regards the emotional basis of a piece of writing as the guarantor of its quality and authenticity, an infallible touchstone by which readers may differentiate between genuine works of art and superficial imitations.[52] In typically ironic fashion, however, Li expresses this idea in metaphors (shivering and groaning) that are themselves clichés in the history of Chinese literature.

Pointedly ignoring this fact, however, Li sets out to persuade readers that his own writings express just such unmediated, authentic emotion. In a biographical essay on his close friend Geng Dingli (d. 1584), Li avers that Dingli never requested or expected that Li would compose such a tribute. Li undertook the project on his own initiative simply because he "truly could not bear *not* to compose the biography for Dingli."[53] Li's explanation of the process by which he came to write it alludes to his being overwhelmed by an insuppressible urge. According to his account, he could not resist the powerful emotions that drove him to put brush to paper. In another letter, Li even more dramatically analogizes his writing to a natural and irrepressible bodily urge. To his friend Deng Lincai (*juren* 1561) he writes, "I have vomited the blood of my liver and gall to give you for your judgment."[54] This phrase characterizes Li's writing as an involuntary spasm. Metaphorically his words transform into drops of blood and bile that, like splashes of ink on Xu Wei's paintings, splatter inelegantly across the page.⁵⁵

Many sixteenth- and early seventeenth-century readers appreciated the immediacy of Li's writings. Jiang Yingke, for instance, opined that Li's "emotions were authentic and his diction was authentic. Every single sentence flowed from his innermost feelings."⁵⁶ Wang Benke, who meticulously collated and edited Li's posthumously published *Another Book to Burn*, affirmed that "in disgorging [his emotions, Li] was like a man who chokes and cannot keep his food down."⁵⁷ Yuan Zhongdao too expressed the opinion that "If [Li Zhi] had something to say, it had to come out." He further asserted, "Guided by his feelings [Li was] . . . quick to say whatever came into his mind. . . . His writing style was not predictable. Brilliant and inimitable, it sprang from his own feelings. . . . When he had ground his ink and spread out the paper, he would throw open his clothing, give a shout, and go to work like a hare darting out of the way of a swooping falcon."⁵⁸ These statements testify to the fact that readers willingly accepted Li's claims that his writings issued from the heart. And like Li, they considered the indexical relationship between Li's powerful emotions and the writings he produced under their sway proof of the writings' authenticity, candor, and aesthetic value.

TRANSPARENT LANGUAGE IN CHINA: MYTHICAL ORIGINS AND THE RECTIFICATION OF NAMES

The conception of literature as the external manifestation of an author's genuine feelings corresponds with long-held beliefs about the inception of the Chinese language. Just as the "Great Preface" to the *Classic of Poetry* posits an indexical relationship between an author's emotional state and the songs, poetry, or other culturally patterned artifacts to which it gives rise, so do the mythic accounts of the origins of Chinese writing impute a direct correspondence between real-world phenomena and the verbal signs used to denote them. And just as Li opined that in his day the relationship between individuals' feelings, their ethical convictions, their actions, and their words had become tainted by imitation and outright deception, so too did he observe that the correspondence between words and their referents—a relationship he, like many of his contemporaries, believed ought to be transparent—was growing increasingly tenuous or murky and difficult to decipher. Whether this pollution of the meanings of words occurred deliberately or inadvertently was not Li's chief concern. Rather, he endeavored to point out the ethical consequences that could arise when the present-day meanings of words deviated from their etymological and phenomenological roots.

According to lore, the graphs of the Chinese language bear an intrinsic relationship to the real-world objects they denote. The myth of the origin of Chinese writing focuses on the legendary figure of Cang Jie, who, in at least one version of the story, possessed four eyes, symbolic of his keen powers of perception.[59] In the account that appears in the preface to the Han dynasty etymological dictionary *Explaining Graphs and Analyzing Characters* (Shuowen jiezi), Cang Jie, the scribe of the Yellow Emperor, invented writing after having "observ[ed] the traces left by the feet and paws of birds and beasts, [and] understood that they could be differentiated by their distinctive principles."[60] This narrative links the shapes of Chinese characters directly to the natural phenomena from which they derive. Like footprints, a paradigmatic example of Peirce's indexical sign, the characters Cang Jie is said to have created *pointed to* the essential properties of the objects to which they referred. In this way, they resembled the eight trigrams of the *Book of Changes* (Yijing), which, also according to legend, came into being when the ancient ruler Pao Xi "observed" (*guan*) patterns in heaven, on earth, and on the bodies of birds and beasts.[61] Together these two etiological myths reinforce the notion that Chinese writing was grounded in—rather than imposed arbitrarily upon—natural phenomena.[62]

Many centuries later, in the late Ming dynasty, however, Li ruefully observed that maintaining this natural connection between words and their referents was becoming increasingly difficult. His writings draw attention to a kind of semiotic slippage or erosion occurring around him, a process by which words were gradually becoming unhinged from the objects they had once designated. He alludes nostalgically to a bygone era when spoken words, like their written equivalents, possessed clear, precise referents. He notices, for instance, that in his own day, the word "disciple" (*dizi*) no longer referred to truly outstanding students, as it had putatively done in the time of Confucius. Li avers that only Confucius's most outstanding disciple, Yan Hui, embodied the essence of discipleship, and so, after his untimely death, the word "disciple" permanently lost its referent. He further explains, "The love of learning died out with the death of Yan. So although the word 'disciple' persisted, there was no longer the actuality of any true disciple."[63] Over time, the meaning of this word grew to encompass a wide array of less worthy students, and during this process of expansion, ambiguity and imprecision increased. Indeed, by the late Ming, this word was even being used synonymously with the term *piaoke* to refer to "whoremongers" and denizens of brothels![64]

Li observes a similarly distressing slippage in the use of the word "friend." In an essay titled "On Friendship" (Pengyou pian), he remarks that the relationships his contemporaries regard as friendship have, in fact, very little to do with the true essence of friendship as practiced by the ancients. Sidestepping any discussion of the graphic origins of the two Chinese characters that make up this word, he simply muses that, as in the case of the word "disciple," common parlance has distended the meaning of this word beyond its proper bounds. Li's own view, grounded in long-standing Confucian precedent, is that true friendship must be lodged in trust and constituted by an ethical and emotional bond between gentlemen of virtue, companions in study, who deeply understand one another and goad one another to pursue righteousness.[65] Yet in recent times, Li notes with dismay, the word "friend" (*pengyou*) has come to connote all sorts of profit-driven associations. Many contemporaries even mistake abject gratitude for friendship and erroneously regard the senior officials who promoted them on the civil service examinations as intimate friends.[66] Li maintains that by expanding the semantic range of the word "friend" these contemporaries have diluted the concept of friendship and warped the word's original meaning.

The notion that the Chinese language, whether written or spoken, had become unmoored from its origins in natural phenomena was shared by many of Li's Chinese contemporaries. The words they used on a daily basis, they felt, had shed much of their intrinsic, etymological affinity to the objects they had once designated and, in taking on new meanings, had strayed far from their roots. The chasm opening up between the basic meanings of words and the miscellaneous definitions they had accrued by the end of the sixteenth century stimulated anxiety and concern, for as Bruce Rusk has argued, they believed that flawed etymologies could distort, obscure, or even pervert interpretations of the classics. In an effort to prevent such distortions, a number of Ming scholars during the Jiajing reign (1522–1566) undertook to compile paleographic dictionaries aimed at recovering, to the greatest extent possible, the sources of Chinese characters.[67]

Others contented themselves simply with remarking upon the discrepancies they observed. The renowned Jesuit missionary Matteo Ricci, who met Li on three occasions and exchanged poetry and gifts with him, pointed out in his treatise on memory, *Mnemonic Techniques of the West* (Xiguo jifa), "As the distance from antiquity increases, characters mutate from their original forms and the natural writing of times past [comes to be considered] strange."[68] Ricci further commented upon the fluctuation in the meanings of words. In his discourse *On Friendship* (Jiaoyou lun), which, like *Mnemonic Techniques of the West*, was published in Chinese, he observes, "Among the ancients, *friend* was a venerated name, but today we put it up for sale and make it comparable to a commodity."[69] Ricci's comments are of particular interest because they resonate strongly with observations made by his fellow Europeans, discussed below, and also by his Chinese contemporaries.

A generation earlier, the well-respected poet and literary critic He Jingming (1483–1521) regretted that the word "teacher," like the word "friend," had wandered from its original, ancient meaning: "the word persists," he affirmed, "but the substance has been lost."[70] And Xu Wei lamented that the word "poetry" too had shed its meaning on account of contemporary poets' excessive reliance on imitation.[71] Writing in the generation after Li Zhi's death, Jin Shengtan also remarked upon the arbitrariness of language, declaring, "I do not know what an 'ink stone' is, but since everyone else calls it an ink stone, I can call it an ink stone too."[72] These sentiments contrast what things have come to be *called* with what contemporaries felt they *truly were* or *ought to be*. They thus highlight discrepancies between the meanings words had come to have by the late Ming and their putatively lost, original essences.

Contemporary anxieties about the indeterminacy of language resonate with the Confucian doctrine of the rectification of names (*zhengming*), the locus classicus of which is *Analects* 12.11: "The ruler rules; the minister ministers; the father fathers; the son sons."[73] Here Confucius teaches that in an ideal society only he who *behaves* as a ruler merits the title of ruler; no discrepancy between words and their referents is permitted. The rhetorical structure of the passage—with its paired repetitions of nouns and verbs—emphasizes the congruency the Master posits between words and the actions and responsibilities they denote. Guaranteeing the etymological purity of words and their indexical relationship to their referents was key to the project of rectifying language, but equally important if not more so were the ethical and political aspects of this doctrine.

The political and ethical connotations of *zhengming* are evident in the homophony between the word *zheng* 正, meaning "straight" or "upright" and carrying the sense of moral integrity, and *zheng* 政, "to govern." Thus the rectification of names means the "straightening" or "putting in order" of names. It may also be translated as "governing names," "governing by means of names," or "bringing about a state in which names are properly governed."[74] In the following statement, Confucius outlines what he believes to be the disastrous political consequences of failing to rectify names:

> When words are not correct, what is said will not sound reasonable, when what is said does not sound reasonable, affairs will not culminate in success; when affairs do not culminate in success, rites and music will not flourish; when rites and music do not flourish, punishments will not fit the crimes; when punishments do not fit the crimes, the common people will not know where to put hand and foot. Thus when the gentleman names something, the name is sure to be usable in speech, and when he says something this is sure to be practicable. The thing about the gentleman is that he is anything but casual where speech is concerned.[75]

From the negative scenario Confucius sketches—i.e. what happens when names are *not* rectified—we may infer the positive implications of rectifying names: what is said may indeed be reasonable, and affairs have a chance of culminating in success. In other words, this passage implies that without precise and accurate language, the ethical and political welfare of the state will be in peril. That Confucius deems correct language a sine qua non for just governance is further emphasized in his assertion that, if entrusted with affairs of state, his first act would be to rectify language.[76] Xunzi too places great emphasis on this concept. He states, "When the king sets about regulating names, if the names and the realities to which they apply are made fixed and clear so that he can carry out the [Dao] and communicate his intentions to others, then he may guide the people with circumspection and unify them."[77]

Although fundamentally the rectification of names addresses the correspondence between a person's title and the actions or role appropriate for him to perform in society, this concept is malleable enough to have been used to elucidate—by analogy—relationships between other sorts of signs and referents. Consider, for instance, Confucius's saying "If a *gu* does not fulfill its function as a *gu*, what kind of a *gu* is it after all? What kind of a *gu* is it after all?"[78] The Qing commentator Mao Qiling (1623–1716) interprets this perplexing dictum as follows: "*Gu* is the name of a wine vessel which can contain two *sheng*. The meaning of *gu* is 'in small quantity.' In ancient times, a measure of three *sheng* of wine was considered just right, five *sheng* excessive and two *sheng* a moderate quantity. Vessels were manufactured accordingly. Hence when making vessels and giving names, the meaning is based on something. . . . Now although the vessel is called a *gu*, it is frequently used to drink large quantities."[79] According to Mao, although the signifier—the word *gu*—remained in circulation unchanged, its relation to its signified changed over time as drinking habits became increasingly immoderate. Whereas the word *gu* initially indicated a small vessel, it both retained this original sense and simultaneously broadened to take on new meanings. The term thus mutated from precision to ambiguity, as the words "disciple" and "friend" did in the late Ming. As John Makeham argues, it is this heightened ambiguity, and the moral degeneracy it implies, that prompted Confucius to remark with scorn, "What kind of a *gu* is it after all? What kind of a *gu* is it after all?" As we have seen, ambiguities of this nature vexed Li, who insisted that, to the greatest extent possible, individual words must seamlessly correspond to the objects they designate, just as entire writings must manifest their author's sincere emotions.

Makeham is quick to point out that "the problem of the [slipperiness of the meaning of the word] *gu* [cannot] be divorced from . . . a breakdown in people's performing their proper social roles; rather [it should be] seen [as] indicative of just such a breakdown."[80] In other words, only in a society in which rulers fail to behave as rulers (or disciples disciples) could there be a *gu* that does not perform its function as a *gu*. The mismatch between the words for objects or roles and the objects or roles themselves, Li would concur, attests to the chaotic and unruly state signification.

Recognizing the ways Confucian thought casts the degradation of language as indicative of social breakdown, we can begin to appreciate the urgency with which Li sought on many occasions to address this problem.[81] From his perspective, halting the insidious slippage that was preventing words from unambiguously designating their referents—as well as the deliberate manipulations that resulted in similar consequences—was essential to restoring the social order. To some extent, Li's advocacy of linguistic transparency runs parallel to and resembles discussions of signification emanating from Renaissance Europe, where linguists and philologists at the turn of the seventeenth century were also registering distress over the gulf they perceived opening up between signs and their referents. Like their Chinese contemporaries in late Ming China, these European scholars aspired to correct linguistic imprecisions and to institute a clearer and more transparent form of language. Independently of the concept of *zhengming*, they surmised that bridging this gap might bring about a harmonious society. And although these utopian language theories on opposite ends of Eurasia failed for different reasons, thinkers in both regions shared the idealistic notion that reforming language might provide a salve for curing the verbal deceptions symptomatic of early modernity.

THE RECTIFICATION OF NAMES AND EUROPEAN LANGUAGE THEORY

As Li and his Chinese compatriots were wringing their hands over the perversions and distortions of the Chinese language as it was spoken and written in their day, contemporaries in Europe were evincing similar dissatisfaction with the imperfections of their many vernacular tongues. They shared the perception that signification had lapsed from an originary, transparent mode and become increasingly misleading and imprecise. This notion, the ethical implications of which I have traced in China to the Confucian doctrine of the rectification of names, had equally deep, although different and culturally specific roots in the philosophical and religious traditions of western Europe. Europe had its own myths of a pristine, original language in which words had conveyed meaning in a precise, unambiguous manner. Mankind's first language in the Garden of Eden was understood to have been based on natural correspondences between the identity of things and the names by which they were known.[82] Michel Foucault describes the situation in these terms: "In its original form, when it was given to men by God himself, language was an absolutely certain and transparent sign for things, because it resembled them. The names of things were lodged in the things they designated, just as strength is written in the body of the lion, regality in the eye of the eagle [etc.]."[83] The relationship between linguistic signs and referents is posited as rooted in perfect identity: Adam, the story implies, calls the lion

"lion" because some mystical essence binds the sound of this word to the majestic beast it designates.[84] As Bruce Rusk rightly points out, whereas early modern Europeans tended to focus on the sounds of language, their Chinese contemporaries paid close attention to both sonic and visual properties. Despite this difference in emphasis, the biblical narrative portrays Adam in a role analogous to that of Cang Jie and Pao Xi. Just as these mythological Chinese figures reportedly based the shapes of the trigrams and the forms of Chinese characters on patterns already existing in nature, so too did Adam merely ratify inherent (nonarbitrary) relationships between signs and referents. Indeed, according to Renaissance interpretations of the Bible, not only did the names Adam conferred upon the animals—and by extension all the words of the Edenic language—dovetail seamlessly with the things they designated, but the whole of creation constituted one perfect interlocking sign system manifesting God's majesty, the "book of nature," which Sir Thomas Browne (1605–1682) described as "that universall and publik Manuscript, that lies expans'd unto the Eyes of all."[85]

Unfortunately, however, as in the case of the Chinese legends examined earlier, this putatively transparent first language, in which meaning inhered in each and every word, did not endure. Genesis tells of a cataclysmic shift that occurred at Babel when God confounded men's tongues as punishment for having arrogantly attempted to build a tower so tall it reached the heavens.[86] From that point on, the pure language of Eden was shattered, its pieces purportedly scattered into the seventy-two languages of the world.[87]

By the end of the sixteenth century, Foucault argues, Europeans began to exhibit cognizance of—and in many cases fascination with—the arbitrariness and conventionality of their many languages. Undoubtedly the rising prominence of vernacular languages called attention to the diversity of human tongues. And earlier in the sixteenth century, the publication of books like Erasmus's trilingual Bible heightened this awareness by raising thorny philological and doctrinal questions concerning the translation of scripture. If, expressed variously in Hebrew, Greek, and Latin, the words of the Bible took on different valences, where exactly did God's truth ultimately reside? While Europeans struggled to make sense of these vexing questions, missionary activity and flourishing trade relations with Asia and the New World introduced scores of foreign words into the vocabularies of European languages, greatly broadening Europeans' linguistic horizons.[88] These factors contributed to the widespread recognition that, unlike the mythical, transparent Edenic language, the modern languages of Europe were incapable of transmitting meaning in a unitary, unambiguous manner. They had changed with use and become contaminated by the deliberate or accidental admixture of foreign elements. Moreover, each language possessed only shards or fragments of the original, Edenic language.

The resultant arbitrariness of language attracted commentary from across Europe. Shakespeare's Juliet famously asks, "What's in a name?," and answers, "A rose by any other word would smell as sweet."[89] And in an essay on glory, Montaigne makes a similar point, which echoes Jin Shengtan's remark on the word "inkstone": "There is the name and there is the thing. The name is a sound which designates and signifies the thing; the name is not a part of the thing or of the substance, it is an extraneous piece attached to the thing, and outside of it."[90] Elsewhere he observes, "Our disputes are purely verbal. I ask what is 'nature,' 'pleasure,' 'circle,' 'substitution.' The question is one of words, and is answered in the same way. 'A stone is a body.' But if you pressed on: 'And what is a body?'—'Substance.'—'And what is substance?' and so on."[91] Statements such as these illustrate Europeans' growing awareness of the discrepancy between the words they habitually used and the essence of the things to which these words referred. Such comments also highlight the perceived difficulty, if not the utter impossibility, of ever achieving clear, unimpeded signification.

But if Montaigne and Shakespeare were content to describe dispassionately the gulf they observed separating signifiers from their referents, other sixteenth-century Europeans urged their contemporaries to endeavor to remedy the situation. In worrying that the reigning indeterminacy of language might lead not only to imprecision but also to ethical depravity, Europeans such as Geofroy Tory (1480–1533) more closely resembled Chinese contemporaries like Li Zhi. In his authorial preface to the *Champ Fleury*, a treatise on language and typography, Tory points an accusing finger at "men who divert themselves by striving to corrupt and disfigure" the French language.[92] Their actions, he chides, not only hamper communication but also reflect poorly on their authors' moral character, since it is the duty of good men to speak clearly and honestly.[93] Tory writes:

> O devoted lovers of well-formed letters, would God that some noble heart would occupy itself in establishing and ordering by rule our French language! By this means many thousands of men would strive . . . to make use of good, honest words. If it is not so established and ordered,

> we will find that from fifty years to fifty years the French language
> will be in large part changed for the worse. The language of to-day is
> changed in numberless ways from the language as it was fifty years since,
> or thereabout.... One could find tens of thousands of ... words and
> phrases abandoned & changed.... I find, further, that there is another
> kind of men who corrupt our language even more. They are the Innovators and Coiners of new words.... Those persons who coin [words] are
> incapable of sound reasoning. However, if our tongue were duly conformed to rule, and polished, such ordure could be ejected. Therefore, I
> pray you, let us all enhearten one another, and bestir ourselves to purify
> it.[94]

Underlying the notion that a language could be purified—or better yet, that the Edenic language itself could be recovered and restored—was the belief that sparks of this original language still inhered in the various languages of the world. The ultimate task, then, was to identify where precisely these fragments lay hidden and, by bringing them together, to reconstruct the language of Adam.[95] In some cases this project of restoring perfect signification even coincided with the utopian aspiration of bringing an end to religious and political discord.[96] For the hope was that if the universal language could be rediscovered, the will of God would be revealed, and peace would reign on earth.

The notion that by rectifying the use of language one could bring about order and social harmony echoes the logic underlying the Confucian doctrine of *zhengming*. Yet the manner in which European language theorists pursued this goal as well as the conclusions they reached differed greatly from Li's advocacy of the rectification of language in Ming China. Neither Li nor his European contemporaries succeeded in restoring pure signification, but Li differed from his European contemporaries in that, unlike them, he regarded the rectification of language not merely as a utopian project—a distant desideratum—but as a feasible goal and a practical guide to ethical conduct. His commitment to this principle is evident in his reluctance to conform to common parlance, his adamant desire to live up to the (often derogatory) names applied to him, and his insistence upon behaving in ways that accorded with his beliefs. These eccentric behaviors bolstered his reputation as a "heretical" figure and led to misunderstandings and even outright hostilities between himself, his peers, and his superiors. By contrast, few if any Europeans interested in analogous problems incurred ill consequences for their commitment to restoring the Edenic language. For them, this quest was primarily an intellectual pursuit, albeit one with ethical ramifications.

Throughout the sixteenth century, European philologists pored over obscure lexicons, seeking to unearth, through studies in comparative philology, traces of the primordial *lingua humana*. By midcentury Guillaume Postel (1510–1581) in France and Theodor Bibliander (1505–1564) and Konrad Gesner (1516–1565) in Switzerland had each undertaken major projects aimed at classifying and systematically comparing the languages of the world.[97] Meanwhile accounts of the Chinese language began to seep into Europe. The Dominican friar Gaspar da Cruz (ca. 1520–1570), who traveled to China in the mid-sixteenth century, reported that the written language of that nation was composed of "a great multitude of characters, signifying each thing by a character."[98] And the Florentine humanist merchant Filippo Sassetti (1540–1588), who traveled to India, opined that Chinese characters each represented a distinct concept.[99] Juan González de Mendoza (1545–1618), in his highly influential *Historia de las cosas mas notables, ritos y costumbres del gran reyno de la China*, concurred, stating that "one figure or character unto them doth signify one thing."[100] Francis Bacon would later repeat this claim in his *Advancement of Learning*.[101] Miraculously, Chinese characters seemed to possess the ability to convey meaning to speakers of diverse languages. The putatively universal validity of this system of signification, along with the "natural" relationship between its graphs and the objects to which they referred, captivated the imagination of Europeans in pursuit of a perfect language. David Porter explains how "a European audience obsessively concerned by the spreading lawlessness of speech" fell under the thrall of "a fixed and unequivocal correspondence between words and the meanings they are taken to represent."[102] Thus in 1586, the French cryptographer Blaise de Vigenère declared Chinese a sacred language whose symbols constituted a "shorthand" for nature, and less than a century later, the Englishman John Webb argued in his *Historical Essay Endeavoring a Probability That the Language of the Empire of China Is the Primitive Language* that Chinese was, in fact, the lost Edenic language.[103]

Looking east to China, these European language theorists believed they had found in the Chinese language a solution to the problem of linguistic instability vexing Europe. To them, the purportedly intrinsic relationship between signifier and signified in written Chinese promised a degree of authenticity and semiotic stability lacking in the languages of Europe. Bacon, for instance, opined that Chinese characters embodied a certain "reality" because, unlike European languages, they expressed "neither letters nor words . . . but things or notions [themselves]."[104]

Moreover, many European language theorists assumed (erroneously) that the shapes of Chinese characters had been preserved, unaltered, for millennia and therefore attributed to this language a primordial purity not entirely unlike the purity Li Zhi and many of his Chinese contemporaries (as well as Ricci) believed had once characterized ancient Chinese, but which their own contemporary discourse no longer exemplified. Ignorant of the historicity of the Chinese language, Webb interpreted Chinese as the repository of an unadulterated, prelapsarian truth.

The European aspiration to restore the correspondence between signs and referents bears comparison to the Chinese project of *zhengming* in that sixteenth-century Chinese and Europeans shared the perception that they were each living in an era of debased signification, imposture, and groundless imitation. Many on both ends of the Eurasian continent believed that the forms of Chinese characters had originally been inspired by nature and therefore that they possessed the ability to convey meaning in a nonarbitrary way. Additionally, they shared the ambition to restore this "natural" signification in the hope of taming the linguistic chaos of the day and bringing about an era of social harmony. Where Li and other sinophone observers of the Chinese language differed from these purely European-trained language theorists, however, was in their insight into the mutability of the Chinese language over time. Unlike the Europeans discussed above, Li recognized that in diverse contexts the same Chinese graphs had the ability to acquire new referents, and in various contexts the same words might take on radically diverse meanings.

But although Li arguably exhibited even greater zeal for the endeavor of stabilizing language than did many European linguists, his writings bristle with flamboyant uses of irony, contradiction, and paradox, which seem to undercut his repeated assertions that words should signify transparently. The unacknowledged gaps between Li's stated theory of language and his practice as an author make it difficult to interpret his pronouncements on the rectification of language. Yet, as the following chapter argues, his embrace of verbal self-contradiction paradoxically attests to the authenticity of his writings and signals his participation in a widespread early modern ethos of indeterminacy.

CHAPTER 2

The Rhetoric of Bluff

Paradox, Irony, and Self-Contradiction

Despite Li Zhi's stated commitment to clear and transparent language, his writings teem with instances of self-contradiction, ambiguity, irony, and paradox. He repeatedly demonstrates the pitfalls of representation but rarely if ever proposes concrete solutions to these problems. A discrepancy opens up between Li's discursive endorsement of the rectification of language and the strongly paradoxical flavor of his prose. Throughout his texts he often expresses mutually incompatible opinions and portrays himself in irreconcilable ways. These self-contradictions, produced by his slippery use of language and by gaps between his words and actions, emerge both in comparisons between his texts and in individual works.

The tendency to baffle and unsettle readers has been identified as a quintessential feature of early modern European texts. Barbara Bowen, a scholar of French Renaissance literature, has traced the source of the perplexities these texts provoke in readers to rhetorical features such as paradox, irony, and self-contradiction, which abound in European literature of the period. Focusing on the *effects* of these and related figures of speech—the fact that they all generate ambiguity and indeterminacy—she classifies them under the broad term "bluff." The flexibility and open-endedness of this concept renders it useful for establishing the grounds on which to compare Li Zhi's writings to works from both contemporary China and early modern Europe.[1] Like diverse symptoms of the same disease, bluff in its multifarious guises pervades the literature of these early modern societies.

Just as the physical world in which Li lived challenged and sometimes entirely thwarted individuals' powers of discernment—for instance, their ability to decipher the meanings of sartorial, numismatic, and textual signs—so too do the contradictions, paradoxes, and ironic statements characteristic of Li's books and many other works of early modern literature disconcert readers and hamper their ability to interpret texts reliably. Thus the rhetorical features associated with bluff may be seen as manifestations of the material uncertainties widespread throughout early modern societies.

This chapter, however, centers on the rhetorical features of Li's writings. I begin by examining a single case in which Li's texts put forth assertions that contradict actions he performed and statements he made elsewhere in his literary corpus. In two letters composed within months of one another in 1588, Li implies both that he is and is not a "heretic," a traitor to Confucian orthodoxy.[2] Studying these discrepant accounts provides an initial glimpse of Li's propensity to undercut his own assertions and to render readers unsure how to construe his words.

If Li truly advocated the rectification of language, why do his writings ring with so many contradictions? Does the bluffing that pervades his texts cast doubt upon his assertions that his works exhibit unmediated self-expression? Do his numerous self-contradictions oppose and ultimately undermine his stated advocacy of precise language? If not, what accounts for the inconsistencies between the style and the content of his writings? Could it be that because the rhetorical bluffing characteristic of his prose resonates with the contradictions of the day, it paradoxically attests to the authenticity of his works? In a contradictory world, perhaps contradictory statements constitute the most accurate expressions of truth. By endorsing incompatible viewpoints and generating doubt as to his true opinions, Li created texts that rhetorically resembled the turbulent state of signification in his society. And the homology between the rhetorical structure of his texts and the social and economic contexts in which they were written raised readers' awareness of the paradoxes everywhere present in the early modern world.

A RECTIFIED HERETIC

Perhaps the most dramatic instance of Li's unsuccessful attempt to rectify language involves his effort to shape contemporaries' perceptions of him. As a member of the literati class and a participant in the civil bureaucracy for over twenty years, he frequently alluded to his Confucian background and occasionally referred to himself and like-minded thinkers as "us Confucians."[3] He even self-importantly compared himself favorably to Confucius's most accomplished student, Yan Hui, the classical embodiment of true discipleship. And yet in a letter to his young follower Zeng Jiquan (n.d.), written in the latter half of 1588, Li ruefully observed, "Most people with no insight regard me as a heretic."[4]

The misalignment between Li's characterization of himself as a Confucian scholar and the name applied to him by others—heretic—troubled him, for it constituted, to his mind, a breach of rectified language. In a letter written to his close friend Jiao Hong several months earlier, in late spring of the same year, Li feigned to mend this gap: "Common people and the entire group of phony Scholars of the Way view me as a heretic. I say it would be better truly to *become* a heretic so that that group will not give me an empty name. How about it? I've already left home [to study Buddhism]; these things are all I have left. So why would I cherish them rather than use them as a means to live up to the name [I've been called]?"[5] The letter to Zeng Jiquan, cited earlier, articulates almost verbatim the same sentiments and, significantly, the same *rationale*. Li states, "[Because] people with no insight regard me as a heretic . . . I've decided to *become* a heretic in order to live up to the title those morons bestowed upon me."[6] The quoted passages from these two letters evince Li's dedication to the mission of restoring the bond between words and actuality, an aspiration he shared with certain European Renaissance language theorists. And the reason he provides is as important as the goal itself: he claims that he sought to become a heretic almost out of a sense of duty—so as to prevent a situation in which name and reality would not align.

Yet a layer of irony emerges when we realize that the chronology of Li's narrative is faulty. By the time he composed the letter to Jiao Hong, he had already forfeited his place in Confucian officialdom by resigning his post as prefect of Yao'an. Hoping to pursue a life of monastic study, unencumbered by familial obligations, he had sent his wife and daughter away permanently to live in Fujian, more than a thousand miles away. And in doing so, he had reneged on his role as husband and father.[7] Additionally, he had for several years been embroiled in a contentious correspondence with Geng Dingxiang (ca. 1524–1597), a Confucian official of national renown and elder brother to Li's recently deceased friend Geng Dingli. Li's affection for Geng Dingli had been so strong that upon retirement from his position as prefect of Yao'an, Li had taken up residence in the Geng household, where he had lived for several years. Yet following the death of his friend, Li's relations with Geng Dingxiang had taken a turn for the worse. In a series of open letters to Geng Dingxiang, Li hurled accusations that this leading Confucian official was arrogant, blind, and hypocritical. These letters, which circulated widely in manuscript and later in print, proved deeply embarrassing to Geng and seriously tarnished his reputation.[8] Thus by the time Li's critics in Confucian officialdom began to refer to him as a heretic, our author had already violated four of the five cardinal Confucian bonds: he had exhibited his disinterest in continuing to serve as a loyal official to his ruler, abdicated his responsibilities as both a husband and a father, and arguably betrayed his friend. The derogatory appellation of "heretic," therefore, did not precede but rather followed from Li's deviant behavior.

Yet the reputation for unruliness, once earned, inspired Li to engage in ever more provocative acts so as to continue to merit the moniker.[9] In late summer 1588, after writing to Jiao Hong and before writing to Zeng Jiquan, Li performed an act so abhorrent to orthodox Confucians that it soon became the cornerstone of his reputation as a heretic: he shaved the hair from his head.[10] By removing his hair, Li departed radically from Confucian doctrine, which requires that the body be kept intact and that hair be neither shaven nor shorn. Li undertook this action voluntarily, fully cognizant of the strong negative reactions it would provoke among contemporary Confucians. It is ironic that a man who compared himself to Confucius's most outstanding disciple could bring himself to do such a deed. And yet the rationale Li articulates in the two letters studied here is clear: he wanted his identity to conform to the name by which he was known.

A second layer of irony surfaces when we consider that the very notion of a "rectified heretic" is itself a contradiction in terms. Since the rectification of names is a central tenet of Confucian thought, a true apostate from Confucian tradition would very likely reject the basic premise that names could or should be rectified. Certainly neither Buddhist nor Daoist thought endorses this view. But in his writings Li seems intent on proving that words, actions, and intentions must indeed be brought into alignment. Thus although his actions explicitly violated Confucian norms, his stated and restated goal was to foster a state of *zhengming* in which his behavior and his title would mutually reinforce one another.

Li's adherence to these contradictory positions resulted in a paradox. Was he a heretic posing as an orthodox Confucian? Or a Confucian posturing as a heretic? In either case, his contradictory claim to be a rectified heretic calls into question his earlier assertions, discussed in the previous chapter, that his writings transparently manifested his true emotions. It further casts doubt on his commitment to the project of establishing language as a clear and reliable medium of communication. Indeed, instead of exemplifying the consistent and precise use of language, Li's self-portrayal as a rectified heretic illustrates the early modern problem that the meanings of words seemed to be growing increasingly indeterminate.

THE RHETORIC OF BLUFF: CONTRADICTION, IRONY, PARADOX

Li's contradictory assertions regarding his status as a "rectified heretic" constitute just one instance of his penchant for undermining his own claims. His writings display numerous examples in which his words and actions conflict with one another, in which he makes irreconcilable statements in diverse writings, and in which he advocates incompatible positions within a single text. Yet all of these self-contradictions differ fundamentally from the acts of deliberate, self-interested deception Li accused contemporary Confucians of perpetrating. According to Li, the phony Confucians of his day crafted webs of false words designed expressly to win them money, accolades, promotions, or prestige. Their verbal tricks were calculated to enrich themselves. By contrast, Li's own self-contradictions, we have reason to believe, never stemmed from the desire to protect himself from censure or scandal, much less to seek or acquire material gain. Instead, they constituted instances of rhetorical bluff.

As a term of literary analysis, "bluff" does not entail duping readers, simply "disconcerting" them.[11] Bowen explains that this umbrella category encompasses a range of rhetorical means used to draw implied readers' attention to or heighten their awareness of the artifice and pitfalls of representation. She writes that instances of bluff "demolish [readers'] card-houses of *idées recues* and *expressions toutes faites*[;] they astonish and shock us . . . [and] leave us puzzled."[12] Bluff may involve the use of self-contradiction, metatheatricality, self-referentiality, paradox, and enigma; it may refer to juxtaposing incongruous styles or themes, or using identical terms to refer to incompatible ideas. In other words, the essence of this concept lies not in the particularity of individual rhetorical elements but rather in their shared *function*, which is to generate ambiguity. The breadth of this category is its strength, for it may be used to facilitate comparisons among far-flung works that take readers off-guard and prompt—and at times even compel—them to revise their previously held views.

Although the full range of strategies of bluff at play in early modern Chinese and European texts is too vast to be detailed in its entirety, it is helpful to examine the histories and etymologies of certain salient Chinese and European terms, such as the words for contradiction, irony, and paradox. This exploration will enrich our understanding of the associations these terms carried in their local cultural contexts and reveal conceptual commonalities and discrepancies among them. Moreover, it will provide the basis from which to compare Li's fascination with the unreliability of language and the ostentatious self-contradictions everywhere present in his writings to the pervasive tone of irony present in works of contemporary Chinese fiction and the sustained wordplay, exaggeration, distortion, and polysemy characteristic of early modern European texts.[13]

A considerable number of Li's writings, no less than his contemporaries', conform to Aristotle's definition of contradiction, for they exemplify "opposition[s] that, of [their] own nature, exclude . . . compromise."[14] As such, these works additionally resonate with the English and romance language etymology of the word "contradiction," which derives from the Latin *contra dicere*, literally "speaking against." If a self-contradiction therefore entails speaking both *for* and *against* the same proposition, Li Zhi's affirmation and simultaneous denial that he is a heretic illustrates this point. As Bowen notes, the clash between such incompatible positions bewilders readers and compromises their ability to construct a unified, coherent meaning from such texts.

The etymology of the Chinese word for contradiction, *maodun*, accords with and amplifies this Western understanding of contradiction. Composed of the graphs for spear (矛*mao*) and shield (盾 *dun*), the word *maodun* derives from an anecdote related by the legalist philosopher Han Feizi (d. 233 BCE): "In the state of Chu, there was a man who sold shields and spears. He used to advertise his shields by saying 'My shields are so strong that nothing can puncture them.'

He similarly advertised his spears by saying 'My spears are so sharp that there is nothing they cannot pierce.' Someone once asked 'What would happen if I were to use your spear against your shield?' The salesman was dumbfounded."[15] The client's confusion and the salesman's flummoxed reaction illustrate the irreconcilability of the contradiction. And the fact that the passage provides no resolution marks it as a consummate example of bluff. The salesman is so disconcerted by the client's question that he is unable to respond. The query punctures his pretense and leaves him speechless.

The concept of piercing or puncturing figures prominently in several Chinese words that describe bluffing techniques that appear frequently in Li's writings. The modern Chinese words *fengci* and *fanfeng*, commonly used to translate the English words "irony," "satire," and "sarcasm," allude explicitly to this action. The graph *feng* means "to ridicule or criticize," *fan* means "to oppose or reverse," and *ci* means "to pierce or puncture." At root the rhetorical strategies of *fanfeng* and *fengci* entail opposing or reversing conflicting points of view so as to puncture or pierce a façade or to ridicule and critique an existing opinion.[16]

The notion that rhetoric can pierce through pretense or expose hypocrisy was well established by the sixteenth century. An anonymous colophon to the sixteenth-century erotic novel *The Plum in the Golden Vase* (Jin ping mei), for instance, asserts that the author used "allegory to puncture [contemporary targets]."[17] Similar allusions to pricking and deflating by rhetorical means may be found at least as far back as Han dynasty criticism of the *Classic of Poetry*. What these devices share is their fundamentally destructive or critical character. In this way, they diverge sharply from the idealistic project of rectifying names. For, if rectifying names entails striving against all odds to restore or reestablish parity between words and things, techniques like puncturing, critiquing, opposing, and reversing simply expose problems. They suggest no remedies.[18]

The essentially negative quality of these rhetorical forms resonates with the etymology of the word "irony," which derives from the Greek root *eironëia*, meaning "interrogation."[19] Irony consists of contrasting the surface meaning of a word or statement with its deeper import. As such, it embodies a kind of contradiction, for, to return to Aristotle, it presents readers with "an opposition that . . . excludes compromise."[20] Contradictions of this sort instill doubt about the correspondence between what is *said* and what is *meant*.

They therefore prompt readers to wonder which layer of meaning to privilege and whether to construe statements literally or in the reverse sense.[21] By raising—and significantly not answering—such questions, ironic statements leave readers perplexed, suspended among contending possibilities. For this reason, like the Chinese techniques of poking and puncturing, they exert the destabilizing effect of bluff.[22]

Another type of puzzling statement that resists resolution is the Chan paradox, a rhetorical element with which Li Zhi was familiar. Paradoxes and logical non sequiturs appear regularly at the end of "public cases" (*gong'an*; Japanese pronunciation: *kōan*), brief dialogues that record students' questions and their masters' often illogical replies. By responding in statements that defy ordinary logic, the masters hoped to catapult students into a state of enlightenment or transcendence, free of the limitations of referential language.[23] The masters' paradoxical comments never reveal the truth; they simply prompt students (or readers of these recorded dialogues) to discover truth for themselves. In this sense, these enigmatic pronouncements accord with a statement by Li Zhi's near contemporary, the English poet John Donne (1572–1631), who declared that paradoxes are "alarms to truth."[24] Donne's metaphor accentuates the catalytic function of paradox: like an alarm, the contradiction inherent in every paradox jolts the reader or listener awake from his habitual somnolence or complacence and propels him into a state of heightened awareness.[25]

Certainly the structure and genre of Li's writings differ greatly from those of Chan *gong'an* literature. Li Zhi was no Chan master; he proudly declared himself "unwilling to serve as teacher for even a single day."[26] Nonetheless, he did at times sternly admonish the monks living at the Temple of the Flourishing Buddha, and it is even reported that he brought about one monk's enlightenment by speaking to him through a Chan paradox.[27] More important, the flagrant self-contradictions that abound in his writings, as well as the discrepancies between his personal comportment and his verbal accounts of his actions, bear comparison to Chan paradoxes in that they goad readers to question the categories through which they habitually interpret the world. Further, they expose the pitfalls and limitations of all forms of representation. As the examples below illustrate, Li's pervasive deployment of the rhetoric of bluff connected him, without his knowing it, to authors and artists scattered across the early modern world. The disconcerting effects these texts elicited attest to the works' participation in an early modern aesthetic.

LI'S BLUFFING IN COMPARATIVE CONTEXT: SELF-APPRAISAL, MISLEADING TITLES, AND COY PREFACES

The early modern period was rife with instances of rhetorical bluff, yet the precise manner in which this bluffing took place varied in local contexts. How, then, do Li Zhi's writings exemplify this characteristic feature of early modernity? What do they share with contemporaneous Chinese and European sources? And what sets Li's uses of rhetorical bluff apart? The following three case studies, Li's "Self-Appraisal" (Zi zan) and the authorial prefaces to *A Book to Keep (Hidden)* and *A Book to Burn*, illustrate the rhetorical means by which his texts bluff their readers. Each case study begins with a close reading of an individual text and examines the rhetorical methods by which it disconcerts the reader, undermines his expectations, or strains his credulity. Next, the interpretations place Li's works in a wider early modern context and investigate their bearing on his assertions that his texts are faithful expressions of his heartfelt sentiments.

Self-Appraisal

Among the most self-contradictory of all of Li Zhi's writings is a literary self-portrait written in 1588 and titled "Self-Appraisal." As a piece of autobiographical writing, this essay demonstrates Li's ability to adopt a layered perspective. As in any self-portrayal, the author plays the roles of both the writing subject and the object of inquiry.[28] And because both of these positions are to some extent fictionalized, readers who encounter this piece must also consider a third perspective, that of the historical author. Brief and pithy, the text is worth quoting in its entirety:

> He was by nature narrow-minded and he appeared arrogant. His words were vulgar, and his mind wild. His behavior was impulsive, and his friends few, but when he got together with them he treated them affectionately. When interacting with people, he took pleasure in seeking out their faults; he did not delight in their strong suits. When he hated people, he cut them off and sought to harm them all his life. His ambition was to be warm and well-fed, but he called himself a Bo Yi and a Shu Qi.[29] His character was fundamentally that of the man of Qi,[30] but he claimed that his belly was filled with the Dao and that he drank of virtue. Clearly he was the type who would not lightly give anything away, and yet he made excuses for himself

by saying he was like Yi Yin.[31] He would not even pluck one single hair to give to another, but then he complained that Yang Zhu was a thief of benevolence.[32] His actions violated the way of the ten thousand things, and the words he spoke conflicted with the feelings in his heart. This is the sort of person he was. The people in the village all hated him. In ancient times Zigong asked Confucius: "What if all the people in the village hate a person?"[33] The master said: "One cannot judge him yet." As for this reclusive scholar, perhaps one can?[34]

The text presents Li as a man of many contradictions. It compares him to Bo Yi and Shu Qi, paragons of Confucian virtue who, according to Sima Qian, opted to starve to death rather than eat grain produced in a state whose ruler they deemed immoral. Yet at the same time, the text asserts that Li valued material comforts. It portrays him as claiming to be virtuous and "filled with the Dao" when in fact he resembled the depraved man of Qi. According to Mencius, this scoundrel tricked his wife and his concubine by bringing them luxury foods and telling them that these tasty morsels had been offered to him as gifts from government officers, when in fact he had stolen the food from gravesites, rendering it taboo to eat.[35]

These inconsistencies take on a distinctly negative moral valence: Li is depicted as a liar and a hypocrite, whose words, actions, and intentions do not properly align for "the words he spoke contradicted the feelings in his heart." By professing to be a liar, Li unconsciously rehearses the famous paradox attributed to Epimenides of Crete: "All Cretans are liars." This paradox involves the logical contradiction "If A, then not-A." If Epimenides, being a Cretan, lies when he says "All Cretans are liars," then the phrase "All Cretans are liars" must be true. Thus by telling the truth, Epimenides has disproved his own thesis, that *all* Cretans (including himself) are liars. Paraphrasing this paradox, Li Zhi's French contemporary Montaigne states, "If you say 'I lie,' but in fact you're telling the truth, you're actually lying."[36] Conversely, if Epimenides's statement "All Cretans are liars" is false—if in fact, some Cretans speak the truth—then he has still contradicted his premise, rendering his initial statement once again false. The paradox cannot be avoided.

Li's "Self-Appraisal" raises similar questions: if it is true that Li's words undercut his genuine feelings, then the truth of all claims in the "Self-Appraisal" must be reevaluated, including the claim "the words he spoke conflicted with the feelings in his heart." But questioning the veracity of this sentence opens up the possibility that the words he spoke *did not* conflict with the feelings in his heart; perhaps his words faithfully and accurately manifested the author's emotions, as he so often claims in other essays. In this latter case, the sentence itself is a lie. Thus Li's "Self-Appraisal" bluffs readers by confronting them with an irreducible logical conundrum.[37]

The text seems to support the hypothesis that the Li depicted in the passage is indeed a liar. After all, he boastfully compares himself to Bo Yi and Shu Qi, even though he craves material well-being. Li the character is thus cast in a negative light because the text exposes his lack of self-knowledge, or worse, his eagerness to deceive others by exaggerating his own righteousness—a failing the historical Li repeatedly associated with phony contemporary Confucians. The allusions to the man of Qi, Yi Yin, and Yang Zhu further reinforce this point: the Li in the portrait is woefully conceited and attempts to mask his many deficiencies with pretentious and misleading allusions to classical antiquity. What makes him even more objectionable is that, despite his blindness to his own failings, he takes delight in seeking out the faults of others.

Yet oddly, as a piece of writing, "Self-Appraisal" fails to exemplify any of the character flaws for which it castigates its subject. If the Li *in* the portrait is characterized as arrogant, self-satisfied, and hypocritical, the Li *creating* this verbal likeness reveals himself as anything but. Instead of covering over his moral deficiencies—as would a man who called himself a Bo Yi or a Shu Qi but desired to be well fed—the narrator of this piece boldly exposes "his" deficiencies to the scrutiny of readers. A gulf thus opens up between readers' firsthand experience of Li the narrator and their secondhand understanding of Li the character: while the latter perpetrates outright deception, the former simply engages in rhetorical bluff. In other words, the Li nested *within* the representation may be a hypocrite, but the Li narrating the account demonstrates (perhaps excessive) humility by obsessively and publicly excoriating the character he identifies as himself.

And yet it would be rash to conflate the authorial persona with the historical Li Zhi. For, as the literary scholar Wai-yee Li has pointed out, the narrator of this piece speaks from a vantage point that mimics that of the detractors of the historical Li Zhi, men who may well have accused the author of exhibiting flaws similar to those the narrator attributes to the character. Moreover, it was a commonplace for Ming scholars to portray themselves in writing as peculiar, eccentric, defiant, or uncompromising, as if casting themselves as nonconformists enhanced their aura of authenticity or reputation for virtue. Indeed, as Wai-yee Li has suggested, Li's exaggeratedly self-critical style both here and in the case of his status as a rectified heretic exhibits a certain "conventional unconventionality" characteristic of the period.[38] For example, Li Zhi's acquaintance Xu Wei describes himself in a tomb inscription as "worthless and lazy, but straightforward," boasts of his tendency to undress in public, and proudly announces that many "people thought ill of him."[39] In the context of Ming scholars' propensity to exaggerate their peculiarities, Li's decision to depict himself as irascible and inconsistent ought not to be seen as a revelation of the true character flaws of the historical Li Zhi but rather as simply another mask, a stereotypical, fictionalized image of an eccentric and, ironically, a bid for authenticity.

Because of the incongruities among the layers of Li Zhi's narrative, neither Li the character nor Li the narrator fully inspires readers' confidence. Like the weapons salesman in Han Feizi's parable, who brags about his impenetrable shields and his spears that can penetrate anything, Li the author displays two incompatible images of himself: one as a humble narrator, the other as an objectionable, hypocritical character. These conflicting personae, the one tucked inside the other, dependent upon it and yet at odds with it, perfectly embody the concept of bluff. Their juxtaposition raises questions about the veracity of both. For it is as inconceivable that one man could simultaneously exhibit sincere humility and hypocrisy as it is that a spear could penetrate anything and a shield could be impenetrable. Thus readers are left dumbfounded, just like the potential client in the parable.

The uncertainty this passage generates calls to mind a host of perceptual tricks and situations of mistaken identity pervasive in literary and visual arts of the period, both Chinese and Western. Li's textual reduplication of himself evokes a favorite strategy employed by the magic monkey Sun Wukong, hero of the sixteenth-century novel *Journey to the West* (Xiyou ji). When confronting a ferocious adversary, Sun plucks several hairs from his hirsute, simian arm and blows on them to transform them into an army of virtual selves. The enemy, unable to distinguish among these identical-looking monkeys or determine which is the real Sun Wukong, is confounded and soon overpowered.[40] Sun's self-multiplication, like that of Li Zhi, raises questions about the singularity of identity and the reliability of representation. But unlike Li's account of himself, which ends without resolving the tensions among the plurality of authorial identities it conjures, the identity of the real Sun Wukong is confirmed and the confusion dispelled.

Cases of temporarily doubled or mistaken identity also frequently appear in drama of the period, since the medium of theater lends itself to questioning the permeable boundary between fantasy and reality.[41] As Shakespeare's Jaques in *As You Like It* and Xu Wei's Mulan in an opera of the same title observe, "Everything . . . is an illusion after all"[42] and "all the world's a stage."[43] Tang Xianzu's popular drama *The Peony Pavilion* (Mudan ting), written in 1598, for instance, portrays a father forced to confront the "strange" (*qiguai*) appearance of a young woman who claims to be—and indeed is—his deceased daughter, returned to life. Denying the possibility that she could have been resurrected, the father concludes that although the young woman resembles his daughter in every respect, she can be nothing more than "a false impersonation by some fair-featured harpy or seductive fox-spirit."[44] He therefore refuses to recognize her or consent to her marriage. A dispute then ensues over the girl's identity: is she human or ghost, real or impostor? The question is referred to the emperor himself for adjudication. And here, as in *The Journey to the West*, the truth will out: the play ends with the solid reestablishment of the girl's identity.[45]

Significantly, in both of these cases it is individual characters within the fictional world—not the audience—who experience confusion over who is who. The same could be said of the several plays by Shakespeare whose plots turn on mistaken identity, among them *Twelfth Night* and *As You Like It*. Although characters on stage experience doubt over other characters' identity, this lack of clarity is confined to the fictional world and functions for the audience as a source of dramatic irony. The audience does not share the characters' bewilderment; rather it looks on, amused. This is emphatically not what happens at the end of Li's "Self-Appraisal." The short essay ends inconclusively and leaves readers distinctly discomfited. The narrator allows discordant images of Li to coexist in tension with one another. The result is a sense of unease that extends beyond the printed page and directly affects readers.

Perhaps a more suitable analogy to Li Zhi's discrepant self-portrayals, then, may be found in the visual work of a Chinese artist deeply influenced by Li's writings. Chen Hongshou's (1598–1652) "Venerating Antiquity" playing cards, created shortly after the fall of the Ming, take their cue from a set of playing cards titled

"Counting Money," which were produced during Li's lifetime. The "Venerating Antiquity" playing cards are decorated with portraits of historical figures, classified into suits based on their attitudes toward and experiences involving money. The highest suit of cards represents individuals who worshipped money, while the lowest suit illustrates men of modest means. In her study of these cards, art historian Tamara Heimarck Bentley has observed that a remarkably large number of the portraits of historical figures physically resemble the artist: they share his bushy eyebrows and slanted eyes.[46] Chen depicts himself both as the wealthy and shrewd official Fan Li (Spring and Autumn pd.), a member of the highest suit of cards, and as the penniless poet Tao Qian (365–427), a member of the lowest suit.[47] By portraying himself in these incompatible guises—as a lover of money and as an impoverished scholar—Bentley observes, Chen raises questions about his own identity. Moreover, Chen's cards, like Li's verbal self-portrayal and unlike the dramatic and fictional works mentioned above, resist resolving these tensions. Instead they allow mutually conflicting aspects of the autobiographical subject to exist side by side.

Chen Hongshou's playing cards arguably showcase divergent aspects of their subject's personality, but unlike Li's "Self-Appraisal," these discordant self-portrayals all occupy a single plane of representation. They can be juxtaposed, but not nested inside one another. Li's text, on the other hand, consists of onion-like layers of representation. In this respect, his essay may be said to resemble the visual technique of mise-en-abîme, in which an image contains within it a smaller version of itself. Richard Vinograd has identified this technique as characteristic of the early modern period.[48] Analyzing similarities between Velázquez's painting *Las Meninas* (Figure 2.01) and the Chinese printmaker Min Qiji's (1580–after 1661) highly original, "metapictorial" illustrations of *The Romance of the Western Chamber* (Xixiang ji) (Figure 2.02), Vinograd focuses on the ways in which both works deploy mirroring, storied framing devices, and trompe l'oeil techniques to create impossible spaces that puzzle viewers and accentuate the artifice of representation. The easel, with its back to the viewer in Velázquez's painting, suggests that it—not the painting viewers actually see—is the *real* portrait. And images of the rolled-up, three-dimensional edges of a hand scroll, printed onto the flat surface of Min Qiji's album leaf illustrations, along with the distorted perspective of the round window in the center of the image, raise further

Figure 2.01. Diego Rodriguez Velázquez (Spanish, 1599–1660), *Las Meninas*, or *The Family of Felipe IV*, ca. 1656. Oil on canvas, 3.18 x 2.76 m. Museo del Prado. Photo credit: Art Resource.

questions about framing: where does the representation end and the world outside begin?[49]

These visual conundrums find literary corollaries in early modern texts that interrogate the boundaries between representation and reality. Among such texts, the contemporary novel *Don Quixote* stands out because, by incessantly calling attention to—and undermining—its own authenticity, this text, like Li's "Self-Appraisal," erodes readers' confidence in their ability to disentangle truth from fiction. Throughout the novel, the narrator

Figure 2.02. Min Qiji (Zhejiang province, Chinese, fl. 1640), "The Beautiful Yingying Writes a Letter." Illustration 18 of the album *The Western Chamber*, ca. 1640. Print, 25.5 x 32.2 cm. Museum für Ostasiatische Kunst. Photo credit: Rheinisches Bildarchiv, Köln.

habitually reassures readers of the veracity of his "history," yet the text crawls with internal contradictions and self-conscious allusions to its own inaccuracies. For instance, in the prologue, the narrator introduces the novel as his child, "born of [his] own brain." But he subsequently backs away from this claim, calling the text merely his "step-child." More strikingly, in one chapter the text breaks off abruptly. A battle is interrupted, the combatants' weapons poised midair. The narrator calmly explains this rupture by alluding to a hitherto unmentioned source text, which he suddenly claims is incomplete. What follows is a lengthy and overtly fictional discursus on the pitfalls of textual transmission. The novel, the narrator now states, derives from a flawed translation of an incomplete manuscript, scrawled in Arabic—a language he does not know—and discovered by chance in a marketplace in Toledo.[50] As the layers of nested narrative become increasingly convoluted, readers grow increasingly perplexed. Their bafflement reaches new heights when the fictional characters refer nonchalantly to an author named Miguel de Cervantes. These self-referential loops in the narrative cause readers to lose their bearings and to doubt the authenticity of the text before their eyes.

While Li's self-description is less elaborate, the paradoxes and contradictions it exhibits elicit a similar effect: they inhibit readers from taking the text at face value. For no matter how readers construe his "Self-Appraisal," they can derive no logically consistent meaning from it. By puzzling the reader as to what he means and whether he is telling the truth when he claims he isn't, Li confounds the prospective reader and stimulates him to reflect not only on the nature of his identity but also on the very possibility of accurate representation in an era of unreliable signs. Thus the form of Li's writings, his refusal to offer solid answers, exemplifies the early modern aesthetic of bluff. Paradoxically, Li's inability to reduce his experience or his depiction of himself to a simple, coherent narrative heightens the authenticity of his prose, even as it disconcerts readers.

Misleading Titles, Coy Prefaces

If "Self-Appraisal" bluffs readers by causing them to doubt the veracity of Li's conflicting narratives, authorial prefaces to his two major literary collections, *A Book to Burn* and *A Book to Keep (Hidden)* go one step further. They extend the bluff into the real-world relationships between text and author, text and reader, and reader and author. These prefaces confront readers with a set of paradoxical claims both about the ways in which the historical author treated his writings and about his expectations regarding readers' interactions with his books. By demanding action on the part of readers yet providing inconsistent indications of what sorts of action are required, these texts create a reading experience that both resembles and accentuates the difficulty of negotiating one's way in the early modern world of shifting and unstable signs.

As noted earlier, the title of Li's immensely popular *Book to Keep (Hidden)* puns on the word *cang*, which can be translated as either "to safeguard, store up, collect," or even "hoard," on the one hand, or "to hide, conceal, or sequester" on the other.[51] In an unmarked context, the title phrase could refer simply to book collecting, a favorite pastime among late Ming literati. Thus an unsuspecting reader might bring to such a volume expectations akin to what a modern reader might bring to Walter Benjamin's essay "Unpacking My Library: A Talk about Book Collecting." But a savvier reader would spot the pun lurking in the title. Indeed, this title seems deliberately crafted to pique readers' interest, since in the saturated book market of the late Ming, authors often used eye-catching titles to attract readers' attention. Pitting two divergent meanings of the word *cang* against one another, the title stimulates readers to consider whether the book conveys wisdom worthy of being preserved for posterity, or transmits frivolities—or worse, dangerous or reprehensible ideas that ought to be kept out of sight. An authorial preface invites readers to consider all of these possibilities:

> It is titled *A Book to Keep (Hidden)*. And why *A Book to Keep (Hidden)*? Because this book can only [constitute] personal pleasure; it must not be shown to other people. This is why I've called it *A Book to Keep (Hidden)*. There's nothing I can do if one or two busybody friends incessantly seek to read it. How could I stop them? But I say by way of warning: if it is to be read, all of you will read it in your own manner; you must not use Confucius' "authoritative edition" as the standard by which to dole out praise and blame.[52]

From the outset, the preface calls into question the relationship between author and reader. What does the former expect of the latter? And by reading even these several lines of the preface, has the reader already violated the author's expectations? The line "this book can only [constitute] personal pleasure" is ambiguous: *whose* personal pleasure? If we interpret this line to mean that the book was written solely for the author's own private enjoyment—an assertion Li repeats elsewhere in his writings—then any reader's attempt to engage with this text might constitute an intrusion. Indeed, a preface to the same volume, composed by Li's friend Liu Dongxing (1538–1601) in 1599, recounts a conversation between Li and Liu that corroborates this claim. Liu reports:

> The gentleman was constantly occupied with books. All day long he would copy them out and annotate them for himself, singing praises and evaluating them for himself. He was unwilling to show anyone [what he wrote]. Considering his behavior peculiar, I [Liu Dongxing] asked him about it, and the gentleman replied: "When I was at loose ends in Yunnan, I had nothing to do but befriend the ancients. . . . I arrived at interpretations that differ substantially from those of the past. How could I dare to discuss them with anyone? So I simply wrote down my opinions and hid them away, waiting for [the right reader, who might appear] a hundred thousand generations hence."[53]

A preface to the same work by another of Li's friends, the distinguished Confucian official Mei Guozhen (1542–1605), articulates a similar rationale: "Knowing he was out of sync with his generation, Li Zhi averred 'I'll just jot down [my thoughts] and hide [this book] for the time being until, one hundred thousand generations from now, it will [finally] find an appreciative reader.'"[54] These statements lend credence to the notion that Li intended *A Book to Keep (Hidden)* to be kept private and not read—at least for several hundred years! Additionally, although Li began work on this text in 1582 and completed a draft by roughly 1588 or 1589, he delayed publication for at least ten years.[55] Li further emphasizes his desire that the book be kept out of sight when he writes in his authorial preface, "There's nothing I can do if one or two busybody friends incessantly seek to read it. How could I stop them?" These lines underscore the author's reluctance to share his writings. It seems it was only with resignation and no little trepidation that he acquiesced to the insistent requests of curious would-be readers.

Yet a letter Li wrote to Jiao Hong in 1588 casts some doubt on this assertion. Here Li may be seen actively inviting Jiao to read his writings: "Please allow me to explain: as for *Li Zhi's Book to Keep (Hidden)*, I only copied it out once. I am submitting it to be read by a special person [namely, you]. . . . *A Book to Keep (Hidden)* should be shut away and made secret. But you may still enjoy its arguments discreetly. And I would like to discuss them with someone who understands me. That is why I'm submitting the manuscript to you."[56] Later in the same letter, Li writes, "It would be absolutely inappropriate for you to allow ordinary, unrefined people [*su shi*] to see it." This passage calls into question the idea that Li viewed all contemporary readers as equally demanding and intrusive "busybodies" and sought to prevent his manuscripts from circulating in any form. Rather, it portrays Jiao as an exceptionally sensitive reader, whose opinions Li valued and actively solicited.

But was Jiao really so exceptional? There is evidence to suggest that during the several years Li spent writing *A Book to Keep (Hidden)*, portions of the manuscript circulated among a circle of his acquaintances, if not more widely.[57] Thus even before the book was published in 1599, the readership of this text extended beyond the "one or two" individuals to whom Li's preface alludes. In fact, the authorial preface acknowledges this wider readership when Li declares, "All of you [*zhu jun*] will read it in your own manner." Additionally, in a 1597 letter to Geng Dinglih (b. 1541), the younger brother of Geng Dingxiang and Geng Dingli, Li articulates far grander aspirations for his book's readership. He writes, "This book of mine conveys timeless [strategies for] peaceful governance; it should be introduced into the emperor's own classroom and used as a means to select scholars on the imperial examinations; it is not mere babble!"[58] These hopes explicitly contradict his statements that the book must be kept tightly under wraps.

Clearly, *A Book to Keep (Hidden)* was never addressed simply to a singular, intimate reader, much less composed exclusively for the author's own amusement. Li sought the work's publication, and by publishing it, he targeted a national, anonymous readership. The discrepancy between his lively involvement in the promotion of his book and the intimate rhetoric evident in the authorial preface establishes from the outset an ironic tone that is amplified in his conflicting insinuations that the book's contents are at once triflingly insignificant, appropriate only for "personal pleasure"; vitally important and deserving of the emperor's attention; and threatening enough to warrant keeping them out of sight of those whom they might contaminate or offend.

The authorial preface to *A Book to Burn*, likely published in 1590, contains many of the same bluffing strategies present in this preface to *A Book to Keep (Hidden)*. However, it is unclear which preface was composed first. *A Book to Burn* was published close to a decade before *A Book to Keep (Hidden)*, yet the preface to the former work alludes to the existence of the latter. Thus it is possible that Li Zhi may have drafted the preface to *A Book to Keep (Hidden)* before he wrote the preface to *A Book to Burn*. Regardless of the chronology of composition, the preface to *A Book to Burn* provides insight into the question of whether Li deemed the contents of *A Book to Keep (Hidden)* serious, trifling, or dangerous. At the same time the preface to *A Book to Burn* complicates the issue of the intended readership of *A Book to Keep (Hidden)*. The preface to *A Book to Burn* opens, "I have written four books. The first is called *A Book to Keep (Hidden)*. It records several thousands of years of good and bad deeds from ancient times to the present. It is not easy for common people with eyes of flesh to read, so I intended [at first] to hide it.[59] I meant for it to be hidden in a mountain to await someone of a later generation, a Ziyun to come."[60] Unlike the authorial preface to *A Book to Keep (Hidden)*, this preface insists upon the ethical value of that volume. It further confirms that *A Book to Keep (Hidden)* is not merely diversionary reading; it is a serious, didactic work. Thus the preface to *A Book to Burn* affirms that *A Book to Keep (Hidden)* should be kept out of sight not because it is of little value but rather because it contains wisdom so profound that it risks being misunderstood by ordinary, undiscriminating readers, readers with "eyes of flesh." It demands a reader as insightful as Ziyun.

The mention of Ziyun alludes to a story involving Sima Qian, the father of Chinese historiography. Fearing that his comprehensive history of China, the *Historical Records* (Shiji), might be misconstrued by the undiscriminating readers of his own era, Sima Qian vowed to "hide" his work away and "store it in a famous mountain" (*cang zhu ming shan*) to await a suitably perceptive reader.[61] This reader turned out to be Ziyun. Thus by invoking Ziyun, Li Zhi tacitly compares himself to Sima Qian, and by extension places himself in a long and illustrious tradition of virtuous, misunderstood scholars stretching back at least as far as the third century BCE poet Qu Yuan. Like these unfortunate, unappreciated scholars and poets of yore, Li Zhi implies, he pours his genuine emotions onto the page, but few if any of his contemporaries grasp the import of his words. The analogy between the *Historical Records* and *A Book to Keep (Hidden)* further bolsters the latter text's bid to authenticity, for when Li contends that "the virtuous sages of antiquity did not write unless they were [morally] outraged," he is quoting the sentiments of Sima Qian.[62] However, this grandiose comparison, far from *hiding* the book, serves instead to advertise it.

And yet this self-aggrandizing analogy is laced with irony. For the text of *A Book to Keep (Hidden)* draws heavily on *The Left Scribe's Record of Deeds and Personalities through the Ages* (Lidai shi ji zuobian), a work by the Ming literatus Tang Shunzhi (1507–1560), which in turn reproduces nearly verbatim large sections of Sima Qian's *Historical Records* along with excerpts culled from other historical writings.[63] Thus *A Book to Keep (Hidden)* follows in direct line of succession from the ultracanonical first comprehensive history of China. Yet throughout his book, Li Zhi continually reverses Sima Qian's time-honored judgments on historical figures and events. Li provocatively praises individuals whom Sima Qian excoriated and reviles those whom he extolled. Indeed, it was Li's highly idiosyncratic interpretations and their potential to subvert orthodox judgments that ignited the rage of the imperial censor Zhang Wenda and spurred him to submit to the emperor a memorial impeaching Li Zhi and recommending the destruction of his books. Thus Li's comparison of himself to Sima Qian, an author whose writings he unrelentingly punctured and critiqued, must be read as largely ironic. But where does this interpretation leave the reader? Surely we are to be distinguished from those blind, fleshy-eyed readers who lacked all powers of discernment. But ought we to envision ourselves as latter-day Ziyuns, readers of exceptional insight? Are readers being flattered or mocked, invited to read or cautioned to keep their distance?

If the allusion to Ziyun is meant to flatter the reader by comparing him to one of the most insightful readers in Chinese history, one may rightly doubt how committed Li really was to hiding *A Book to Keep (Hidden)* or, for that matter, to burning *A Book to Burn*. And yet the authorial preface to the latter text insists that readers should literally incinerate the book: "[In] *A Book to Burn* . . . my words get right to the point and criticize the intractable errors of today's scholars. Since I get right to the heart of their terminal illnesses, they certainly will wish to kill me. So I want this book to be burned. I mean that it should be burned and abandoned; it must not be allowed to remain."[64] If the preface to *A Book to Keep (Hidden)* conveys Li's hope that his writings will merely be concealed, the preface to *A Book to Burn* expresses the more violent—and indeed prophetic—wish that the work be totally destroyed. In 1602, the Wanli emperor, responding to Zhang Wenda's memorial, issued an edict ordering the destruction of all Li's writings along with the wooden blocks used for printing them.[65] When Li composed his preface, he surely could not have foreseen these events. In fact, his letters attest that he actively sought the publication of this book. In the preface to *A Book to Burn* he even announces that the wood blocks for printing the volume have already been carved.[66] This preface, then, raises questions similar to those posed by the preface to *A Book to Keep (Hidden)*: if the author knew his books were being published—if he *wanted* them to be published—why did he incite readers to ignore or destroy them? The discrepancy between the author's calls for his books' destruction and the active role he took in their distribution constitutes an act of bluff, for it generates grave doubts about the sincerity of Li's words.

This gnawing sense of doubt is heightened by a further equivocal remark in the authorial preface: "What was to have been burned is no longer to be burned, and what was to have been hidden is no longer to be hidden."[67] Poised on the threshold between the paratext and the text proper, these words both beckon and withhold. They seem on one level to imply that Li has finally overcome whatever reservations he once had about his texts being widely read. Yet on another, they reify these concerns by obsessively repeating them.

What, then, *is* the desired relationship between reader and author? Are these texts meant to be perused, discarded, or secreted away? The books' titles themselves invite ambiguity. *A Book to Burn*, which may also be construed as an imperative, *Burn This Book*, assails the reader with a stark decision: Should he obediently incinerate the volume as the title exhorts—and as Li Si, the advisor to one of Li Zhi's heroes, China's first emperor, Qin Shihuang, would have recommended—or should he disobey this command and read it? Either choice entails a violation, for he who burns the book breaks the implicit "pact" between reader and text; but he who reads it transgresses the explicit order stated in the book's title.[68] The convoluted rhetoric of the prefaces further amplifies these contradictions.

The coy style and tortured ambivalence of Li's authorial prefaces set them apart from many other late Ming authorial prefaces, in which authors more typically belittle their own scholarly achievements and beg the reader's pardon for any potential errors or omissions. However, comparable examples may be cited from early modern Europe. Authorial prefaces by Rabelais and Montaigne resemble Li's in that they too establish ambivalent, uncomfortable, and at times even hostile relations among authors, readers, and books. The preface to Rabelais's *Gargantua*, composed in 1534, features a fictitious narrator, Alcofribas Nasier, who seems to lean off the page and enter directly into the reader's space. He tauntingly addresses his anonymous readership as "high and mighty guzzlers" and individuals afflicted with venereal diseases.[69] These insults combine with a complex series of analogies and allusions designed to draw readers in. Alcofribas self-importantly insinuates that his book contains hidden within it the wisdom of Socrates and that readers must not be fooled by its humble appearance. Instead, they should grapple with the text tenaciously like dogs gnawing on a bone. They should "crack it open" and suck out its "nourishing marrow."[70] But paradoxically this invitation is retracted almost as soon as it is issued, for Alcofribas immediately denies that the book is anything other than "charming nonsense" produced by his "cheesy brain."[71] Among the strategies of bluff present in this preface, we may notice parallels to Li's suggestion that the contents of *A Book to Burn* are both trivial and weighty.

Li's tacit comparison of himself to Sima Qian also echoes Rabelais's invocation of Socrates. Undoubtedly the Greek philosopher and the Chinese historian occupied different positions in their respective cultural histories, but both were revered as authoritative figures from antiquity. So by allying themselves with these towering cultural icons, both sixteenth-century authors were attempting to bolster the authority of their own texts. Additionally, both prefaces teeter on the brink between fiction and reality and establish an ambivalent push-and-pull relationship between the reader and the authorial persona: mingling flattery with insults, they simultaneously lure prospective readers in and thrust them out.

Perhaps even more suitable for comparison is the brief introduction "To the Reader," which precedes Montaigne's *Essays*. Like Li's preface, it declares that the author wrote the *Essays* only as a form of personal amusement and did not intend it to be read. But Montaigne, like Li, undercuts this position by making a pretense of addressing his reader directly, in the second person. What's more, although he employs the intimate, informal pronoun *tu* rather than *vous* and affirms that the book should serve as nothing more than a memento mori for his "relatives and friends, so that when they have lost [him] they [might] . . . recover some features of [his] habits and temperament," historical documentation affirms that he endorsed the book's dissemination to a wide and anonymous readership, and even likely participated in the publication process.[72] Thus Montaigne, like Li, engages readers in a coy exchange that seems to invite them into the text and simultaneously to ward them off. Montaigne even quips at his implied reader, "You would be unreasonable to spend your leisure time on so frivolous and vain a subject. So farewell!"[73]

This closing line—which is paradoxically also an opening—raises questions akin to those generated by Li's prefaces. Do the authors genuinely doubt the worthiness of their subject matter? Or are their warnings simply ruses designed deliberately to attract readers' attention? No conclusive answer to these questions can be reached. And it is this open-endedness, this resistance to definitive interpretation, that so provokes and delights readers. What Li's prefaces share with these European prefaces, then, is the deployment of paradox and self-contradiction to confound and provoke readers, and ultimately to spark their interest. From the very outset, these texts inform readers that they are not what they appear to be. Because of this, they alert readers that some utterances should be taken with a grain of salt, others swallowed whole, but these particular texts never direct readers how to ingest—let alone digest—even one line.

Throughout his writings Li Zhi denounces guile and condemns anyone who would intentionally misrepresent himself in order to deceive others. He claims that words, deeds, and intentions should dovetail smoothly with one another and that his own writings exemplify such stable, transparent signification. The origins of these sentiments lie deep in the Confucian concept of *zhengming*, the rectification of names, which posits the existence of an intrinsic bond between correct language and ethical conduct. Verbal deceptions of the kind Li observes—and decries—among the Confucians of his day create ambiguity, which threatens to blur categories and undermine the social order.

Yet his prose is saturated with contradictions, ironies, paradoxes, and inconsistencies—examples of rhetorical bluff. Thus despite Li's insistence upon his own openness and honesty, his texts present neither a consistent nor a coherent worldview. The author's convoluted and disconcerting style links his writings to an aesthetic of indeterminacy evident in writings from early modern China and Europe. Despite the widely divergent religious and philosophical traditions of these cultures, the literature and arts of both places playfully tangle truth and falsehood, reality and illusion. That Li's texts so strongly exemplify this tendency casts doubt upon the author's self-proclaimed adherence to transparent signification. And this in turn leaves us to wonder why an author who claims to endorse transparent *manifestation* of emotion would engage in bluff at all. Why not express himself directly, in straightforward language? Why not say precisely what he means?

Like many of his contemporaries, Li Zhi was infected by the rapid and unpredictable changes taking place throughout the early modern world. For this reason the rhetorical bluffing symptomatic of the age may be understood as an indexical sign, a manifestation of the tempestuous state of signification in early modern societies. By allowing contradictory layers of meaning to proliferate in his book, by fluctuating among discrepant viewpoints, and by adopting framing techniques that obscure his own opinions, Li's writings illustrate the difficulty of deciphering meaning under these circumstances. And yet his texts are no mere mirror of society, un-self-consciously reflecting the semiotic turmoil of the day. They are the works of a consummate commentator: through the rhetoric of bluff, Li both mingled in the general melee and simultaneously responded to and honestly critiqued it.

CHAPTER 3

Sartorial Signs and Li Zhi's Paradoxical Appearance

Li Zhi's physical self-presentation was as provocative and difficult to decipher as his writings. Like them, it too may be read as a grand act of bluff. In the summer of 1588, shortly before moving from the Vimalakīrti Monastery in Macheng to the Cloister of the Flourishing Buddha on the bank of Dragon Lake, Li shaved the hair from his head in compliance with Buddhist custom, but incongruously allowed his long beard to remain.[1] Additionally, he seems to have habitually garbed himself in traditional Confucian robes and headgear. Although he may not have maintained this peculiar appearance consistently throughout the rest of his life, the odd figure he cut deeply impressed itself upon contemporaries and elicited numerous comments. Li's ambiguous appearance and contradictory accounts of his motivations for cultivating it stand out against the dual backdrop of his endorsement of transparent signification and his rejection of self-serving duplicity. The textual record describing Li's appearance and the reactions it generated, as well as the author's own diverse and inconsistent justifications for presenting himself in this manner, document paradoxes that, like those found throughout his writings, reveal his multilayered and ambivalent identity. What appear as contradictions—the clash between the author's long beard and Confucian robe on the one hand, and his shiny shaved head on the other—should be understood not as clumsy attempts to declare unwavering allegiance to any ideological position or to endeavor to improve his social standing but rather as evidence of his painful choice to express his complex identity.

At first, Li's deviation from norms of dress and hairstyle may seem typical of the era in which he lived, a time when sumptuary laws designed to differentiate clearly among people of different social classes and ethnicities were frequently flouted.[2] However, the manner in which Li violated these expectations, as well as his motivations for doing so, differed fundamentally from those of the vast majority of his contemporaries. Whereas many in the late Ming dressed "aspirationally," imitating the attire of the upper classes, very few tampered with their hairstyle as radically as did Li Zhi.[3] Indeed, unlike others of his generation, Li violated conventions of self-presentation in ways that rendered his identity either illegible or downright offensive to his peers.[4] Thus rather than gain him admittance to elite circles, Li's self-presentation made him the object of ridicule and perhaps even physical attack. He boldly assumed this odd appearance in an effort to make his body and clothing accurately reflect his paradoxical position both within and outside Confucian official culture and to dramatize the struggles that occupying this position caused him.

Li's writings demonstrate familiarity with the idea, first articulated in ancient texts and still well-known in the Ming, that one's physical self-presentation—which included both hairstyle and garments—ought ideally to mirror one's words and actions as a manifestation of one's moral character and corresponding social status. Accordingly, his writings register chagrin over the fact that many of his contemporaries wore clothes designed to conceal their social status. The pretense inherent in these men's choice of clothing mirrors the verbal deceptions they perpetrated. The following discussion focuses on the cultural and philosophical underpinnings of the idea that one's physical appearance may express identity in ways similar to one's words and actions. It also touches briefly on contemporary European discourses on the meaning and import of clothing, as well as its uses and abuses, for Renaissance Europe, like late Ming China, was home to sumptuary laws that were often honored in the breach.[5] Both discussions pave the way for my analysis of Li's unusual self-presentation and my examination of the contradictory justifications he and his biographers provide for why he presented himself in this manner.

CLOTHING AS A MANIFESTATION OF IDENTITY

Since earliest times, ritually correct clothing was associated in China with maintaining social order. Along with a host of interrelated semiotic signs, including standard weights and measures, and appropriate music, garments that revealed their wearer's personal character, social standing, and identity were viewed as consonant with a harmonious, well-regulated society. According to the *Book of Rites* (Liji), the rulers of the Zhou dynasty (1046–256 BCE) toured the countryside every five years, stopping in each feudal state to examine all aspects of everyday life, including clothing. Wherever practices deviated from the government-sanctioned norm, punishments were meted out accordingly: "Where there [was] neglect of the proper order in the observances of the ancestral temple, [this] was held to show a want of filial piety and the rank of the unfilial ruler was reduced. Where any ceremony had been altered, or any instrument of music changed, it was held to be an instance of disobedience, and the disobedient ruler was banished. Where the statutory measures and the (fashion of) clothes had been changed, it was held to be rebellion, and the rebellious ruler was taken off." Moreover, the *Book of Rites* states, any individual caught "using licentious music; strange garments; wonderful contrivances and extraordinary implements" was put to death, since such behaviors were seen to "rais[e] doubts among the multitudes."[6] Corroborating this account, the *Zuozhuan* threatens, "Clothing that does not correspond to one's inner state will bring disaster upon one's person."[7] And Xunzi (313–238 BCE) warns of the perils that may befall a society when transgressions of sartorial propriety become ubiquitous: "The evidence of a chaotic age is that men wear brightly colored clothing; their demeanor is effeminate; their manners are lascivious; their minds are bent on profit; their conduct lacks consistency.... An orderly age is the opposite of this."[8] Implicit in these statements is the understanding that in ancient China clothing held both social and political significance.[9] Texts—whether wrought of words and music or fashioned of fabric—were perceived not simply as symbolic manifestations of personal virtue but also as signs of social and political well-being. As such, semiotic disturbances were seen to figure instabilities in the social world.

But what constituted appropriate dress? Since before the Han dynasty, sumptuary laws were used to distinguish among individuals of various ranks. For instance, the Han political theorist Jia Yi (201–169 BCE), in his "Discourse on Dress" (Fuyi) states, "Different styles and patterns are applied to classify the upper and lower [strata of society] and to differentiate [between] the noble and the [base]. Therefore, if people's status [is] different, their titles, their power, their authority, their banner symbols, the certificate of their orders, the greetings and favors they receive, their ranks and salaries, their hats and shoes, their robes and ribbons, their ornaments and decorations, their vehicles and horses, their wives and concubines, their benefits and bestowals, their palaces and houses, their beds and mattresses, their utensils, their drinks and foods, their sacrifices, their funerals, all are different."[10] These rules are endorsed in the *Guanzi*, a Han compilation of texts dating back to the Warring States period: "Let clothing be regulated according to gradations in rank.... In life, let there be distinctions in regard to carriages and official caps, clothing and positions, stipends and salaries, and fields and dwellings.... Let no one, even if worthy and honored, dare wear clothing [that] does not befit his rank."[11] Following in this tradition, sartorial statutes featured prominently in Chinese legal codes and were preserved and reinforced over the centuries.[12] Ming sumptuary regulations were particularly strict, since the dynastic founder, Zhu Yuanzhang (1328–1398), held that the previous dynasty (Yuan/Mongol, 1271–1368), had marked a rupture in this transmission of vestimentary norms. According to a member of Zhu's court, one reason the Yuan dynasty had collapsed was that it had failed to maintain proper sartorial distinctions between commoners and nobility.[13] In an effort to rectify this problem, reinstate order, and assert its own legitimacy, the new dynasty implemented rigid sumptuary laws. The Ming legal code thus set forth in painstaking detail the various types of costume to be worn by individuals of each social class.[14] Additionally, the *Great Ming Commandment* (Da Ming ling) stipulated, "There is a hierarchy in the colors of clothes, official ribbons, houses, and vehicles and horses used by officials and commoners; people in the upper rank can use those for the lower rank, but no reverse practices [will be tolerated]."[15]

Sojourning in China in the late sixteenth century, Li's acquaintance, the Jesuit missionary Matteo Ricci, was struck by the detailed regulation of official regalia. Although he was familiar with sumptuary laws from his experiences in Italy, Ricci remarked with fascination in his journal:

> All mandarins, whether high or low, whether of the military or civil branches, have the same hats of black material and with two flaps on either side.... They all also have one type of robe, boots of the correct style..., a large belt with various patterns only proper for officials, and two squares embroidered with varying figures, one on the chest and the other on the back. The girdle and these squares have

significant differences and enable one to distinguish higher and lower ranks. . . . The girdles differ according to the standing of the wearer.[16]

The law's minute attention to every aspect of an official's attire from head to toe was designed to enforce distinctions between social classes. Yet these regulations also betray profound anxiety over the potentially destabilizing phenomenon of social mobility.

Unsurprisingly, despite tight legal prescriptions, boundaries between social classes did begin to blur. The Zhengde reign (1506–1521), which ended just shortly before Li Zhi's birth in 1527, saw a steep rise in violations of sumptuary statutes, and these transgressions grew only more numerous and more flagrant during Li's lifetime as international and interregional trade networks expanded.[17] By his young adulthood, it was not uncommon to see nobles, wealthy merchants, and even eunuchs dressed illegally in garments reserved for imperial use.[18] We hear reports of commoners impersonating scholars, servants sporting outfits so luxurious they rival those of their masters, and women parading about in facsimiles of gowns designated for imperial concubines.[19] Li himself alludes to "great bandits who wear [Confucian] caps and clothes."[20] Examples of such violations equally permeated the fiction and drama of the period, which portray a population living in open disregard of sumptuary legislation.[21]

Li Zhi was keenly aware of violations of sumptuary statutes, and he shared with many of his contemporaries the desire to reinstate more reliable forms of signification. His essay "Adorned with Every Mark of Dignity" (Wu suo bu pei) traces the process by which garments and ornaments worn on the body gradually became detached from the virtues, skills, and character traits they had once putatively designated. Li's essay opens with a quotation from the Eastern Han scholar Wang Yi's (fl. 130–140) commentary on "Encountering Sorrow" (Li sao), a poem in which the poetic speaker-cum-author, Qu Yuan (ca. 340–278 BCE), repeatedly describes "adorning" (*pei*) his body with flowers and herbs representing his many virtues.[22] Li quotes Wang Yi: "People whose conduct is pure and clean are adorned with fragrant orchids. Those whose virtue is bright and radiant are adorned with jade. People who can untangle difficulties are adorned with a *xi* hook made of bone, and those who can resolve doubts are adorned with a *jue* disc made of jade."[23] Wang's statements corroborate the established Chinese narrative that in antiquity each person wore the token that accurately and appropriately corresponded to his character and abilities. Li affirms this view, then contrasts the hypothetically perfect, transparent semiotic system of antiquity with the very real and confusing state of affairs evident in the late Ming:

> In ancient times, when a man went out, he did not part from his sword or his ornaments. When he travelled abroad, he did not part from his bow and arrow. Day or night, he did not part from his *xi* or his *jue*. . . . [But] people of later generations lost sight of the substance of these talismans; they saw in them nothing more than beautiful adornments to be cherished. . . . From that moment on, the custom of using these talismans began to fall into disuse, and their ornamental and protective functions became disassociated. It's not merely that civil officials no longer know how to use a weapon; even military men making ordinary social rounds imitate the attire of civil officials, wearing loose garments and wide belts. How refined and proper they appear! But as soon as there is danger, could it be that only civil officials have their hands tied? Even the military men, what use are they?[24]

Li's remarks draw attention to the widening gap between signs and the objects they purport to designate. He perceives that by his own era the connection between how a person *looked*—the objects with which he adorned himself—and what he actually *was* had all but dissolved: appearances had become as unreliable and potentially misleading as words. Consequently, he believed he was living in an era of decline, a far cry from the mythic past when clothing and ornamentation revealed the identity, character, and corresponding social status of the wearer as transparently as words manifested what was "on [the speaker's] mind intently."

The notion that words and clothing ought ideally to signify in concert is rooted in the concept of *wen*, meaning "patterning," "ornamentation," and by extension "literature" or "writing." The eclectic Han rationalist philosopher Wang Chong (27–91), for instance, explicitly analogizes clothing to words and stresses that both semiotic systems, when operating smoothly, render visible inner qualities of the speaker or wearer. He asserts, "*Wen* (patterned words) and virtue are the garments of mankind. . . . Expressed sartorially, [words and virtuous deeds] become garments."[25] Strengthening the connection between clothing and words, he further declares, "Garments [should] serve to denote the rank of worthies; worthies may [also] be distinguished by their literary abilities."[26] These statements imply a normative view that words and clothing alike should constitute outward expressions of inner virtue.

Taking this notion one step further, Li's intellectual forebear, the eccentric philosopher Wang Gen (1483–1540), founder of the radical Taizhou branch of Wang Yangming's School of the Mind, to which Li adhered, fashioned for himself an outfit that complied exactly with the vestimentary prescriptions recorded in the *Book of Rites*.[27] Seeking to justify his decision to adopt such strange antiquarian robes, which visibly deviated from contemporary fashions, he asked rhetorically, "How can I speak the words of [Sage King] Yao and act as Yao did without also wearing his clothes?!"[28] Wang Gen's peculiar sartorial choices stemmed not merely from his desire to draw attention to himself but also, importantly, from his sincere belief that words, deeds, and clothing should signify in concert. And his behavior may have prefigured Li's own exotic self-presentation, for each man strove, in his own odd way, to maintain harmony between his inner convictions and his outer appearance.

Li's support for the view that clothing should manifest one's inner qualities may be observed in an essay he wrote praising his acquaintance Liu Xie (fl. 1570), a native of Macheng who served as district magistrate in Jiangxi. This humorous essay subtly analogizes the verbal hypocrisy widespread among late Ming Confucians to the practice of dressing aspirationally. Li condemns both forms of social imposture and laments that in his day clothing, like words, was more often used to mask an unsavory interior than to reveal the wearer's true character. To make this point, Li recounts a (likely fictitious) exchange between the titular character and a pretentious "gentleman from the School of Principle" (*daoxue xiansheng*), who garbed himself in Confucian raiment and peppered his discourse with allusions to authoritative texts. Li writes, "There once was a gentleman from the School of Principle who wore dignified platform shoes and walked in large strides. He dressed in a generously long-sleeved robe with a wide sash. With the obligations of morality as his cap and the principles of human relations as his garments, he sprinkled his writings with one or two phrases picked up from the classics, and on his lips he always had several passages from orthodox texts. On this basis he claimed that he was a true disciple of Confucius."[29] The passage charts the pretentious gentleman's unsuccessful attempt to appear respectable by decking himself in Confucian paraphernalia both sartorially and verbally. Yet because he lacks the requisite ethical foundation, his efforts end in failure. The perceptive Liu Xie quickly recognizes that the man possesses only the external trappings of virtue; like the poetic imitators and Ciceronians mentioned in chapter one, his veneer proves fake. Li mocks the superficiality of the pretentious gentleman and praises Liu for his incisiveness.

Li Zhi was not alone in opposing misleading sartorial signs. Similar sentiments were often voiced in both China and Europe. Writing on the phenomenon of social imposture, the scholar Li Le (*jinshi* 1568) insisted, "Caps and garments are the means by which individuals exhibit their [social] position; they are not mere decorations."[30] And Fan Lian (Ming, n.d.) complained, "When slaves vie to dress splendidly, it is hard to be noble; when ladies copy the fashion of prostitutes it's hard to be decent."[31] Another Ming literatus, Hong Wenke (Ming, n.d.), went so far as to petition the emperor to establish a bureau of "fashion police" to inspect and monitor the level of sartorial rectitude throughout the land.[32] For his part, Li Zhi declared, "Ever since the Song royal house fell from its position of dominance, the world has been topsy-turvy, just like a person wearing his hat on his feet and his shoes on his head. Sages occupy inferior positions, unworthy people superior ones."[33] Echoing these sentiments, the narrator of the early seventeenth-century Chinese novel *Marriage Destinies to Awaken the World* (Xingshi yinyuan zhuan) comments nostalgically that although in ancient times clothing accentuated distinctions among individuals of different ranks, "today, dark damask and silk gauze, embroidered shoes and cloudy footwear are worn by all people without discerning their social status, fortune, seniority or gender." "How," the narrator laments, "could these things not anger Heaven and Earth and exasperate ghosts and spirits?"[34]

Similar reports, both official and anecdotal, abound from across contemporary Europe, where efforts to enforce sumptuary laws met with little compliance. The Diet of Worms in 1521 advocated "the urgent need for sumptuary legislation in order to maintain the visibility of social status as manifest in attire," and the Diet of Augsburg in 1530 drafted new sumptuary laws "to ensure that each class should be clearly recognized." Additionally, the English "Enforcing Statutes of Apparel," a proclamation dating from 1566, described the "disorder and confusion of the degrees of all estates . . . and . . . the subversion of all good order."[35] These official statements were seconded by personal accounts. Describing his visit to Augsburg in 1580–1581, Montaigne averred, "It's not easy to distinguish who is noble because everyone wears velvet hats and carries a sword,"[36] and the Italian Stefano Guazzo (1530–1593), writing in 1574, opined that based on a person's attire, "a man can discern no difference in estates."[37] The fiery British Puritan preacher Philip Stubbes (ca. 1555–ca. 1610) passionately voiced similar concerns: "Now there is such a confuse mingle mangle of apparell in England, and such horrible excesse thereof, as euery one is permitted to flaunt it out, in what apparell he listeth himselfe, or can get by any meanes. So that it is hard to knowe, who is noble, who is worshipfull, who is a Gentleman, who is not."[38] In words that recall those of Xunzi, quoted earlier, the Spanish Franciscan Juan de Santa María (d. 1622) invoked Sallust's warning that sartorial confusion signaled social erosion: "When a kingdome . . . [exhibits such] corruption of manners . . . that men do pamper and apparel themselves in curious manner, like women, and make no reckoning of their honestie, but deal therewith as with any other thing that is vendible . . . [then the] Empire [may] be given [up] for lost."[39] These numerous complaints—Chinese and European alike—share the understanding that the practice of concealing one's true identity under borrowed robes had become shockingly widespread on both ends of the Eurasian landmass. And the deceit inherent in such behavior spawned both noisy denunciations and urgent warnings that, in the words of Rabelais, "the hood does not make the monk."[40]

But what made these frequent sartorial transgressions so keenly distressing was not merely that they interfered with the legibility of a semiotic system intended to accentuate the boundaries between social classes. More disturbing still, they seemed to signal—or perhaps even to trigger—actual changes in behavior. For, as Li suggests, by cloaking themselves in scholars' robes, military men ultimately lost or forgot their martial skills.[41] When danger struck, they no longer knew how to react. Implicit in this statement is the assertion that changing one's clothes corresponds to or perhaps even brings about an unsettling shift in identity.

The suggestion that clothing could effect such a fundamental change may seem implausible. Yet several historians' investigations into the role and function of clothing in Renaissance Europe help to explain this assertion. Bronwen Wilson, for instance, has traced Renaissance European understandings of clothing to the etymology of this word in Romance languages: "Derived from the Latin *habitus*, or aspect, the [Italian word *habiti* and also the French word *habit*] signified the ways in which apparel invested bodies with meaning through . . . the tradition and conventions attached to dress. The [Italian] word is also defined as *contegno*, meaning attitude and behavior and thereby conveying those attitudes to which people are inclined habitually or innately."⁴² In other words, clothing was perceived to possess the ability both to *express* the status and disposition of the wearer and also to *confer* status and attitudes upon the wearer. Writing about Renaissance European understandings of the relationship between clothing and identity, Ann Rosalind Jones and Peter Stallybrass aptly capture the idea that clothing may mold or shape the wearer. Tracing the English word "fashion" to its Latin root, *facere*, "to make," they analyze the extent to which clothing was perceived truly to *make* the man: "[In Renaissance Europe] clothes [were understood to] permeate the wearer, fashioning him or her from within. This notion undoes the opposition of inside and outside, surface and depth. Clothes . . . inscribe themselves upon a person who comes into being through that inscription."⁴³ Thus clothing, which once had revealed differences in station, had come to blur not only the *representation* of these differences but also the fundamental differences themselves. To wit: the military men Li describes ceased to behave as military men when they no longer wore the appropriate raiment.

The phenomenon of garments that disguise, conceal, or, most unnervingly, alter the identity of the wearer signaled incipient social decline, and as such mirrored the linguistic erosion evident in Li's China. The parallel between social and linguistic deterioration finds expression in the words of Li's British contemporary, Ben Jonson, who, drawing on Thucydides and Horace, wrote, "Wheresoever, manner, and fashions are corrupted, language is. It imitates the public riot. The excesse of Feasts and apparrell, are the notes of a sick State: and the wantonnesse of language, of a sick mind."⁴⁴ These words, which resonate with the etymology of the word "text"—from the Latin *textere*, "to weave"—were intended to describe a situation far removed from Ming China. Yet in fact they point to a shared perception in early modern China and Europe that society was unravelling and that this process was finding equal expression in the unruliness of language, the lawlessness of clothing, and the malleability of social identity.⁴⁵ Yet Li Zhi's deviations from sartorial convention, like his pervasive use of verbal bluff, do not exemplify but rather resist this trend toward debased signification. For unlike his contemporaries, who strove to impress their superiors by speaking in inflated language and donning showy attire that either misrepresented them or distorted their identity, Li opted for an anomalous guise that, like his paradoxical language, accurately manifested his conflicted identity and, in the process, won him not social acceptance but suffering and infamy.

LI ZHI'S UNCONVENTIONAL APPEARANCE

Li's incongruous appearance posed a riddle to anyone who heard about it or saw him, for it bucked every Chinese sartorial convention. Having served in the Confucian bureaucracy for nearly thirty years as a fourth-tier official, Li was entitled to wear scholars' robes and the square headdress appropriate for middle-ranking officials. This sartorial choice is mentioned by Li himself and by several of his biographers.[46] What was striking about Li's self-presentation, then, was not his clothing alone but rather the juxtaposition of his Confucian attire and his shaved head. Bai Yinzhang (1584–1658) declared that Li "was bald but dressed as a Confucian."[47] And He Jiaoyuan (1558–1631) stated, "He shaved his head but kept his beard; and often wore the *jinxian* cap befitting a worthy and accomplished scholar."[48] Wang Keshou (d. 1620) further confirms that "he wore a Confucian cap to cover his monk's pate."[49] These accounts point to the peculiar combination of traditional Confucian attire and a shaved head.

In premodern China, hair, like clothing, served as a semiotic marker registering an individual's social station and religious or ideological commitment. Confucian filial piety required that, in deference to one's parents, one maintain one's entire body intact.[50] For this reason scholars and officials typically abstained from cutting their hair or altering their body in any way.[51] Despite the many syncretic borrowings from Buddhism that had seeped into Confucian thought since the Song dynasty (960–1279), Ming Confucians continued to observe these practices conscientiously.[52] As one sixteenth-century European visitor to China remarked of the mandarins he encountered, "They are proud to have a great head of hair. They let it grow long and coil it up in a knot on the crown of their head. They then put it in a hairnet . . . [to] fix the hair in position, wearing on top of it a bonnet. . . . This is their ordinary headgear . . . [and t]hey take a good time each morning in combing and dressing their hair."[53] But if Confucians considered thick, well-groomed hair a sign of respect to parents and elders, Buddhists viewed it as a symbol of attachment to the mundane world. And because removing one's hair visually deemphasized one's gender identity, shaving one's head was taken to represent a monk's abstention from sexuality, and by extension his renunciation of familial ties.⁵⁴ Thus a tonsured head signaled a monk's or nun's rejection of Confucian filial duties. In this way, Confucian and Buddhist attitudes toward hair stood starkly at odds.

Indeed Confucian critics of Buddhism often pointed out in disdainful terms the putatively heretical hair-related practices of Buddhist devotees. Although Li himself showed great sympathy for and knowledge of Buddhism, his writings contain several such anti-Buddhist jibes. In an essay on the *Diamond Sūtra*, written in 1593, he derides Buddhists for "disfiguring ... their appearance, ... changing ... their robes, abandoning ... the kindness of rulers and family, and personally rebelling ... against [Confucian] teachings." The essay ends ironically with Li urging readers to cultivate "the mind of nonabiding[, since] with this mind, one can carry on conversations with those disloyal, unfilial, head-shaving, strange robe-wearing monks in person!"⁵⁵ Although these critical remarks should not be read as reflective of Li's personal views on head shaving—they were most likely written while his own head was shaved—they do at least evince his awareness that Confucian doctrine regarded the practice of hair removal as taboo.⁵⁶ A letter dating to 1588, the year in which he first shaved his head, extends this argument one step further. Li states wryly, "To disfigure my appearance by shaving my head is distasteful not only to Confucian scholars but to everyone."⁵⁷ And yet, cognizant of the negative responses his decision might provoke, one hot summer day Li took a razor to his head.

The many and contradictory motivations attributed to Li Zhi, by both himself and others, will be examined below. For now, I will focus on the reactions his extraordinary appearance precipitated in those who saw him or heard about his behavior. Had Li thoroughly abandoned one identity for another—had he cast off his Confucian robes and donned in their stead the simple frock of a Buddhist monk to match his shiny pate—his identity might have discomfited his contemporaries slightly less. What rendered Li's appearance so profoundly disturbing and so challenging to interpret was the mixture of two seemingly irreconcilable ideological positions. A tomb inscription for Li Zhi, composed by the promising young scholar Wang Keshou, attests to the incomprehensibility of Li's appearance. The document records an encounter that took place between the two men the year after Li first shaved his head: "In the year 1589 I [Wang Keshou] first encountered Li Zhi at Dragon Lake. At the time, two or three friends were also present. The old man [Li Zhi] emerged with a shaved head and a beard. I said 'You have shaved your head, yet your beard remains. It seems, sir, as if you've not finished the job.'"[58] Wang's bemused reaction is telling. He seems at a loss for how to interpret Li's appearance and can only surmise that he has caught Li in medias res, in the fleeting moment between our author's rejecting one identity and fully espousing another. Wang scarcely imagines that this paradoxical appearance could be anything other than transitory.

A similar opinion is expressed by Geng Dingxiang, whose alleged hypocrisy Li unrelentingly attacked throughout *A Book to Burn*. Upon learning that Li had recently shaved his head, Geng assumed that Li had also adopted Buddhist attire and leaped to the conclusion that our author had wholeheartedly embraced the Buddhist religion.[59] Geng's deduction makes a certain amount of sense, for it was not uncommon in this period for men—especially those who had fulfilled their Confucian familial obligations—to join monasteries late in life.[60] Hearing the news about Li's bald head, Geng immediately dashed off a letter to the two men's mutual friend Zhou Sijiu (*jinshi* 1553), stating, "Those who are bound by Confucian thought will be shocked and consider his behavior strange, but those who put their faith in Buddhism will be delighted by Li's action."[61] Li's friend Deng Yingqi (*jinshi* 1586) was so appalled by Li's conduct that he related the story to his mother. And the mother, regarding Li's decision to shave his head as proof of his apostasy from Confucian values, registered such concern that she was unable to eat for days and piteously implored Deng to persuade Li to grow his hair back.[62] These remarks show that Wang, Geng, Deng, and even Deng's mother viewed Li's hairstyle as a rejection of his allegiance to Confucian values. Despite the ethos of religious syncretism prevalent in the late Ming, they could not conceive that Li would deliberately cultivate a composite identity inclusive of incompatible Confucian and Buddhist elements.

Wang's narration of an encounter that took place between himself and Li in Tongzhou in 1601, shortly before Li's death, further bolsters this point. Here Wang displays continued shock that Li persisted in presenting himself in such an unconventional guise:

> [Li] wore a Confucian cap to cover his monk's pate and greeted us with proper decorum. In *surprise*, I asked him "Why so reverent?" He replied "I used to read Confucius' books, but I was unpersuaded. Recently I've been perusing the *Book of Changes* and I've realized that Confucius' teachings are worthwhile after all. How dare I fail to follow their ritual prescriptions?" I *paused* then replied, "It seems

that in the past you were still caught in the snares of [attempting to distinguish] right from wrong." The old man answered, "These matters do not concern me alone; they affect everyone. As long as we have hands, how could we refrain from striking when there are people who deserve to be struck; and as long as we have mouths, how could we refrain from rebuking those who deserve to be rebuked?" I *laughed* and said "You've not changed a bit, Li Zhuowu!" [Emphasis mine].[63]

Wang's hesitation and laughter are characteristic responses to bluff. They highlight his surprise and register his uncertainty how to respond to a ritually correct Confucian greeting issuing from a bald man residing in a monastery. Surely such a peculiar, even monstrous appearance would have provided ample reason for contemporaries to have difficulty classifying Li neatly as either a Confucian or a Buddhist.

Yet by choosing to present himself in this manner, Li was arguably dramatizing his conflicted inner convictions.[64] He was manifesting his complex identity. Having studied Buddhist texts seriously for close to a decade, Li was well versed in Chan and Pure Land teachings and held both in high esteem. On many occasions both he himself and his contemporaries referred to him as a monk (*heshang*).[65] He wrote commentaries on several major Buddhist texts and spent years at the Cloister of the Flourishing Buddha. However, he took no religious vows, resisted submitting to monastic discipline, and by some accounts abstained from taking part in prayer services.[66] To the end of his days he adhered to a vegetarian diet only sporadically and was ultimately accused of entertaining women on the premises of the Cloister of the Flourishing Buddha, in flagrant violation of Buddhist law.[67] At the same time, he viewed core tenets of Confucian doctrine with abiding respect and raged against their perversion by phonies styling themselves Confucians. His incongruous appearance dramatized these ambivalences, and in doing so raised disturbing questions. What manner of man was he? The identity of this idiosyncratic "Confucian monk" seemed to defy classification.[68]

If Li's enigmatic appearance provoked laughter from Wang Keshou, clearly not all of his contemporaries responded to it with such good humor. According to one account, when Li shaved off his hair "everyone was shocked and considered [such behavior] strange; rumors arose from every direction. The prefect [of Huangzhou] and a military officer in that region declared that because Li Zhi was behaving eccentrically and confusing the multitudes, he must be arrested immediately."[69] Another contemporary account leveled similar charges: it asserted that Li was "behaving eccentrically, deceiving the multitudes, and wreaking havoc upon the world."[70] As if harkening back to the passage from the *Book of Rites*, which proclaims that those who wear "strange garments . . . raise doubts among the multitudes" and therefore deserve to be put to death, Li anticipates in the preface to *A Book to Burn* that his opponents will wish to kill him.[71]

Li's unconventional appearance did not result in his immediate assassination. However, it did arguably provoke at least one act of violence. In 1591, during a trip to Wuchang to view the Yellow Crane Pavilion with his friend Yuan Hongdao, Li was accosted by an angry mob that accused him of "behaving eccentrically and muddling the multitude" and drove him out.[72] A letter Li wrote to his friend Zhou Sijing (d. 1597) outlines this disturbing experience. Immediately following the description of the event, Li pledges, "That very same day, I put on my [Confucian] cap [and resolved to] grow out my hair and resume my original appearance." The tone of the letter in which this assertion appears is highly ironic, so one may well doubt whether Li actually acted on this intention.[73] Yet the very assertion itself demonstrates that on some level Li connected the violence perpetrated against him not only to the provocative rhetoric in *A Book to Burn*, likely published just one year earlier, but also to his physical appearance. Whether serious or ironic, his oath to grow back his hair so as to avoid such violent episodes in the future implies that Li, for one, perceived a link between his appearance and the aggressive actions of the mob.[74]

If Li's incongruous appearance truly stimulated such a violent response, what prompted him to cultivate and sustain this look? Perhaps unsurprisingly, writings by and about Li Zhi provide contradictory accounts of his motivations for shaving his head. And the confusion generated by the plurality of conflicting explanations mirrors the original difficulty of interpreting Li's appearance. The result is a double bluff, a situation in which interpretation is hampered simultaneously on two levels: making sense of the motivations that stimulated Li to remove his hair proves as challenging as attempting to decipher the meaning or meanings of the resultant look itself. Nonetheless, in what follows I examine several rationales and endeavor to extract meaning from them.

A biographical sketch of our author written by Yuan Zhongdao, the tomb inscription by Wang Keshou, and several other sources portray Li as simply reacting impulsively to physical discomfort. Yuan's "Biography of Li Wenling" (Li Wenling zhuan) states, "One day, exasperated with having an itchy head and tired of combing his hair, [Li] shaved it off, but allowed his beard to remain."[75] An entry in a Qianlong-era (1735–1796) local gazetteer from Li's home town of Quanzhou, Fujian, reiterates this rationale. It explains, "One day his head was itchy and he was tired of combing his hair, so he shaved it off and covered his bald head with a [Confucian] cap."[76] Wang's tomb inscription, the wording of which is repeated almost verbatim in Liu Tong (Ming, n.d.) and Yu Yizheng's (Ming, n.d.) *Survey of Scenery and Mountains in the Imperial Capital* (Dijing jingwulue), broadly restates this rationale but provides additional detail:[77] "The old man [Li Zhi said]: 'How could I have meant anything by shaving off my hair!? Last summer my head felt hot, and I was always scratching my white hair. It emitted a smell like rotting flesh, so foul I couldn't stand it! Then I *happened to come across* a monk who had just shaved his head, so I thought I'd give it a try. Having shaved my hair, I felt happy, so I *made a habit of it*.' He then stroked his beard and remarked 'as for this, I couldn't part with it'" (emphasis mine).[78] These passages all describe Li's shaving as an unpremeditated response to scorchingly hot weather. Omitting any mention of the ideological significance of his action, they focus on the putatively spontaneous nature of the deed. In this way they correspond to Li's descriptions of his own writing: just as Li analogizes his process of literary composition to "vomiting forth" his feelings in a torrent of emotion that "cannot not be stopped," these narratives characterize him as responding to an almost insuppressible somatic urge. His decision not to shave his beard, outlined in the tomb inscription, seems almost equally arbitrary—the result, perhaps, of some ineffable sentimental attachment to his whiskers. Moreover, the remarks this document attributes to Li seem flippant and unpersuasive, for they deny the gravity of the action he took and provide no compelling rationale for it.

Li's own writings offer a number of different motivations for his action, and in characteristically paradoxical fashion, few of his accounts corroborate one another. In an essay titled "Reflections on My Life" (Gankai pingsheng), written in 1596, Li refutes the claim that he shaved his head impulsively. Instead he avers, "The matter of shaving my head . . . was something I had contemplated for a long time before I actually went ahead with it."⁷⁹ Here he characterizes his action as a conscious, premeditated, and reasoned, although painful, decision and one against which the county magistrate of Macheng, Deng Yingqi, had cautioned him. "Alas!" Li sighs. "Writing about this [action] I am in tears."⁸⁰ The letter continues, "It was by no means easy for me to shave my head! I did it only for the reason that I could not bear submitting to the control of others. Shaving my head was by no means easy!"⁸¹ These statements testify to the fact that Li acted deliberately, not impulsively.

Throughout this essay, Li emphatically repeats the assertion that he consciously chose to shave his head. The reason, he states, was to liberate himself from the authority of other people. He lists in detail the purportedly onerous responsibilities scholars must shoulder, from displaying proper obedience to teachers to deferentially carrying out supervising officials' orders. Additionally, he outlines how many times during his official career of more than two decades he became involved in conflicts with his superiors. His statements betray a tone of weariness and evince a deep desire to be rid of these petty entanglements once and for all.⁸² Indeed, more than a decade earlier, in 1580, the very year he would have been due for a promotion, Li so ardently desired to quit his post as prefect of Yao'an that he implored his superiors for permission to resign. His comments in "Reflections on My Life" exhibit his exasperation with the culture of hierarchy and blind conformity he associated with the Confucian bureaucracy.

However, in a letter written in 1588 to his follower Zeng Jiquan, Li provides a rather different rationale for shaving his head. Never mentioning the burden of official obligations, he attributes his action to his aspiration to avoid familial responsibilities. He writes, "The reason I shaved my head was that various people of no importance from home were always expecting me to return home [to Fujian]; moreover, they were constantly visiting me from afar and urging me to attend to my lay responsibilities. So I shaved my head to demonstrate that I would not return and that I certainly would pay no more heed to secular matters. Additionally, many people think of me as a heretic, so I decided to *become* a heretic in order that they not give me an empty name."⁸³ Because of the ironic tone with which this excerpt concludes, one wonders whether the statements made here can be taken seriously. Yet Li insists that it was to avoid fulfilling his familial duties—not to escape from professional obligations or to find a refuge from social hypocrisy—that he shaved his head. These practical considerations were not insignificant, for, as the most distinguished and accomplished member of his clan, Li would have been beset by requests and demands from relatives near and far.[84]

The concatenation of discordant motives and methods these writings display results in a double bluff. Not only did Li's physical self-presentation perplex and disorient those who saw him, but his verbal explanations of his behavior also confounded those who read about them. On one level, the nature of these paradoxical self-presentations, the one visual, the other verbal, may seem to differ. The visual contrast between Li's shiny bald head and his venerable beard and Confucian robes produced an immediate reaction of shock, whereas the discrepancies among his verbal justifications for presenting himself in this manner unfold gradually over time as readers encounter each successive explanation. Nonetheless, the incongruous aspects of his physical self-presentation parallel his contradictory verbal accounts. In each case the "truth" being manifested turns out to be greater than the sum of its parts. For it would be just as inaccurate to classify Li as a Buddhist practitioner on account of his shaved head, or as a Confucian scholar on account of his long beard and attire, as it would be to attribute primacy to any one of the reasons he mentions.

Just as his eccentric appearance manifested his simultaneous adherence to and rejection of elements of both Confucian and Buddhist thought, so too, it seems likely, did all of the various reasons he cites play some part in catalyzing his action. One could well imagine that Li wished to escape both from his familial responsibilities and from his professional obligations and that although he had been considering this decision for some time, he impulsively took action one swelteringly hot summer day in 1588. Thus simultaneously on varying levels, Li's texts exhibit the complex constellation of factors that motivated him to take action and the paradoxical appearance that resulted. As if to cap these various nested paradoxes, Li writes in a poem, "I shaved off my hair and became a monk," but elsewhere he counters, "Although I shaved my hair and became a monk, I am, in fact, a Confucian."[85] Together these statements encapsulate the complexity of Li's identity.

In a society in which sumptuary laws were growing increasingly difficult to enforce and social imposture was on the rise, the expectation that garments could or would reveal the identity of their wearers became ever more unrealistic. Yet the idealistic hope of restoring the intimate bond between inner identity and outer manifestation persisted. Li's stubborn insistence on cultivating an appearance that he deemed expressive of his conflicted allegiances exemplifies his conviction that garments must expose the identity of the wearer just as words must exhibit the speaker's genuine feelings.

The difficulty of differentiating among individuals based upon their often misleading external appearances resembled both the kinds of challenges that readers experience as they endeavor to make sense of Li Zhi's bluff-laden works and the sorts of challenges typical of life in the early modern world. These included identifying and negotiating among counterfeit and legitimate currencies, and discerning false from authentic book editions. In each of these cases, a system of representation is thrown into disarray. And just as the indistinctness of social categories raised concern and placed social actors on guard against deception, so too did the verbal, material, and ideological slipperiness of Li's texts provoke in certain readers a wary attitude toward what they read and a corresponding need to take on the weighty task of making judgments for themselves.

CHAPTER 4

Money and Li Zhi's Economies of Rhetoric

Anxieties over the blurring of social distinctions caused by increases in the number, variety, and significance of fashions paralleled contemporary financial concerns. Economically developing regions of China and Europe, linked by increasingly complex international maritime trade routes, were home to both a wide array of goods whose prices varied erratically and a great number of currencies, some of questionable legitimacy, whose value and even legal status also rose and fell unpredictably.[1] In China, sales were conducted in an astounding multitude of currencies, including barter, cowrie shells, copper coins, unminted silver, and even counterfeit coins. Thus commercial transactions often required that their participants negotiate among a wide array of monies, old, new, domestic, foreign, legitimate, and false, and that they stay alert to rapid alterations in price. Needless to say, these circumstances posed steep challenges and necessitated that individuals exercise caution and keen judgment.

Li Zhi's writings demonstrate his awareness of the precarious economic conditions under which he lived. Despite his somewhat insulated position working in the civil bureaucracy, our author, like many officials of the day, drew only a meager salary. According to one account, he experienced long years of severe poverty interrupted by temporary periods of plenty, but never accumulated any savings.[2] And in midlife he found himself so destitute that he was unable to prevent two of his children from dying of starvation.[3] He himself also went hungry on occasion.[4] Yet his writings seldom explicitly address the economic tribulations of the day. More often they do so obliquely, via analogy.

In this period, "the economic" was not considered a distinct sphere of activity; concepts such as value, predicated on trust and authenticity, permeated both everyday life and literature.[5] As Sandra K. Fischer has argued with respect to early modern Europe, all forms of social activity were understood to fall "under the aegis of economic exchange," and even verbal interactions carried an economic valence, as the value of words could be inflated or their meaning falsified.[6] The interpenetration of the economic, the verbal, and the social evident in Li's texts both resembles and diverges from the intersection of these domains in the writings of several of his European contemporaries. Like him, these writers struggled to make sense of the economic and numismatic uncertainties confronting them. Consequently, texts by Shakespeare, Donne, Cervantes, Rabelais, and Montaigne, among others, frequently refer to the inflation of language, the counterfeiting of virtue, and the cheapening of reputations.[7] These overtly economic metaphors highlight the ways in which questions about value came to color early modern perceptions of language and social relations.

The intermingling of these concepts seems appropriate, for money is more than just a medium of exchange; it is, as one scholar aptly puts it, an "emotionally charged object."[8] Money makes powerful truth-claims about the value of objects in the world, and for this reason price instability and disturbances to the monetary system such as sudden demonetizations and rampant counterfeiting, which were common occurrences in early modern China and Europe, may provoke unease or stimulate distrust in the very notion of communicating value accurately. Moreover, as a system of signs, money resonates analogically with other semiotic systems. Hence misgivings about the ability of money to convey value reliably may prompt further queries into the possibility that words or actions may adequately express intentions or ideas.[9] It is in these subtle extensions of the discourse on value that Li's economic thought is most clearly visible.

Unlike his European contemporaries, whose texts abound in explicitly economic metaphors, Li rarely employed blatantly economic terms. His writings' engagement with the current economic situation was far more indirect and is evident less in what his texts *say* than in what they *do*. By using words in unpredictable and unconventional ways, Li encourages his readers to regard his texts with the same discerning eye with which they might view money of unstable value or merchandise of uncertain worth. Thus even when Li addresses subjects far removed from "the economic" narrowly defined, his rhetoric nonetheless often prompts readers to reflect upon the shifting values and potential falsification not only of salable objects but also of words, identity, reputations, and social relationships. In this way Li's writings subtly approximate in language the challenges of appraising the values of currencies and commodities in the early modern world.

Mutability of value was a major theme in both Europe and China at the turn of the seventeenth century, but the trajectories along which these regions' financial systems were progressing differed greatly. Perhaps the most striking disparity lay in the trend to embrace or reject highly symbolic forms of money. The majority of European economies, which had previously relied on precious metals, were gradually beginning to adopt increasingly symbolic forms of currency such as fiat monies, promissory notes, and bills of exchange, whereas China had long since experimented with and rejected purely symbolic currency, paper bills. Paper currency had been introduced as early as the Yuan dynasty but was abandoned in the mid-Ming on account of spiraling inflation. By Li's lifetime, many Chinese viewed symbolic media of exchange with skepticism. Instead, the market trend, which government policy only partially endorsed, was to reduce dependence on symbolic currencies and, to the greatest extent possible, to determine value via weight. Thus copper coins often changed hands at values unrelated to the inscriptions they bore, and even lumps and ingots of unminted silver circulated freely. As the examples in this chapter attest, Li's opinions of the metaphorical economies of sincerity and virtue reflect the strong current of cultural mistrust toward symbolic representation evident in the late Ming. Further, they exhibit the author's nostalgic desire to reestablish reliable, durable standards of value that correspond to his views on the rectification of language.

But paradoxically—if unsurprisingly—Li's writings abound in acts of bluff, which themselves parallel the phenomena of fluctuations in monetary value and commodity prices, proliferation of media of exchange, and counterfeiting. The economic ideas nestled in Li's writings subtly manifest the repercussions of these disturbances on late Ming society. Li himself, like many of his contemporaries writing from Europe, was only dimly aware of the development of global networks of international trade and their effects upon the particular economic crises he experienced. Yet his texts evince some ways in which local economic conditions, which were enmeshed in much larger, intercontinental trade relations, affected both social relations and verbal self-expression.

PROLIFERATION OF CURRENCY, FLUCTUATION IN VALUE, AND LI ZHI'S RHETORIC

As early modern societies in China and Europe came to rely increasingly on commercial exchanges, money began to play a more significant role in their economies. And the sheer number and variety of currencies in use in early modern urban centers posed stark challenges for appraising value. By one estimate, Europe in 1600 was home to as many as four hundred different kinds of coins, which circulated so broadly that even an obscure Norman nobleman noted in his diary that he had learned to recognize nearly three dozen sorts of coins.[10] And the narrator of the early sixteenth-century German chapbook *Fortunatus* carefully reports to readers the value of the many currencies his protagonist handles.[11] Reports from contemporary China likewise document individuals using coins from a wide array of dynasties and reign periods alongside contemporary issues and unminted silver. As the editor of the Norman gentleman's diary remarks, "One can judge by this [variety] what familiarity and what care one had to take in handling so many types of money in order to count exactly and avoid errors detrimental to either the buyer or the seller."[12]

After 1567, when China lifted its ban on private international maritime trade, vast quantities of New World and Japanese silver started flowing into China, and this precious metal came to be regarded as the preferred store of value as well as the medium in which taxes were collected.[13] Silver played such an important role in the economy that the succeeding century came to be known as China's silver century. However, despite its ubiquity, silver was considered too valuable to be used for most everyday purchases. For this reason copper coin remained the medium of choice for small transactions. The weight, inscriptions, color, and metal content of Chinese copper coin varied tremendously. Coins were made from copper of varying quality, extracted from mines in diverse regions of China, and cast by artisans of varying skill levels. As a result, even coins of the same denomination and dating from the same period were not uniform. This was especially the case during the Wanli reign.[14] And due to the vagaries of the market, the value stamped upon these coins often provided only an unreliable indicator of the coin's exchange value. One Ming author describes having traveled to the capital as early as 1518, where he found that poor quality copper coins, known in local slang as "boards," were being exchanged at a rate of only half their face value.¹⁵ Reports from Europe also attest to alarmingly high rates of inflation.¹⁶

To make matters still more complicated, a large number of coins circulating in sixteenth-century China were not Ming issues at all. For nearly a century, from 1436 to 1503, the state closed all mines and halted the production of copper coin.¹⁷ This meant that contemporaries came to rely on coins from earlier periods, many of which had aged and thinned by passing through many hands. Gu Yanwu's (1613–1682) *Records of Daily Knowledge* (Rizhi lu) reports that as a child, the author frequently encountered coins from the Northern and Southern Song dynasty, and even a few Tang issues.¹⁸ These antique coins differed from one another in size, weight, and purity. And in the intervening centuries since their manufacture many had been clipped or shaved, diminishing their value. Distinguishing among these coins and attributing to each its proper value was surely no simple matter.

International trade further compounded the situation of numismatic complexity. As foreign coins, notably Spanish pieces of eight, entered China in increasingly large numbers, discrepancies arose between the face value of a coin and its exchange value.¹⁹ For instance, the value of a Spanish *real* in Fujian or Taiwan was determined on the basis of its weight in silver, not its legal tender value in far-off Europe.²⁰

Similarly across Europe, although governments endeavored to cope with an influx of foreign monies by imposing values on them by fiat, these values did not always reflect either the coins' metallic content or their legal value in their distant country of origin.²¹ As a result, such efforts to impose value often proved ineffectual: royal decrees were disregarded, leaving vendors and licensed money changers free to appraise value according to market trends.²² As the relationship between the face value and exchange value of coins grew increasingly tenuous, the responsibility of assessing value moved further away from the jurisdiction of the law and came to rest more heavily on the shoulders of individuals. Weighing and assaying money became an unremarkable part of everyday life, as attested by European paintings of the period (Figure 4.01).²³ Such scenes were even more widespread in China; for instance, a Jesuit traveling in Macao and in the bustling international port city of Quanzhou, where Li Zhi spent his formative years, exclaimed in wonder that even Chinese children excelled at appraising the quality and purity of silver.²⁴ Unsurprisingly, weighing and assaying silver likewise feature prominently in contemporary Chinese fiction and drama.²⁵

Figure 4.01. Johannes Vermeer (Dutch, 1632–1675). *Woman Holding a Balance*, ca. 1664. Oil on canvas, 39.7 x 35.5 cm. Widener Collection (1942.9.97), National Gallery of Art. Photo credit: Art Resource.

The open conflict between two incompatible systems of interpretation—face value and metallic content—vying for the authority to determine the exchange value of coins highlighted the state's failure to guarantee the value of money. And the uncertainty of its value undermined the basic viability of the currency.[26] For, as the Han dynasty monetary theorist Guanzi recognized, a currency's ability to function effectively rests upon the confidence and respect it commands as a legally sanctioned instrument of exchange. Building on this idea, the late Ming monetary thinker Jin Xueyan (fl. 1570) punned cleverly on the words for "coin" and "power" and pronounced that "coin is synonymous with power" (*qian zhe quan ye*). He concluded that in order to retain control over the country, "rulers should wield power over [the country's] wealth."[27] This requires inspiring the people's trust in the value of money. If ever a government loses its ability to command this respect, the symbolic power of money—its capacity to represent value—is compromised, and confusion, ambiguity, and lawlessness ensue as individuals scramble to reassign value on an ad hoc basis. This was precisely the situation in late Ming China.

In response, the Ming state endeavored at many junctures to reassert its authority to regulate the value of coins. But laws restricting or prohibiting the use of certain types of coin were often unenforced and quickly repealed.[28] And Chinese monetary policy changed course so unpredictably throughout the sixteenth century that the chief grand secretary Gao Gong (1510–1578) was moved to comment, "The people [live in] fear that the coin they obtain today will be worthless tomorrow."[29] The mere rumor that a new monetary decree would be issued could incite market crises of panic buying or hoarding. One contemporary Chinese observer described the situation in these words:

> With each recoinage the financial assets of shops and money changers suddenly were rendered worthless. . . . [Merchants] usually held their tongues and liquidated their inventories. . . . But the petty shopkeepers and peddlers, having lost their stock of capital, expressed fear and doubt to each other. . . . Villainous rogues seized the opportunity to spread rumors; some warned that "baked lacquer" coins would be demonetized; others predicted that "gold reverse" coins would be demonetized; still others confidently asserted that Jiajing, Longqing, and Wanli issues would all circulate simultaneously. The people did not know whom to believe. Households that had stored up coin would sell their stock cheaply, recouping a mere 10 percent of the value of their holdings. A hundred coins containing a full twelve *liang* of copper would fetch a mere 0.03 tael of silver.[30]

Needless to say, such monetary instability spawned confusion and anxiety.

Compounding these concerns was the related issue of price instability, which afflicted both contemporary China and Europe. In Europe, massive influxes of New World silver throughout the second half of the sixteenth century led to dramatic price hikes that alarmed contemporaries and later came to be known as the Price Revolution.[31] In

China, several Qing dynasty authors recollected that unsteady prices had contributed to a general sense of unease in the late Ming. One such report from the early Qing states, "Price instability has existed from ancient times, but ... over the past thirty-several years the price of a single object has sometimes risen by ten or a hundred times. From dear to cheap and cheap to dear, prices have been erratic and unpredictable (zhanzhuan)."[32] Another author traced the origins of the prevailing economic concerns back even earlier: "[At] the end of the Zhengde and beginning of the Jiajing reigns ... prices fluctuated. Only the capable were able to succeed. Those who were a bit slow were ruined. The family on the east might become rich while the family on the west became impoverished. As the equilibrium between those of higher and lower status was lost, everyone struggled over paltry sums."[33]

Li Zhi personally experienced the effects of these tumultuous economic conditions. Comments scattered throughout his writings allude to price hikes and sudden fluctuations in the value of currency. In one missive he wrote, "When the situation gets to the breaking point, the price of a grain of rice, a single unit of silver, and even a respectful glance increases in value tenfold." "In times like these," he ruefully noted, "if one can pay one coin and truly receive one coin's worth of goods one will truly love and the 'father-and-mother' official [i.e., the district magistrate, who takes care of the populace as parents care for their children], and things will surely be different from the way they normally are [in such uncertain times]."[34] Elsewhere he reported that when his native Quanzhou fell prey to pirate raids in 1560, "no amount of money could purchase rice or corn."[35] In another text he poetically remarked, "The situation these days is like chess; it changes in the blink of an eye."[36]

It stands to reason that, buffeted by such uncertainties, Li would have supported policies conducive to economic stability. Although he refrains from addressing this topic directly, remarks culled from the preface to the chapter "Famous Ministers who Enriched the Country" of *A Book to Keep (Hidden)* support this inference. Here he praises two celebrated finance ministers of the past, Sang Hongyang (d. 80 BCE) and Wang Anshi (1021–1086), both well-known for instituting price regulation along with their ambitious programs of economic reform. Li explicitly commends the former for setting in place policies designed to promote the equitable distribution of grain and for controlling the price of this commodity so effectively that the people's needs were satisfied and government coffers filled.[37] He equally lauds another well-known figure from Chinese economic history, Liu Yan (716–780), who in Li's words "weighed the ten thousand goods and saw to it that nothing under heaven was excessively expensive or inexpensive, and that commodity [prices] remained stable."[38] By invoking figures like Liu, Wang, and Sang, Li signals his approval of a bygone system of fair pricing and stable monetary value.[39]

Li's sober financial outlook is consonant with many of his stated opinions on language. In both cases he opposes fluctuation in value or meaning and favors constancy. As discussed in chapter one, Li's writings express his consternation over the discovery that the meanings of words shift over time and his desire to restore and maintain their original significance. He was particularly disturbed to observe that by the late Ming, the word "friend," for instance, no longer connoted a cherished confidant but indicated merely a common acquaintance. To be sure, the process by which the meanings of this and other words became diluted (or polluted or eroded) differed from that which caused the value of money or goods to fluctuate. Nonetheless, the phenomenon of a word seeming to mean less and less over time or carrying vastly different connotations in different contexts may be said to resemble the situation of objects selling for discrepant prices or even, arguably, coins moving in and out of the legal economy or being exchanged for different values. The commonality lies in the strain that all these situations place on acts of interpretation. Under such circumstances, participants in verbal and financial transactions alike must be alert to the variable value or meaning of the tokens being exchanged—coins, objects, or words. Failure to recognize that in late Ming common parlance the word "friend" no longer necessarily connoted an intimate companion could result in as disastrous a misunderstanding as the inability to discern that a coin that had once been legal tender had subsequently lost value or even been demonetized.

The verbal economy of Li Zhi's texts frequently demands that readers exercise precisely this sort of discrimination, in other words, that they choose among conflicting interpretations of a single word or phrase. Even when he does not employ explicitly economic diction, Li's revaluation of words resonates with the monetary instabilities of the day. A letter he composed to his close friend Liu Dongxing exemplifies this phenomenon: "The problem with worthies is that they love reputation. If you don't use reputation to seduce them, they'll never listen to what you say."[40] The meaning of this short passage hinges on the ironic and highly idiosyncratic use of the word "worthies" (*xianzhe*). As any reader with common sense would concur, *true* worthies would not need to be "seduced" by means of reputation. Thus the word "worthies" cannot be interpreted literally here. Rather, in this context, Li uses the term to refer to the antithesis of true worthies, people who deceptively present themselves as men of virtue and are widely (though erroneously) heralded as such by those too ignorant to be able to tell the difference. Li's crafty manipulation of language leads to a discrepancy between readers' expectations of what the word "worthies" is *likely* to mean—that is, what they feel it *ought* to mean—and what it *actually* means in this particular context. The notion that the meaning of words is flexible and must be reinterpreted in varying contexts mirrors the understanding that even familiar types of coin may have discrepant values in individual transactions or that the price of everyday items may unpredictably change. In this way, the passage illustrates the malleability of the significance of words, which parallels the shifting value of coins and the context-dependent price of commodities. These situations all stimulate readers of various kinds to exercise their powers of discernment.[41]

Li's bluff-laden writings further reflect the unreliable economic conditions by presenting their author in a variety of guises. His use of rhetoric reinforces the notion that the economic uncertainties of the day not only affected practical, financial exchanges but also influenced language use and the construction of identity. By opting to present himself and his views alternately as orthodox and heretical, Li demonstrates the mutability of his own persona and encourages readers to adopt different attitudes toward him in different moments. This vacillation between legitimating and censuring his own views tacitly parallels the movement of coins in and out of the legal economy. For, just as fluctuations in the legality of a coin made users continually reassess the value of money, so too does Li's protean and paradoxical dramatization of his ideas—as alternately legitimate and unlicensed, important and insignificant—compel readers to assess and reassess them. The internal inconsistencies in his writings invite readers at times to reject the very ideas they had formerly accepted, and conversely to accept ideas they had once rejected.

In a letter to his friend Jiao Hong, Li explicitly thematizes the fluctuation of his own identity. Referring to himself by one of his many monikers, Zhuowu, Li writes, "The person you have seen is merely the former Zhuowu; you do not know that the Zhuowu of today is entirely different. The person you're fond of is the Zhuowu of days past. You do not realize that the former Zhuowu was very flimsy and weak. If you felt glad for the Zhuowu of the past, then you will definitely pity the Zhuowu of today. For if the Zhuowu of the past was like that, how did it come about that the Zhuowu of today turned out like this?"[42] In this passage Li evinces genuine wonder at the changes that time has wrought upon his own identity. His inability to fathom the forces motivating these changes echoes contemporaries' bewilderment at the erratic changes to monetary policy and the concomitant fluctuations in the value of money. And just as demonetizations stirred rumors and engendered disquiet and even panic, so too did Li's unconventional behavior and variable literary self-presentations give rise, as we have seen, to scandal and unrest among those who knew of him.

Nonetheless, the analogy of Li's chameleon-like identity to the shifting values of money and goods must not be overstated. While participants in the economy stood to lose their fortune through the frequent demonetizations of coins, surely no reader's livelihood hinged on the reliability of Li's authorial self-presentation. Additionally, unlike coins or commodities, which, being mere objects, lack the agency to enhance or reduce *their own* value, our author exerted creative control over his self-presentation and literary works. As we have seen, he deliberately chose to cast himself alternately as rebellious dissident and staid Confucian scholar. Despite these factors, his multifaceted self-presentations challenged readers' interpretive abilities in ways that echo the difficulties of assessing more concrete forms of value in the late Ming.

Yet Li insisted at every turn that these multifarious self-presentations all constituted accurate expressions of his ever-changing self. He passionately averred, "Although I shaved my hair and *became* a monk, I truly *am* a Confucian."[43] The copulas in each half of the sentence attest to Li's sincerity. They imply that in the moment of writing he embraced the identity of a Confucian as fully as he had previously espoused that of a monk. Neither identity was feigned or counterfeited. His ideological position had undergone a genuine change.[44]

MONETARY AND METAPHORICAL COUNTERFEITING

This insistence on authenticity was especially important, since as early as the Yongle reign (1402–1424) counterfeiting had become a major, inescapable part of the Ming monetary landscape. Although the severity of the problem waxed and waned in subsequent reign periods, the practice persisted beyond the dynastic collapse. This scourge likewise troubled the economies of western Europe and became so widespread that, according to one scholar, it affected contemporaries on a daily basis.[45] In France, as early as the reign of François I, complaints were heard that the unsanctioned alloying of coins was degrading the quality of money in circulation. One mid-sixteenth-century source, for instance, condemned the fact that "many people indiscriminately take and alloy coins of gold and silver, both French coins and foreign ones."[46] And in England the high number of laws prohibiting counterfeiting in the early seventeenth century testifies to the prevalence of this activity and the government's inability to curb it.[47]

Counterfeiting likewise flourished in China throughout Li's lifetime. Not only did individuals mix base metals into the unminted silver taels that circulated as money, but, because the Ming government did not manufacture adequate supplies of copper coin or ensure consistent standards of quality, many even cast their own "private" coins.[48] According to contemporary reports, "in cities, people indulged in such roguery to their hearts' content."[49] Unsurprisingly, a discourse grew up mocking and condemning the widespread practice of counterfeiting, and this discourse gradually made its way analogically into literature of the period.[50]

The Chinese government attempted sporadically to curb the widespread use of "private monies." Starting early in the dynasty, dire warnings were published advertising penalties for different types of counterfeiting. Punishments ranged from costly fines and beatings to death by strangulation or beheading.[51] But the government's message was not systematically enforced. In fact, the Jiajing emperor, acknowledging the ubiquity of counterfeiting and his impotence to rectify the situation, took extraordinary measures: he legalized the use of counterfeit coins and published tables establishing official exchange rates among them.[52] This policy, however, lasted only several years before it was revoked and the use of counterfeit money was once again outlawed. Throughout the mid- and late Ming, the national copper mines were shut down and reopened several times, sometimes after a lengthy hiatus. Following each closure, the mints would lay off artisans skilled at producing coins, and many of these individuals would ply their trade on the black market. Similarly, when the mints eventually reopened, the state often resorted to employing notorious former counterfeiters since they possessed the requisite skills.[53] With legitimate coins and counterfeits made by the same pairs of hands, distinguishing between them posed daunting challenges.

Li's writings implicitly address the problem of counterfeiting through their scathing critiques of hypocrisy and social imposture. Li cites numerous examples of mere acquaintances who pose as true friends and ignoramuses who masquerade as scholars and teachers.[54] In each of these situations, one thing is passed off for another. And what rankles Li most are the cases in which the perpetrators, like counterfeiters of money, deliberately scheme to defraud the unsuspecting and to enrich themselves at the expense of gullible people. In illustration of this point, Li recalls the opportunism of "people who pass for friends today." They cozy up to powerful and influential people and shamelessly exploit their inferiors. If they see a person in difficulty, they "stretch out their arms to snatch away his food, and rain stones upon him to plug up his mouth."[55] Once they have achieved their objective, however, they lose all interest in these relationships: "As soon as a teacher loses his position as an official, his students abandon him, and as soon as he has no wealth, his students scatter."[56] With a tacit nod to Mencius, who famously scolded King Hui of Liang for elevating "profit" (*li*) over "righteousness" (*yi*), Li chides the false friends of his generation for likewise placing excessive emphasis on gain.[57]

Perhaps the most stunning example of such deceitful, self-serving relationships appears in an anecdote Li tells about a poet, calligrapher, and painter he calls simply Student Huang.[58] Throughout the narrative, Li characterizes Huang as a devious fellow who epitomizes the hypocrisy of contemporary Confucians. Having met Li on several occasions in the past, Huang appeared unannounced at his doorstep one day, claiming to be accompanying an illustrious gentleman on a pilgrimage to the mountains. Li soon discovered, however, that Student Huang's visit was no coincidence; it was part of an elaborate ruse designed to extract a sizable gift of money from Prefect Lin Yuncheng of Runing, a town near Macheng. Knowing that Student Huang had already visited Prefect Lin three times and each time wheedled out of him a generous monetary gift, Li deduces that Student Huang intended to call on Lin once again. Huang's visit to Li was nothing more than a pretext so that, when Huang later arrived at Lin's home, he could convey to Lin greetings from the famous Li Zhi. Thus by using Li's name as an entrée, Student Huang hoped to insinuate himself into the prefect's good graces. This at least is how Li construes the situation. With disgust, he comments, "Prefect Lin and I both nearly fell prey to [Huang's] tricks without knowing it. How clever! [What passes for] the Study of the Way is no different from this!"

Following the discussion of Student Huang's sly ruse, the letter proceeds to deride as ethically corrupt both self-proclaimed recluses and worthies. Couching his condemnation in economically tinged language, Li declares:

> [Today's Confucian scholars who] fluctuate back and forth (*zhan-zhuan*) [between calling themselves recluses and worthies] use cheating people to obtain profit. [Student Huang and his ilk] call themselves "recluses," but their hearts are identical to those of merchants. In their mouths they speak of "virtue," but their aspiration is stealing. Now to call oneself a "recluse" but to have the heart of a merchant is itself disgraceful. But for him to conceal the fact that he was trying to sponge off of [Prefect Lin], and to say instead that he was going [on a pilgrimage] to Mt. Song and Mt. Shao, to say that people can be taken in and tricked, this is particularly despicable.[59]

In this passage, Li does not condemn Student Huang for seeking an emolument. In hard times, Li himself was not too proud to request financial assistance from friends and patrons.[60] He did so on numerous occasions, and this practice was not at all uncommon for unemployed or itinerant scholars. Rather, what angered Li was Huang's deceit—his mendacious attempt to counterfeit his identity and pass himself off as a humble recluse when in fact he wanted money.

At stake are the connotations of the term *shanren*, translated here as "recluse." The term literally means "mountain man," and it connotes an ethical discourse with deep roots in the Confucian tradition. Confucius advised, "When the Way does not prevail, go into reclusion."[61] Taking this advice seriously, generations of scholars, exasperated with the political intrigues of their day, fled to the hills in an effort to preserve their integrity. Chinese history is replete with examples of such righteous "mountain men" who sought to escape the polluting influences of society by taking refuge in remote mountain sanctuaries. Indeed, Li's decision to resign his official post and retreat first to the Vimalakīrti Monastery and later to the Cloister of the Flourishing Buddha is reminiscent of such a stance, especially since the image of the righteous recluse or mountain man, an individual of lofty ethics and untainted ideals, gained widespread currency in the late Ming, an era in which eunuchs dominated court politics and corruption flourished unchecked.⁶² Ironically, this period also witnessed the phenomenon of false mountain men, hypocrites who, like Student Huang, pretended to lead the lives of recluses but actually engaged in worldly affairs.⁶³

As Li's letter reveals, Student Huang embodied this contradiction: his verbal claim to instantiate moral purity resembled the shiny, misleading surface of a counterfeit coin or the deceptive garments of the "pretentious gentleman" mentioned in the previous chapter: it masked a base interior. And this deliberately crafted discrepancy between outer representation and inner substance incited Li's rage. In the letter he curses Student Huang, calling him "a hungry dog scheming about the day-old shit [he plans to eat]."⁶⁴

Moreover, in his wrath Li overgeneralizes; extrapolating wildly from Student Huang's example, he hyperbolically condemns as hypocrites *all* people who talk of virtue. He writes, "The people these days who discuss virtue and nature-and-life *all* 'travel to Mt. Song and Mt. Shao.'"⁶⁵ This blanket accusation illustrates Li's perception that Student Huang's ruse is no isolated example; it is indicative of deceptions pervasive throughout late Ming society. In other essays, Li also opines that men "of real talent and intelligence are truly few," whereas a great number of "today's scholars . . . frantically scheme about securing profit and avoiding harm. They have departed from reality and cut themselves off from the root."⁶⁶ His belief that his entire society is riddled with duplicity provokes Li to fits. In another letter he exclaims, "Every time I see people planning to cheat heaven and entrap people I want to grab a blade and chop off their heads!"⁶⁷ These violent fantasies of retribution for social imposture echo government warnings that monetary counterfeiting will be punished by beheading. And in his fantasy, Li endows himself with the authority to arbitrate between falsity and authenticity.

The emotional intensity of Li's response to Student Huang's deception and the alacrity with which he generalizes from one instance of duplicity and condemns all "men who talk of virtue" may strike readers as extreme or even paranoid. But these reactions begin to make sense if we regard them as psychological symptoms associated with living in a culture of widespread counterfeiting and hypocrisy. Richard Doty explains that often "when any one [coin] is proven false, every other one will be suspect."⁶⁸ In other words, the bond of trust on which the monetary system rests, once broken, is not easily restored. A similar logic governs human relations, grounded in trust (*xin*) and expressed in words. So, just as counterfeit coins attack our deeply ingrained assumptions about monetary value, Student Huang's social imposture stirs up unsettling questions about the reliability of verbal communication and even, perhaps, identity. It prompts readers to question how much credence we can or should put in an individual's ability to represent himself in words.

In an essay titled "On Loftiness and Cleanliness" (Gao jie shuo) Li describes his personal experience of having been deceived repeatedly by people who represented themselves in misleading words. "Time and again," he writes, I exerted myself to the utmost in serving ... 'men of intelligence and talent' with sincere respect, but in the end they did not reciprocate my sincerity." He tells how, in exasperation, he simply removed himself from circulation: "I had no other choice but to separate myself from them. Since they were not only insincere but also treacherous, I had no choice other than to keep my distance. . . . In the end I was unable to maintain relations with anyone."[69] According to this narrative, Li was driven into reclusion because his interactions with other people had become intolerable. Naïvely taking at face value his interlocutors' claim to be "men of intelligence and talent," Li responded by lavishing sincerity upon them. But again and again these phonies defrauded him, for they offered in exchange only superficial semblances—counterfeits—of respect.

Thus metaphorically Li's decision to remove himself from social intercourse corresponds to what economists refer to as Gresham's law, namely that "bad money drives good money out." This economic principle states that where alloyed, damaged, or counterfeit coins abound, this low-quality currency will become the preferred medium of exchange and full-bodied coins will go out of circulation; they will be hoarded for their enduring value. By analogy, then, Li's retreat to the monastery in Macheng can be interpreted as a kind of self-hoarding, an assertion of his ethical superiority and a rejection of anyone who would counterfeit virtue.

However, as the English etymology of the word "currency" indicates—from the Latin *currere*, "to run"—currency must *circulate*. And human beings too must engage in social interaction. Li recognized the disadvantages of remaining forever holed up in his monastic retreat. Despite the solace he took in Buddhist reclusion, his writings document his yearning to return to social circulation, a need so strong it seemed at times to prompt him to reconsider the motivations that had driven him into reclusion in the first place. He writes:

> Although I keep the door closed all day, I have the unceasing desire to meet someone whose virtue surpasses my own. For a full year I have sat alone, and for a full year I have endured the sorrow of not meeting anyone who could deeply understand me.... Hearing footsteps in a deserted valley or even seeing a face that looks as if it might belong to a countryman brings delight.[70] Yet [people who misunderstand me] say that I do not wish to see anyone. How could this be? I just regret that so far no one resembling a human being has stopped by. Even if a shadow slightly resembling that of a human being paid a call, I would immediately do obeisance, giving no heed to whether the person was of lowly status. I would run toward him, giving no heed to whether the person was of noble status. In every case, I would perceive his strengths and overlook his shortcomings. Not only would I overlook his shortcomings, but I would also, with the utmost respect, serve him as my teacher. How much the more so, given that I am "biased" in favor of such people![71]

In this passage Li expresses several discrepant views; he begins by evincing the desire to meet someone whose virtue exceeds his own. Yet, as he continues, he presents himself as increasingly desperate. By the end, he seems ready to forgive the duplicity he so violently condemned and to settle for the company of "shadows" that only "slightly resemble . . . human beings." While extreme loneliness may have driven Li to express such sentiments, I would venture that the criteria on which he chose his interlocutors did not in fact waver much. It is telling that the concessions Li considers making with regard to the kind of companions with whom he would interact pertain to "status" and "noble rank," *external* factors that have no necessary bearing on an individual's sincerity of heart. In fact, Li continued to place a premium on genuineness of spirit. This inclination to value authenticity is affirmed in another essay, in which Li repeats that his friends and associates must all "appreciate virtue."[72] It seems, then, that his standards remained more or less constant: he sought acquaintances on the basis of their genuine ethical fiber and was willing to overlook their social position, status, or outward appearance.

He did, however, lament the fact that his contemporaries often misunderstood his values and construed his behavior as "biased and unfair."[73] He relates that they accused him of inhospitably turning guests away from his door or "failing to receive them with courtesy."[74] He also reports that one friend ignorantly inquired, "You are fond of friends, but these past two years I haven't noticed that you've had associations with anyone. Why is that?"[75] These anecdotes demonstrate the extent to which Li felt that the majority of his educated peers failed to comprehend his motivations or to acknowledge the gap between his own authentic sentiments and other people's phoniness.

Indeed Li's writings often excoriate his contemporaries for what Li identifies as their failures of discernment. On the economic plane, their inability to discriminate between sincerity and superficiality echoes the difficulty many sixteenth-century Chinese and Europeans experienced distinguishing between legitimate coins and counterfeits. The analogy I have been proposing places Li in the position of the valuable, full-bodied coin and explains his reluctance to interact with inferior people as unwillingness to degrade his own value. This analogy finds support in a comparison Li draws between social and economic exchanges. In his essay "On Five Types of Death" (Wu si pian), Li commends men who sacrifice their lives for the sake of a soulmate who fully appreciates their value. This valiant act Li describes as doing "big business" (*da maimai*). In the same breath, he denigrates men who give up their lives for false friends who fail to recognize their worth. This foolish act he characterizes as making a "petty sale" (*xiao maimai*).[76] His point is that only those who die for a true friend "sell" their lives for an appropriate price. Yet too many of his contemporaries, Li implies, lack the perspicacity to tell the difference.

The comparison of friendship to a financial exchange helps to explain the indignant reaction many of Li's actions provoked among contemporaries. For, just as a person who lacks the discrimination to distinguish between legitimate currency and counterfeit might cry foul when a counterfeit coin is rejected in a transaction, Li's contemporaries bridled at his refusal to interact with men of feigned or superficial virtue. Unable to differentiate between genuine sagacity and its counterfeit, these ignorant men accused Li of being excessively finicky in his choice of companions and interlocutors.

Li was deeply troubled by what he construed as his contemporaries' inability to understand him, their failure to distinguish between genuine articles and fakes—real virtue and its mere semblance. Nonetheless, one can easily imagine that Li's peculiar and erratic behavior may truly have baffled many of his contemporaries. The unpredictability of his behavior and the uncertainty it generated may even be compared to the haphazard monetary policy pursued by the Ming government. By alternating between legitimating and outlawing counterfeit coins, the government created a situation in which discriminating between authentic and false coins was extremely difficult. Similarly, the multiplicity of positions among which Li's prose frequently shuttles provided opportunities for readers of these texts to practice the skill of discernment.

The widespread practice of counterfeiting in the late Ming affected more than the monetary economy alone; it resonated with and perhaps even amplified wide-ranging cultural reflections on the reliability of representations of all sorts—especially verbal representations. And it provided fertile ground for musings on the difficulty of discerning between genuine articles and fakes. Traces of these discourses may be found in writings on subjects far removed from money per se. Li's remarks on the debasement of virtue, the perversion of language, and the prevalence of social posturing provide telling examples; his condemnations of phoniness and praise of authenticity, as well as his sophisticated use of rhetoric, obliquely mirror and comment upon the unstable economic conditions of the late Ming. Most interestingly, the literary nature of his text permits Li the freedom to approach this subject from incongruous, even contradictory perspectives. Thus whereas Li speaks out strongly against the counterfeiting of identity, he nonetheless at times perpetuates duplicity through his rhetoric. By simultaneously condemning counterfeiting and perpetrating a sort of deception on his readers, Li's text exemplifies the magnitude, complexity, and widespread repercussions of this problem.

CHAPTER 5

Dubious Books and Definitive Editions

The volume and diversity of sixteenth-century book editions, both legitimate and forged, called upon individuals to exercise powers of discrimination analogous to those required for judging the value and authenticity of money and spoken words. In urban centers across late sixteenth-century China and Europe, literacy and print culture were on the rise.[1] As early as 1522, one Ming scholar commented that "books [have become] as numerous as the sea is vast."[2] And four years later, Erasmus wondered whether there was "anywhere on earth exempt from these swarms of new books."[3] For his part, the Spanish skeptic Francisco Sanchez (ca. 1550–ca. 1623) estimated that "ten million years would not suffice to read all the books there were."[4] A comical image from 1511 illustrates the situation. Visually comparing the manufacture of books to the baking of bread, the German artist Albrecht Dürer suggested that by the early sixteenth century, printed books had become as widely available as loaves of bread—a staple of early modern intellectual life (Figure 5.01). The technologies of book printing, as well as the means for ensuring the literal accuracy of texts—to say nothing of the doctrinal purity of their contents—differed in China and Europe. Matters of ideological orthodoxy and deviancy and their effects upon readers will be discussed in the following chapter; this chapter focuses on book editions as material objects that may be printed with or without the consent of the author, pirated, forged, augmented, expurgated, or misattributed. More specifically, I examine questions that arose as readers, editors, and book collectors attempted to sift through the jumble of contending book editions and differentiate between reliable and spurious texts.

As Ming dynasty printers and book sellers knew well, the trenchant style and scandalous opinions associated with Li Zhi meant that any work bearing his name would surely attract a buyer. Eager to cash in on his reputation, they freely borrowed his name and appended it to works by other authors, hoping thereby to increase sales. The deliberate misattribution of books and commentaries to Li Zhi began during our author's lifetime and grew more flagrant after his death.[5] While forgery and piracy of Li's works were particularly widespread, due in large part to his national notoriety, these phenomena were scarcely unique; in both Europe and China, a great many early modern authors' books appeared in editions both legitimate and unsanctioned.

What is striking is that the material falsification of books in this period—an era in which the very notion of intellectual property rights was in its infancy in both China and the West—mirrored the themes of counterfeited identity characteristic of many early modern texts. As we have seen, Li's writings repeatedly denounce the discrepancies between surface appearances and underlying realities and exhort readers to beware of hypocrisy and lurking deception. Yet when Li discussed his own practice of reading, to which he dedicated his retirement, he rarely if ever voiced concern that the book editions to which he had access may have been faulty. Neither did he decry the unauthorized printing of his own works. Indeed it is uncertain whether he was even aware that the books he had authored were appearing in spurious editions. His genuine writings and personal opinions therefore play a secondary role in this chapter; my primary concern is the question of authenticity that vexed readers and collectors struggling to differentiate between reliable and fraudulent editions. When hack writers and unscrupulous printers meddled with Li's texts by adding to them, subtracting from them, imitating Li's style, or printing works under his name without his permission, they created a situation in which, ironically, books that deplored deception may themselves have been fakes. And books that extolled the virtues of clear judgment required readers to exercise their own judgment to determine whether these very editions were accurate or inauthentic.

The growing role of books and printing in everyday life in China and Europe in this period is well documented, as are the frequent abuses of this medium of textual transmission. In both regions,

Dubious Books and Definitive Editions

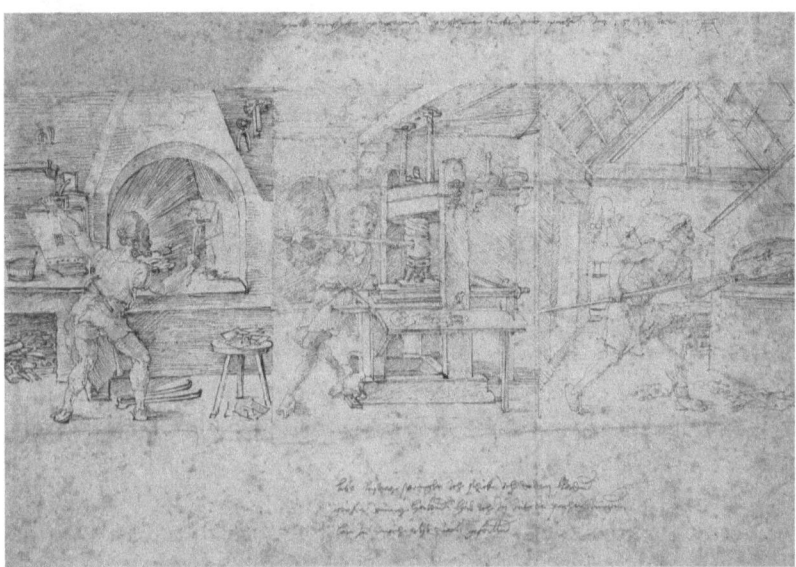

Figure 5.01. Albrecht Dürer (German, 1471–1528). Satirical subject; study of three laborers. 1551. Pen and ink drawing, 20.4 x 29.8 cm. NI 1288; AI1517. Art Resource. Photo credit: René-Gabriel Ojéda.

ineffective checks on authors' control over the dissemination of their works generated unease among authors and readers alike. And contemporary scholars and book collectors registered their suspicion that they or others might lack the ability to identify incomplete, forged, or misleading volumes. The prefaces to Li's posthumously published *Another Book to Burn* attempt to quell such concerns. As personal friends and disciples of the author, the preface writers sought to overcome readers' anxieties by discrediting earlier, illegitimate editions and elevating their own edition as the single, true, authentic one. I analyze the rhetorical bids for authenticity made in these several prefaces and compare them to techniques used by Montaigne's female disciple, Marie le Jars de Gournay (1565–1645), in her posthumous prefaces to the French author's *Essays*, published in 1595, 1598, 1600, 1602, 1604, 1617, 1625, and 1635.[6] These case studies exemplify Chinese and European editors' efforts to establish the credibility of their own editions and to allay readers' fears about the mutability of texts.

PROLIFERATION OF EDITIONS AND FAULTY, UNRELIABLE BOOKS

By the turn of the seventeenth century, more than ever before in either China or Europe, books had become an indispensable part of everyday life. Sold at increasingly affordable rates, especially in China, books were small and portable, and they addressed every subject imaginable.[7] There were merchants' manuals, travel guidebooks, materia medica, almanacs, encyclopedias, poetry and essay anthologies, collections of epistolary correspondence and adages, political pamphlets, religious tracts, songbooks, erotic albums, narratives of voyages to exotic lands complete with accounts of foreign costumes and customs, morality books, study guides, handbooks on refined taste, editions of classical literature, Bibles, and, of course, books on how to distinguish genuine books from fakes!

While the majority of the population in China and Europe remained illiterate during this period, the number of readers increased substantially, especially in China.[8] As early as the fifteenth century, the Chinese literatus Ye Sheng (1420–1474) averred that in his day the consumers of books included farmers, workers, merchants, peddlers, and women.[9] In 1488, a Korean visitor to China remarked that south of the Yangzi River even "village children, ferrymen, and sailors" could read.[10] While these descriptions are likely exaggerated, by the end of the sixteenth century in China, semiliterate commoners, so-called "ignorant men and women" (*yu fu yu fu*), constituted an emerging class of readers for genres such as vernacular fiction and encyclopedias for everyday use.[11] Reading publics in Europe were also on the rise, albeit more slowly, as literacy gradually spread beyond the ranks of scholars and clerics, to include jurists, doctors, and a growing number of shopkeepers. In 1516 Erasmus already imagined a society in which "even the lowliest women [could] read the Gospels and the Pauline Epistles . . . [and] as a result, the farmer [could] sing some portion of them at the plow, the weaver hum some parts of them to the movement of his shuttle."[12]

As scholars have shown, the quantity of volumes produced, the speed at which books were manufactured, and the numbers of individuals engaged in making them all rose significantly in this period. These developments led to similar problems of quality control, even though the structures of the book printing and selling industries differed in China and Europe. Because European movable type technology required a considerable initial outlay of capital, printing in Europe was concentrated in urban centers. By 1470 nineteen European cities had invested in printing presses, and by 1500 this number had grown to 255.[13] According to one estimate, the business of printing in Europe expanded sevenfold over the course of the sixteenth century, and during this span Venice, one of Europe's premier printing centers, was home to an estimated 453 individuals working as printers, publishers, booksellers, and bookbinders.[14] To maximize efficiency, teams of workers simultaneously set type, proofread, and operated the printing presses. This piecemeal production style often generated editions marred by copious errors.[15]

In China, the relatively low cost and minimal equipment required for woodblock printing allowed printing to take place throughout the empire. Although in the late Ming the large-scale commercial printing industry was concentrated in Li Zhi's native Fujian province, craftsmen could be employed wherever was convenient—in urban workshops such as those of Hangzhou and Suzhou, in government offices, even in private residences.[16] These artisans carved entire texts onto wooden blocks that could be printed and reprinted at will. The economic incentives for commercial publishers to print books swiftly were arguably even more intense in China than in Europe, although economic pressures afflicted European publishing too. Fujian printers were notorious for hiring careless craftsmen who valued the volume of their output over accuracy.[17] Using cheap ink that smudged or bled through gossamer-thin sheets of paper, these workers produced volumes littered with typos, misprints, and indecipherable passages, which Li's contemporaries deplored.[18] Xie Zhaozhe (1567–1624), for instance, griped that printers from the urban printing center of Jianyang in Fujian "produced the greatest number of books, but used the lowest quality wood blocks and paper."[19] And the playwright Shen Zijin (1583–1665) railed against "absurd printer's typos" like accidentally replacing the character 亥 (hai) with 豕 (shi).[20] In subsequent centuries, Qing scholars judged the shoddy craftsmanship of Ming volumes even more harshly, claiming, "When people of the Ming dynasty produced a book, they killed it."[21] These remarks all find corollaries in statements by European contemporaries, including

Jean Bouchet (1476–ca. 1558), Clément Marot (1496–1554), Robert Burton (1577–1640), and Pierre de Ronsard (1524–1585), the last of whom protested that the number of typos in contemporary editions was so high that even "the many eyes of Argos would not see clearly enough" to detect them all.[22]

The confusion generated by errors and misprints was compounded by the fact that the same texts could often be found in discrepant versions. Whether in China or Europe, few early modern authors viewed printing as the culmination of their literary labors; rather, they continued to revise their writings long after the initial publication. Perhaps inspired by the etymology of the word "author," derived from the Latin *augeo*, "I augment," countless European authors, including Erasmus, Bodin, Ronsard, Bacon, and Montaigne, continually added to their texts. Citing the fact that he was perpetually accruing new experiences, Montaigne swore to amend his essays "for as long as there [were] paper and ink in the world."[23] The covers and title pages of the resultant second and third editions typically celebrated the books' "updated," "improved," or "expanded" status. For example, the title page of the third (1625) edition of Bacon's *Essays* boasts that it is "newly enlarged."[24] And the title page of the 1588 edition of Montaigne's *Essays* reads, "Fifth edition, expanded by a third book and six hundred additions more than the first two."[25] The 1595 edition of the same work further proclaims its status as a "new edition, taken from the one found after the author's death, revised and expanded by a third more than the previous impressions."[26]

The decision to bring out these subsequent editions rested on more than the authors' accretionary practice of writing. Practical, financial factors also played a part. In most European countries, censorship laws required that prior to issuing any title, printing houses had to obtain official permission, generally in the form of a royal privilege bestowing exclusive printing rights upon a particular publisher for a delimited period of time. It is no accident, then, that second editions often appeared precisely when the first royal printing privilege was slated to expire. By collaborating with authors to publish revised editions, European printers sought to renew their printing privileges and thereby secure future profits.

In late Ming China the government did not exercise prepublication censorship, although it had attempted to do so in the Song dynasty and, by some accounts, even into the early Ming.[27] In 1009 the Song emperor Zhenzong issued an edict requiring private individuals to submit their manuscripts to local officials prior to publication. However, these regulations were difficult to enforce, and by the late Ming censorship primarily occurred after a work was published, as in the case of Li Zhi's writings.[28] The Ming state did reserve for itself the authority to print certain types of material, including astronomical texts, natural histories, and calendars, and it established standard, orthodox editions of the Confucian classics. But these exclusive rights were not always respected, and even when they were, they affected only a minority of texts, leaving printers at liberty to print or reprint other works. Consequently multiple and inconsistent editions of essays, novels, epistolary anthologies, poetry, and drama flourished unchecked, and printers freely festooned the covers and title pages of updated editions with the phrases "revised," "re-carved," and "corrected." Like their European counterparts, early modern Chinese authors generally regarded printing as a provisional step in the process of a book's development. Li's peers thought nothing of publishing and republishing—or adding to—versions of their own and their friends' writings.[29]

While the extant evidence does not allow us to conclude decisively that Li Zhi augmented his works between the publication of successive editions, comments culled from his letters suggest that, like his peers, he was continually revising, editing, and supplementing his works. In one letter, written in 1588 to his friend Jiao Hong, who would later compose a preface for *Another Book to Burn*, Li confides, "*A Book to Burn* is already more than a hundred pages long. I do not know how much more I shall add to it."[30] Elsewhere he writes, "I'm seventy-five years old. I'll die any day now, but I still dwell among books; my brush is always moist, and my ink stone always wet."[31] More tellingly he declares, "My hand writes down whatever crosses my mind, and as I write, I publish; this process cannot be stopped."[32] Together these remarks imply that like many of his contemporaries in Europe, Li did not view publication as the culminating stage in a book's production but rather as a moment in the long and complex process of creating a text.[33]

Another factor contributing to the coexistence of contending editions of individual titles was that in an era before the notion of intellectual property had fully matured, it was not uncommon for Chinese printers to produce unauthorized editions of popular works. Having obtained a copy of a text, they could have a set of wood blocks carved, print copies, and profit from the proceeds, even if they had taken no part in the intellectual labor of authoring the text. In an effort to thwart such "promiscuous reprinting" and protect their products, certain printers added to the covers and front matter menacing phrases like "Book pirates will be prosecuted."[34] But these warnings were rarely enforced and ultimately served little more than a rhetorical function. As a statement by Li's patron Ma Jinglun (1562–1605) attests, a large number of editions of Li's works were printed under such shady circumstances:

> The books that circulate as Li Zhi's in the world today, such as the Shaanxi edition of *Nanxun lu*, the Changlu edition of *Longxi ji*, the Huizhou edition of *Sanjiao pin*, the Jining edition of *Daoxue chao*, the Yongping edition of *Dao gu lu*, and the Shanxi edition of *Ming deng lu*, are all works by people who did not know the gentleman; they simply enjoyed reading his books and took delight in printing them. The gentleman had no knowledge of this. What's more, booksellers, greedy for profit, saw that by printing his books they could make a killing. So whenever they could get their hands on one of the gentleman's manuscripts, there was nothing they would not bring out in print.[35]

Unsurprisingly, the textual accuracy of these pirated editions was dubious. Yet remarkably certain authors not only tolerated but even championed the production of such works. The seventeenth-century Chinese publisher Zhang Chao (1650–ca. 1711), for instance, claimed that many authors were so delighted to have their works reprinted that they didn't care who printed them.[36] In Europe, Erasmus, whose books were also notoriously pirated, is known to have turned a blind eye toward the unsanctioned reproduction of his writings. His actions suggest that no matter how many errors these illegitimate editions contained, he believed they would further the broad dissemination of his ideas.[37] Montaigne even proudly took credit for the five editions of the *Essays* that appeared during his lifetime, although only four of them were printed legally.[38] According to Ma Jinglun, Li Zhi remained ignorant of the unauthorized reproduction of his writings. Yet one wonders whether, had he been aware of these rogue editions, he would have self-righteously denounced their fraudulence or, like Montaigne, endorsed them. One can even imagine Li mischievously titling a volume *A Book to Pirate*.

If Li himself was ignorant of or unfazed by the widespread phenomenon of book piracy, others of his era were not. The illegitimate reproduction of books brought with it a host of complications, for woodblock printing and movable type each endowed printers with the ability to tamper with, alter, and expurgate texts for their own ends. And commercial printers on both continents, eager to boost revenue, took great liberties with the texts they produced: they removed, inserted, and rearranged passages at whim. Li's senior contemporary Lang Ying (1487– ca. 1566) was among the many who decried this practice: "Bookshops have only profit as their aim, and every time they chance on the good books printed in various provinces, should these books be expensive, the Fujian bookshops will immediately reprint them. The number of fascicles and the table of contents will be exactly the same, but the contents [of the books] will be greatly diminished without anyone knowing, thus one book can be sold for the price of half a book, and people fight to buy it."[39] According one of the prefaces to *Another Book to Burn*, studied below, Li's books were "counterfeited and muddled" in precisely this manner.[40] Li's friend Yuan Zhongdao (1570–1623) testified that editions of Li's works were also "regrettably augmented" by miscellaneous materials.[41]

The liberties Chinese publishers took with texts were in no way unusual. European printers routinely disregarded the royal privileges that, in theory, protected rival shops' exclusive printing rights. Instead printers would obtain books manufactured by their competitors, have the type reset, and run off editions or partial editions of their own. If they reduced the typeface or deleted portions of text, these volumes could sometimes be sold for a fraction of the book's original price.[42] Textual manipulations of this kind were widespread throughout seventeenth-century Europe and are recorded in the comments of the Englishman Richard Head (ca. 1637–ca. 1686): "If one Bookseller printed a book that sold, another would get it printed in a lesser Character, and so the book being less in bulk, although the same in matter, would sell it for a great deal less in price, and so undersel [sic] one another: and of late there hath been hardly a book but it is epitomized, and for the most part spoiled, only for a little gain: so that few books that are good, are now printed, only Collections and patches out of several books."[43] While infringements of this sort were exceedingly common in China as well as Europe and clearly affected Li's writings, the abuse most strongly associated with our author was forgery—that is, the production of new texts deliberately misattributed to Li Zhi. Knowing that books bearing Li's name could turn an enormous profit, printers habitually affixed his name to works blatantly written by other people in imitation Li's style. So frequently was Li's name co-opted for such commercial purposes that the phenomenon was well documented soon after Li's death. As his friend and admirer Yuan Zhongdao confirms, "Li Zhi's books have been sold under the names of other people and adulterated."[44] Concerns about the forgery of Li's texts also feature prominently in the prefaces to *Another Book to Burn*.

The works most commonly attributed spuriously to Li Zhi were fiction and drama commentaries. One modern scholar has identified at least eleven editions of fiction and drama that list Li's name as commentator, even though there is no strong evidence that he actually authored any of the remarks in these books.[45] In at least one case, two discrepant sets of commentaries sold under Li's name seem to undermine one another's authenticity: in 1614, Li Zhi's name was appended to a 120-chapter edition of the contemporary novel *Outlaws of the Marsh*, although it had already been listed four years earlier in association with the 100-chapter version of the same book. The substance of these two sets of comments was entirely different, which suggests that one or both texts was likely a fake.[46] These works and the uncertainty surrounding their authorship generated doubt about the authenticity of editions bearing Li Zhi's name.

Li was unquestionably among the late Ming authors whose works were most frequently forged. Yet it was common practice for Chinese book merchants to affix the names of best-selling authors to less alluring texts. Some near contemporaries whose works were also frequently forged for commercial purposes were Chen Jiru (1558–1639), Yuan Hongdao, Feng Menglong (1574–1646), and Zhong Xing (1574–1625).[47] The renowned editor and publisher Yu Xiangdou (fl. 1596) is known to have reprinted and sold the same historical treatise under the names of no fewer than three different well-known contemporary authors within a ten-year span. Perhaps he was trying to test empirically which "brand name" would sell the greatest number of copies.[48] The names and reputations of famous authors were also used to sell various other products. By one account, Chen Jiru's name appeared on a certain delicious kind of bean cake, and his portrait was found adorning the signs hanging from wine shops and teahouses with which he had scarcely any connection. Apparently the mere association with a well-known man of letters, no matter how tenuous or even invented the connection may have been, lent these establishments an air of refinement.[49]

Problems of mislabeling and misattribution pervaded the early modern world and affected all spheres of cultural activity. In China, paintings, calligraphy, antiques, and collectibles as well as ancient and modern books were all routinely forged, copied, and misattributed. The notorious book forger Feng Fang (1493–1566) used ancient-style characters to fabricate editions of canonical works such as the *Book of Changes,* the *Book of Documents,* the *Classic of Poetry,* and the *Spring and Autumn Annals,* which he then attempted to pass off as earlier, more authentic versions of the classics than the copies widely in circulation at the time. Feng's forgeries took their place alongside similar hoaxes by Yang Shen (1488–1559) and Wang Shizhen, who also produced editions of "lost, ancient" books.[50] Antique objects and both ancient and contemporary artwork were also often objects of forgery.[51] One biographer of the artist Chen Hongshou declared that his prints had been forged by thousands of hands.[52] Although this number is obviously inflated for dramatic effect, these accounts help to situate the counterfeiting and piracy of Li Zhi's works in their cultural context. These acts of falsification were not isolated phenomena; such illicit reproduction formed an inescapable part of the early modern cultural landscape.

ON BOOK COLLECTING AND THE PROBLEM OF FINDING RELIABLE EDITIONS

Did anyone care? Were contemporaries perturbed by the abundance of unreliable editions? Or were early modern readers content to consume whatever editions were close to hand, regardless of their accuracy? Art historian Craig Clunas, who has meticulously studied late Ming manuals of taste, avers that his sources rarely mention books as objects of connoisseurship, even though these texts devote considerable space to detailing the criteria by which to discriminate between genuine and false antique ink stones, incense burners, and other material objects.[53] Ming readers certainly displayed remarkably catholic taste in the subjects about which they chose to read, and a great many readers, including Li Zhi himself, were also unperturbed by the poor quality or inaccuracy of the book editions they may have consulted or owned. But despite this indifference on the part of some, certain discriminating book collectors did take care to distinguish rigorously among credible and questionable editions of books. Moreover, regardless of readers' actual behavior, authors and editors strove to promote readers' awareness of the discrepancies among editions and to establish their own editions as unassailably authoritative.

The late Ming dynasty saw a spike in the numbers of individuals involved in collecting books as well as in the size of the collections they amassed. Whereas in the Northern Song dynasty, a collection of 50,000 fascicles would have been impressively large, Ming book collectors amassed collections exceeding 80,000 fascicles.[54] And although Li Zhi was likely exaggerating, he boasted that even in his remote mountain retreat at the Cloister of the Flourishing Buddha he had access to "thousands of fascicles."[55] In urban pockets across Europe, book collections also grew as members of the increasingly literate bourgeoisie sought to improve or affirm their cultural standing. By the mid-seventeenth century it was not unusual for European doctors and lawyers to possess over a thousand volumes, and some, including the Spanish author Francisco de Quevedo (1580–1645), owned as many as 5,000 tomes.[56] Li Zhi's contemporary Hu Yinglin (1551–1602), drawing upon a distinction first made by the Song dynasty painter Mi Fu (1051–1107) with regard to collectors of paintings, classified the growing numbers of Chinese book collectors into two types. True connoisseurs (*jianshangzhe*) possessed genuine aesthetic or scholarly appreciation of the objects in their collections, while mere enthusiasts (*haoshizhe*) used collecting instrumentally as a means to exhibit their social status.[57] In early modern China, the latter category was sharply on the ascent, its numbers swelled by upwardly mobile merchants seeking to flaunt their newly acquired affluence and leverage it to obtain positions of cultural prestige.[58] Yet individuals of both kinds had a strong incentive to avoid purchasing phony publications: true scholars eschewed them out of concern that faulty texts might distort their understanding of the content and meaning of the texts at hand, and mere enthusiasts shunned these volumes because, by doing so, they demonstrated their refinement and discriminating taste.

On both continents consumers with social pretensions were as eager to avoid laying out great sums for spurious or incomplete texts as they were to avoid paying dearly for false objects such as bogus antiques and counterfeited coins. As early as 1522, the Italian jurist Giovanni Nevizzano of Asti (d. 1540) complained of the difficulty of distinguishing between reliable and spurious volumes: "The great number of books makes it difficult to find individual ones. . . . Take care which books you should buy; and you, bookseller, take thought about which list to give to your customer, in what order the books should be printed, and how the fascicles gathered."[59] Remarks like these also resounded throughout sixteenth-century China. An author who referred to himself as The Old Man of Five Lakes (Wuhu laoren) wrote, "Between heaven and earth, it is difficult to find an authentic man, and it is also rare to encounter an authentic book."[60]

In both regions, savvy readers began to develop sophisticated strategies for negotiating among conflicting editions, as well as methods for identifying forgeries. So sustained and meticulous were European collectors' efforts to differentiate between authentic and bogus texts and to catalogue them comprehensively, that the European historian Anthony Grafton has observed, "In the Renaissance . . . forger and critic marched in lockstep."[61] European bibliophiles were assisted in their efforts by the relatively strict regulation of book publication there. Although this system was imperfectly enforced, the fact that, at least in theory, books had to be cleared with the authorities prior to publication enabled European collectors to assemble comprehensive (or allegedly comprehensive) bibliographies of all the books circulating within a certain jurisdiction. These lists could then be annotated with researched or anecdotal evidence of which volumes had been pirated.

Early in the sixteenth century, Renaissance humanists pioneered elaborate philological methods of textual comparison in an effort to establish standard editions of classical texts, both pagan and Christian. Building upon this foundation, the great Swiss bibliographer Konrad Gesner undertook the monumental task of assembling his *Bibliotheca Universalis*, a comprehensive catalogue of all extant works in Latin, Greek, and Hebrew. In the preface to his magnum opus, Gesner outlined the purpose of his project: "I have prepared this list not for learned persons alone, but for everyone, so that even persons with little education might be informed as by a mute teacher, about the reliability and usefulness of every book, or the lack thereof."[62] Gesner envisioned a reading public deeply concerned with not only the textual accuracy but also the material authenticity of books. More striking, for him the problem of verifying texts' authenticity extended beyond elite circles of readers; it affected all individuals' interactions with books.

In the following generations, prominent bibliophiles such as Josias Simler (1531–1576), Jacob Fries (1541–1611), and François Grudé de La Croix du Maine (1552–1592) elaborated upon Gesner's work. In an authorial preface to la Croix du Maine's monumental, multivolume *Bibliothèque françoise*, written in 1584, the Frenchman declared,

"Many people usurp and attribute to themselves the labors of others, and this [my] book will uncover [their vices]." He further avowed, "I detest and abhor [book forgers and pirates] as much as anyone else living in my century."⁶³ With these concerns in mind, he designed his *Bibliothèque* to empower readers to distinguish between legitimate and illegitimate recensions of ancient texts and also to differentiate between accurate and unreliable editions of contemporary texts. He described his project in these words:

> I have not contented myself to put in these Latin and French bibliographies [merely] the catalogue of works written by each author, but in addition I have included by whom they were printed, as well as the size of the margins and the dimensions of each book, how many pages it contained, and above all the name of the person to whom it was dedicated. This I have done without omitting any of the books' qualities. And furthermore, I have noted down the beginning or the first line of each work and composition, and provided some information on when the authors lived, as well as many other minute details, which I will not enumerate here, but which nonetheless I have observed in these Catalogues.⁶⁴

La Croix du Maine also sternly cautioned readers of the prevalence of fake editions. One entry, for instance, bore the following warning: "[Michel de Nostre-Dame] wrote an infinite number of Almanacs and Prognostications, which were so well received and which sold so well that many people imitated them and borrowed the name of the aforementioned Nostredamus so that they could achieve greater renown and reputation."⁶⁵ In China, the absence of laws requiring prepublication censorship would have made it impossible to compile a bibliography as comprehensive as that of la Croix du Maine. However, despite the vast scale on which books were being produced, contemporary Chinese continued valiantly to attempt to catalogue them. Yet the amount of care taken in distinguishing authentic from phony publications differed greatly depending on the genre and cultural status of the works in question. Needless to say, there was much more at stake in securing reliable editions of canonical texts than there was in obtaining the most authoritative edition of a joke book or popular drama. For this reason, the government sponsored lists of authorized editions of classical literature but left the rest unclassified. Some publishing houses printed catalogues of their inventories, and a few dedicated bibliophiles made lists of the books they owned or knew of. For instance, Li's close friend Jiao Hong, who served as a compiler for the Ming dynastic history, published an extensive bibliography recording the titles of both extant and lost books, and the renowned book collector Huang Yuji (1629–1691), who also served as a compiler for the state history, recorded the titles of over 15,600 works, most of which dated from the Ming dynasty. The quality and type of the information these privately produced catalogues purveyed varied considerably, yet even the most accurate records did not provide such detailed information as did Gesner's *Bibliotheca Universalis*. It was not until the eighteenth century, under the influence of evidential scholarship (*kaozheng xue*), that significant numbers of Chinese bibliographers began to regard information about the editions of contemporary books as worthy of careful documentation.[66]

The Ming bibliophiles who expressed concern over forgery and piracy seem to have done so in relatively general terms. In his widely read *Unofficial Gleanings of the Wanli Era* (Wanli yehuo bian), Shen Defu (1578–1642) warned of "cunning rogues who forge texts or print only half of them so as to deceive gullible buyers." He insisted that "there were hundreds of such volumes," but unlike la Croix du Maine, Shen did not have the resources necessary to detail their precise dimensions or list their exact publication information.[67] Like Shen, the book collector and author Hu Yinglin also alerted readers to the prevalence of book falsification and urged his fellow collectors to act with caution.[68] But Hu went one step further; he listed the titles of several contemporary books he believed were falsified. Another late Ming literatus, Qian Xiyan (fl. 1612), entered into greater detail. The "False Books" (Yan shu) chapter of his *Playing with Flaws* (Xi xia) mentions Li Zhi by name and provides information on which specific works by Li were published illegitimately. He even exposes the identity of the forger, Ye Zhou (fl. 1595–1624), an erudite and often inebriated young playboy who hailed from Liangxi, near Suzhou, and published with the Hangzhou publishing house Rongyutang.[69] The text supplies similar, though less detailed information on the unauthorized printing of a work by Yuan Hongdao.[70] Qian's account is considerably more specific than those of Shen and Hu, yet unlike contemporary European bibliographies, which aimed for comprehensiveness, Qian's text remains selective, unsystematic, and anecdotal.

The thoroughness of Chinese and Europeans' responses to the onslaught of unreliable editions differed: Europeans produced lengthy and detailed catalogues that aimed to account for works in all genres, while their Chinese contemporaries assembled distinct government-sponsored lists for canonical works and privately assembled lists for noncanonical and contemporary works. Regardless of the genres being classified, Chinese bibliographers tended to pay far less attention to the physical characteristics of volumes than did their European contemporaries. Nonetheless, in both places in the sixteenth century, concerned collectors strove to point out and warn consumers against the proliferation of unauthorized books. The most vociferous critics of book forgery and piracy, however, were not readers or collectors, but authors and editors, who felt that greedy printers were unfairly cashing in on *their* reputations and profiting from their literary labors.

ESTABLISHING A DEFINITIVE EDITION

The preface writers to *Another Book to Burn*, Li Zhi's friends Jiao Hong, Zhang Nai (*jinshi* 1604), and Wang Benke, were all deeply troubled by the abundant falsified editions of Li's works.[71] Each of the prefaces argues for the authenticity of this work, a compilation of writings left behind upon Li's death, lovingly collated by Wang, and published in Wanling, Anhui in 1618. Acknowledging the prevalence of spurious editions of Li's works, the preface writers exhibit varying degrees of doubt in readers' ability to distinguish among them. Their bid for the authenticity of their own volume rests primarily on claims of Wang's personal familiarity with the author and on assertions of the care and meticulousness with which he edited the text.

These criteria for authenticity closely mirror those invoked by Montaigne's disciple Marie de Gournay in her posthumous prefaces to the French essayist's magnum opus. Like Li's preface writers, Gournay compiled the writings Montaigne left behind after his death, in 1592. These consisted of additions to and revisions of the author's existing essays, not entirely new works, as was the case for Li in 1602. Nonetheless, Gournay's task resembled that of Li's preface writers insofar as, like them, she took a keen interest in denouncing spurious editions and establishing the authority of her new edition. Two editions of the *Essays* had appeared between 1593 and 1595 and omitted whole chapters or retitled them.[72] Thus the preface writers to *Another Book to Burn* and the *Essays* shared the aspiration to discredit such misleading editions and to inspire readers' confidence in the reliability of their own editorial work.[73]

All three preface writers to *Another Book to Burn* were painfully aware that Li's works had been widely falsified. While they shared the conviction that their own volume was unassailably authentic, they differed in the degree of confidence they placed in readers' abilities to recognize its value and to discriminate accurately between false and authentic editions. Jiao was the most optimistic. He proclaimed, "There are many apocryphal editions [but] those in the know scorn them."[74] Wang and Zhang, however, remained slightly more skeptical. In a passage that rings with ambivalence, Wang opined:

> Within our four seas there is no one who does not read Li Zhi's writings, no one who does not aspire to read all of them. They read them without stopping, and even read forgeries. Those who counterfeit Li Zhi's works, imitate his style, and forge his commentaries want to deceive people. But they cannot deceive people incapable of being deceived. The world does not lack people of insight; undoubtedly *they* can tell the difference [between authentic and spurious editions]. Yet down to the present day, every play, lewd joke, and fiction commentary that you see in bookstores is marked with the words "By Master Zhuowu." People gullible enough to believe whatever they hear are enthralled by these editions, which inflict considerable damage on people's hearts and minds. Li Zhi's spirit must be in deep anguish. This is what I greatly fear.[75]

Wang's uncertainty of readers' powers of discrimination is unmistakable. On the one hand he ardently hopes and even asserts that readers do indeed possess the perspicacity to distinguish true Li Zhi editions from false ones: forgers "cannot deceive people incapable of being deceived." But on the other hand, he worries that readers may ultimately lack the necessary judgment to tell Li's real works from fakes, for he avows that forgers already "inflict considerable damage on people's hearts and minds." Zhang's preface expresses even graver misgivings:

> Because Zhuowu's books are important, both real editions and fake editions circulate in the world. In this world, few people have eyes. For this reason, they are not able to discover the intention behind the real editions; and when they read the fake editions, they are misled.... Today commoners surpass Li Zhi's outrageousness and indulge in wanton acts; they take pleasure in behaving like petty, unscrupulous men. At the slightest provocation, they pick up their brushes and throw into confusion the writings Li Zhi left behind, and they claim that *their* works are his lost manuscripts. For instance, if reading an ancient book, someone with a solid foundation [in learning] might investigate the evidence and establish a definitive edition. By doing so, he would "dot the eyes of the painted dragon" [i.e., add the crucial touch that would bring the authentic work to life].[76] But

people who lack this foundation comment at random; they are only "marking the gunwale to show where the oar sank" [i.e., using fruitless and illogical methods].[77] Alas! How can I find a person with eyes to read Zhuowu's book?[78]

Zhang's preface seems to register his despair over the lack of readers endowed with sufficient judgment to distinguish between authentic and phony editions of Li's works. Yet he concludes by asserting that the fake editions are "not worthy of discussion," praises Wang for attempting to establish definitive editions, and affirms that Wang has succeeded in "preventing the authoritative editions from rotting away."[79] Jiao sees the situation in a more positive light. His comments imply that Wang's volume is so irrefutably authentic that its publication will ensure that "those who publish false editions will no longer be able to do so."[80]

The preface writers anchor the authority of Wang's editions in two major criteria, both of which find parallels in Gournay's prefaces to Montaigne's *Essays*. In each case, authority rests on the editor's personal familiarity with the author and on the care the editor took in compiling the manuscript. Wang's preface opens with a detailed description of his close relationship with Li Zhi. This recital, which is corroborated by Jiao's preface, functions rhetorically to shore up Wang's position as uniquely capable of making editorial decisions regarding Li's work. Implicit in Wang's and Jiao's remarks is the observation that since rival compilers and printers did not know Li personally, their editions cannot possibly be as reliable as Wang's own. Wang writes, "I, [Wang Ben] Ke, followed the late gentleman [Li Zhi] for nine years. Day and night I kept him company and never left his side for even a moment. No one served him for as long as I did, and no one was in a better position to know his true nature than I."[81] Wang's claim to have produced *the* authentic edition of Li's remaining writings draws subtly on the ancient Chinese concept of the soul mate, literally "the one who knows the sound" (*zhi yin*). This concept derives from the tale of the mythological zither player Bo Ya and his close friend and sympathetic listener Zhong Ziqi, who always uncannily knew just what was on Bo Ya's mind as he was plucking or strumming his instrument.[82] The image of the compassionate friend who "knows the sound" was adapted by the literary critic Liu Xie (ca. 465–ca. 522) in his *Literary Mind and the Carving of Dragons* (Wenxin diaolong) and came to refer to a "singularly understanding reader." Such a reader would possess prodigious powers of empathy that would enable him to gain access to the author's intentions, which, although manifested in the structure and wording of the text, may not be fully perceptible to obtuse or novice readers, let alone those with "eyes of flesh." By allocating to himself the role of Li's "singularly understanding reader," Wang rhetorically establishes a pipeline to Li's authorial intentions and in so doing lays claim to the perfect authenticity of his edition. Yet, as illustrated in the following chapter, Wang's theory of hermeneutics—his understanding of where meaning resides and how it is to be accessed—accords only partially with Li's own.

Independently of the concept of "the one who knows the sound," Gournay employed a similar technique: though unrelated to Montaigne by blood or marriage, she repeatedly referred to herself as the essayist's "daughter" (*fille*), and alluded to him as her "father" (*père*).[83] Defending her intellectual progenitor against accusations of impiety, Gournay's preface invokes her special relationship with her "father," stating, "It is I who have the right to speak in this regard, for I alone was perfectly acquainted with that great soul, and it is I who have the right to be trusted."[84] So close was the spiritual bond she claims to have shared with Montaigne that she even self-aggrandizingly dubbed herself "another himself."[85] This phrase strengthens her claim to privileged access to the author's thoughts, for its diction echoes the manner in which Montaigne, in his well-known essay "On Friendship" (De l'amitié), described his soul fused to that of his boon companion Estienne de la Boëtie. Through rhetorical techniques designed to accentuate her personal acquaintance with the author and her unique understanding of his character, Gournay, like Wang, angled to solidify her credibility and to strengthen readers' confidence in the faithfulness of her text to the original.

The second method these editors used to bolster the credibility of their editions was to describe the care they took in collecting and reviewing materials for inclusion. Here again Wang's remarks are less copious than those of Gournay, though their import is analogous. Wang modestly squeezes the narration of his editorial process into a single sentence: "I collected the unpublished manuscripts of *A Book to Burn* and *On the Four Books*, and collated them along with my elder brother Bolun."[86] This terse statement is corroborated by Jiao and Zhang, each of whom remarks upon Wang's meticulousness as an editor. Jiao writes, "Wang of Xin'an followed [Li Zhi] for ten years and gathered together his scattered writings, leaving none behind."[87] And Zhang lauds Wang for the great service he did Li by "establishing definitive copies of his real books, providing them with tables of contents, and transmitting them to people throughout China."[88]

Gournay's preface accomplishes the same end in significantly more words. Displaying what one critic has characterized as "virtually paranoid anguish" over proving the legitimacy of her edition, she devotes several full pages to denigrating devious or careless printers as "plunderers and filchers of books," all the while praising her own painstaking editorial efforts.[89] Among other virtues, she announces proudly that her edition "follows [Montaigne's original text] more than exactly."[90] These were no hollow boasts: Gournay's 1595 edition contains significantly fewer typographical errors than any edition of the *Essays* appearing during Montaigne's life.[91]

By invoking the editor's intimacy with the author and calling attention to his or her scrupulous attention to detail, these preface writers attempted to shield the works at hand from contamination and to quell readers' fears that the present editions could be tainted. Yet ironically the editors' insistence on the accuracy of their texts only highlights the ubiquity of the problem of fraudulence in both cultures. As the European book historian Adrian Johns has noted, "With piracy regarded as an omnipresent hazard, no individual was automatically immune from the label of pirate, and no book too grand to be called a piracy."[92]

The editors' goal of persuading readers of the authenticity of their editions contrasts sharply with the rhetoric of bluff, which I have identified as paradigmatic of the early modern period. Unlike Li Zhi, whose writings assail readers with a variety of paradoxical and incongruous opinions, the preface writers to these texts take on an overtly suasive role vis-à-vis readers. Far from challenging each reader to exercise his own judgment and trusting him to arrive at his own conclusions, the preface writers act as brokers of authenticity; they present readers with ready-made assessments and endeavor to impose upon them an interpretive scheme, which they expect readers to accept uncritically. Yet the passive role these preface writers envisioned for readers accounts for only one facet of Li's far more complex ideas on the production and location of textual meaning. The following chapter examines Li's contradictory statements on the relationship between reader and text, his own eccentric interpretive practices, and historical readers' reactions to his texts. Motivating this inquiry is the desire to find out whether his texts, like their prefaces, encouraged readers to accept authoritative judgments or provoked readers to draw their own boldly idiosyncratic conclusions.

CHAPTER 6

Provoking or Persuading Readers?

Li Zhi and the Incitement of Critical Judgment

An avid and omnivorous reader as well as an acerbic critic, Li Zhi was one of China's most incisive and provocative interpreters of his generation. His comments on all manner of texts consistently opposed conventional views and overturned orthodox judgments. In considering his practice as a reader, his theory of reading, and the responses his works elicited from contemporary readers, two major questions arise. These are, first, whether meaning is fixed, determinate, and singular, or flexible, subjective, and open-ended. In other words, does the true meaning of a text reside deep within it, waiting to be extracted by a perceptive reader, or is meaning constructed—and sometimes willfully imposed—by subjective, independent-minded readers? The second question, related to the first, is whether Li's adversarial commentary and eccentric interpretations functioned persuasively or provocatively. Did his judgments on the texts on which he commented inspire their first readers to trust his opinions as true, or did they goad readers to follow his example and come up with their own original ideas?

The meaning of a text can never be reduced simply to the author's intention or the reader's interpretation; it is necessarily produced in the dynamic interaction between the two.[1] Nonetheless, authors may, and often do, attempt, through rhetoric, to control the meaning of their works or, conversely, to delegate to readers the responsibility of *making* sense of their writings.[2] What is perplexing about Li's texts is that they do both. When describing his own method of reading, he sometimes claims to be able to penetrate to the core of a text he has read and expose its latent meaning, while at other times he denies that doing so is even possible. Li's contradictory attitudes, which perplexed his initial readers, signal his participation in a trend perceptible in both early modern China and Europe in which some bold readers gradually liberated themselves from authoritative interpretations and began to trust themselves to arrive at their own conclusions.

The preface writers to *Another Book to Burn* consistently clung to the more conservative view, grounded in Confucian hermeneutics, that textual meaning was firmly anchored in the author's intentions and that the role of the editor was to persuade readers of the authenticity of his edition. At times Li valorizes the notion that textual meaning is determinate. He boasts, for instance, that his superior vision allows him to perceive nuances of meaning hidden from more obtuse readers. His sparkling fresh commentaries on texts of all kinds may be understood to corroborate this view: by bringing to light unnoticed aspects of the source texts, they demonstrated his unerring insight and positioned themselves—and him—as credible sources of authority.

For this reason, they have been seen as prefiguring the inventive and unconventional fiction and drama commentaries of Jin Shengtan and other late imperial commentators on popular culture. These commentators, it has been argued, deployed an arsenal of rhetorical strategies aimed to convince readers of the acuity of their readings and to shore up their authority as reliable "brokers of meaning."[3] To the suggestion that their floridly subjective interpretations might have been designed, on the contrary, to provoke readers to develop their own views, the literary scholar Martin Huang cautions, "Despite all the seeming . . . advocacy for the 'reader,' the traditional commentators [such as Jin] were ultimately concerned with 'the correct reading' or 'the control of meaning.' They would have certainly shunned the 'non-hierarchical' idea that each reader is entitled to his own reading."[4] These remarks suggest that Li, like Jin, may never have questioned the premise that texts possess a stable, durative meaning. Even though his own judgments bucked all convention, some late Ming readers interpreted Li's writings as purveyors of sound judgments to be absorbed and accepted. And even more readers worried lest others, less discriminating than they, might assent to his views uncritically.

Yet to emphasize Li's attempts to control the meaning of the texts on which he commented or to convince readers to endorse his outlandish judgments risks overlooking a more important aspect of his writing. On several occasions Li explicitly undermines the notion that meaning inheres in texts. He contradicts the assertion that a reader's task is to drill down and reveal authorial intentions. On the contrary, he opines that the meaning of a text is forever expanding as each successive reader negotiates his own relationship with the work. This attitude resembles what literary theorist Robert Scholes refers to as "centrifugal reading," for it releases readers from the "centripetal" task of attempting to reconstruct authorial intentions.[5] Instead it encourages each reader to approach the text playfully, perhaps even irreverently, always mindful that future readers may disagree with his interpretations.

Understood in this light, Li's peculiar judgments on the textual tradition on which he was reared are best regarded not as dogmas for readers to accept but as catalysts that incite them to follow his example by exercising their own critical faculties. Surviving comments of late Ming and early Qing readers of Li's books demonstrate that quite a few of them rose to meet this challenge. Emboldened by the bravura with which Li himself reversed canonical judgments, these readers turned the same methods against Li's writings and questioned the validity of his pronouncements.

Independent-minded readers, even cheeky ones, have always existed, but the early modern period provided a particularly fertile ground in which they could develop their subjective, appropriative strategies of reading and give free rein to their interpretive agency. Surrounded by misleading appearances and unstable linguistic, sartorial, numismatic, and bibliographic signs, growing numbers of readers began to recognize that textual meaning was not monolithic but open to interpretation—indeed manipulation. Under these conditions, the idea that meaning could be pinned to a single, unchanging point of view such as a traditional gloss putatively transmitting the author's intent became increasingly untenable, and readers accordingly took upon themselves the responsibility for passing contingent, subjective judgments on the texts they encountered. Although on some level Li still yearned for a stable system of signification (illustrated in chapter one, as well as in his endorsements of the centrality of authorial intentions), his extravagantly inconsistent, bluff-laden texts exemplify his bold attempts to cope with a changing reality. By daring to impose meaning on the world around him, Li produced writings that echo texts composed by increasingly self-assured readers from across early modern Europe.

Li's books managed to dislodge some contemporary Chinese readers from their habitually compliant, author-centered manner of reading, and impelled them to develop new strategies for *making* sense. However, this fact does not imply that Li consciously intended to produce this effect, nor that all or even most of his readers responded in this way. Some readers approached Li's volumes as reverentially as they did orthodox commentaries on canonical works. Nonetheless, in an era of increasingly indeterminate meaning, the ability to assess critically for oneself signs of all varieties was swiftly gaining importance, while the habit of relying on others' fixed judgments was growing ever more dangerous. The fact that Li's works sparked controversy over how best to interpret them marks them—along with clothing, money, and book editions—as manifestations of the troubled state of signification in early modernity. Yet by using rhetoric that prompted some readers to hone their powers of personal judgment, Li's texts served not only as symptoms of an unruly age but as strategies for addressing and perhaps even overcoming these symptoms.

LI ZHI AS A READER

Li pored over books throughout his life and consecrated his retirement to quiet study. In the preface to his poem "On the Joy of Reading" (Du shu le), composed in 1596 in the seclusion of his monastic retreat at the Cloister of the Flourishing Buddha, he avers, "From my early days to my old age, I have . . . devoted myself single-mindedly to reading."[6] He even describes reading as the single pleasure remaining to this solitary septuagenarian:

> If I pack up the books on my shelf,
> Where will I find my happiness?
> Refreshing my spirit, enjoying myself
> For me lies precisely in nothing but this.[7]

Li's devotion to reading, especially in his final years, attracted his contemporaries' attention. Liu Dongxing reported that "the gentleman was constantly occupied with books. All day long he would copy them out and annotate them for himself," and Jiang Yihua (fl. Wanli period) confirmed that Li "read day and night, summer and winter, never ceasing."[8]

Always curious, Li perused books of every genre. As Jiang Yihua attests, "All his life he read widely in [Confucian] documents and histories. . . . He also was familiar with Buddhist scriptures and classics on divination."⁹ Yuan Zhongdao's biography of Li corroborates this account, stating that Li's reading included "tales of the Daoist immortals, Buddhist religious works, the *Li sao*, the historical writings of Sima Qian and Ban Gu, the poetry of Tao Qian, Xie Lingyun, Liu Zongyuan, and Du Fu, as well as the more remarkable among fictional writings and dramas by famous Song and Yuan playwrights."¹⁰ Yet for Li, reading was no passive enterprise. He read actively, even aggressively, with brush in hand, and, in the words of Jiang Yihua, "his critical comments never ceased."¹¹ Although I am not aware of any extant manuscripts that preserve Li's marginalia, he reportedly adorned his volumes with copious comments. Yuan Zhongdao writes, "On snow-white paper, with red annotations, [his] neatly ordered characters marched down the page between precise margins, original ideas constantly bursting forth."¹² These statements demonstrate Li's passion for reading and point to the critical attention he lavished on the texts he studied.

Li made no secret of his eclectic tastes or his penchant for sharp critique. He is credited with having published annotated editions of both canonical texts and works of lowbrow fiction and drama. And his name is associated with incisive commentaries on everything from orthodox Confucian texts such as *The Four Books* and *The Book of Changes* to Sunzi's *Art of War*, the Buddhist *Record of Causes and Effects* (Yinguo lu), and popular literature such as *The Romance of the Western Chamber* and *Outlaws of the Marsh*. Although, as noted in the previous chapter, many of these annotated editions are likely apocryphal, there is no doubt that for Li analyzing, dissecting, and recording his opinions on what he read—not merely absorbing the ideas passively—were fundamental to his practice of reading.¹³

Li's interpretive practices often accentuated "oppositional reading" (*fandu*), a strategy that the literary scholar Yang Yucheng defines as "a kind of reading against the grain, the most striking aspect of which is its ironic, mocking character."¹⁴ Li regularly recast the meanings of well-known phrases, radically reappraised the ethical status of historical figures, and overturned orthodox judgments. Yet the motive underlying these virtuosic interpretive moves proved difficult for some readers to discern. Did Li conceive of his works as presenting readers with conclusive, binding, and irrefutable judgments, or did he expect the unprecedented opinions he voiced to stimulate readers' doubt? In his authorial preface to the first part of

A Book to Keep (Hidden), Li dispassionately acknowledges several possibilities:

> It would be fine for one to say that the judgments of right and wrong presented here are just the views of one person—me, Li Zhuowu. And it would also be fine for one to say that they are the collective judgments of millions upon millions of generations of great sages and worthies. It would be fine for one to say that I have overturned the judgments of right and wrong established through millions of generations, and then [in turn] for one to overturn *my* judgments of right and wrong. But it would also be fine for one to put one's trust in my judgments.[15]

In this passage, Li elaborates several incompatible ways readers may approach his writings; these range from the most passive, reverent acceptance of his claims to far more aggressive techniques. Yet despite the incongruences among these stances, Li seems to value them all equally, judging them all "fine" (*ke*). The conflicting responses he imagines his books may elicit from readers foreshadow the very real debates that would ensue in the late Ming and early Qing as the first historical readers struggled to figure out how best to construe the meaning of his texts. Yet before analyzing contemporaries' reactions to Li's works, I will examine the contradictory postures Li himself adopted toward the works he read, as well as the steps he took to incline readers to accept his judgments and the measures he used to induce them to reject them.

PENETRATING VISION

Li's preface to the poem "On the Joy of Reading" details the many advantages he enjoyed, which enabled him produce such astute interpretations of all he read: his eyes, his disposition, his feelings, and most important his insight and his audacity. His emphasis on these last two faculties hints at his endorsement of Confucian hermeneutics, according to which a discerning reader must probe the text before his eyes, seeking to discover latent traces of the author's intent. In the passage below, Li does not question the basic validity of this paradigm of reading; rather, he claims to possess such extraordinary insight that he can perceive textual subtleties that would elude less attentive readers. His own acute observations, he maintains, lead him to draw conclusions that boldly depart from established norms. He explains:

My insight is a blessing, for when I look into a book I can see the person who wrote it, and moreover I can see the state of that person's whole being. Of course, a great many writers since antiquity have read books and commented on the affairs of the world. Some of them see the visage; some of them see the body covered with skin; some of them see the blood vessels; and some of them see the muscles and bones. But the bones are as far as anyone ever goes. And although some of these scholars claim to have burrowed into the internal organs, in fact they have not even penetrated the bones. This [ability to see straight into the marrow of the author's bones] is what I consider to be the foremost of my blessings.

My audacity is a blessing, for those who were envied and admired in earlier ages so much that they are regarded as worthies, I myself have mostly regarded as fakes. I have mostly regarded them as old-fashioned, worthless, and useless. Yet those who have been despised, abandoned, reviled, and spit upon, I truly believe could be entrusted with our country, our families, and ourselves as individuals. My sense of what is right and wrong, as in this instance, gravely transgresses what people in earlier ages used to think—so what could I do without audacity? This is the next most important of what I call my blessings from heaven.[16]

If texts manifest their author's aspirations or intent (*zhi*), then reading becomes a process of following the author's words back to their source. As Mencius states, "We use our understanding to trace [the meaning of a text] back to what was [originally] in the writer's mind—this is how to grasp it."[17] Or, as Liu Xie elaborates in his fifth-century treatise on literary criticism, "The reader opens the text in order to enter the feelings [of the author]."[18] Although texts cannot "mis-manifest" their author's intent, a gap always separates the fullness of the author's pre-articulated feelings from the necessarily incomplete expression of these feelings in words. As the "Appended Sayings" (Xi ci zhuan) to the *Book of Changes* states, "What is written does not give full expression to what is said; what is said does not give full expression to the concept in the mind."[19] Thus the more adept or "insightful" the reader, the more nimbly he will traverse this gulf and accurately reconstruct the author's intended meaning. The understanding that the reader must strive to reconstitute authorial intent prevailed throughout late imperial times.[20]

Li's assertion "When I look into a book I can see the person who wrote it, and moreover I can see the state of that person's whole being" corresponds to this understanding of reading as decipherment. The difference he posits between his own interpretive skills and those of other people is one of degree, not kind. And since the notion that an adept reader would conjure an image of the author in his mind's eye was widespread in both sixteenth-century China and Europe, the method of reading Li describes conforms to a model familiar to contemporary readers.[21] Li asserts that what distinguishes him from other readers is nothing more than the penetrating vision he claims to possess. His insight, he avows, enables him to see more deeply than anyone else into the metaphorical "bodies" of the texts he studies, and therefore to grasp their true, intended meaning. As he arrogantly declares elsewhere, "When it comes to reading Confucian texts . . . truly no one is more skilled than [I,] Master Zhuowu!"[22] Guided by his powerful vision, Li proclaims, he arrives at judgments that "transgress" (*li*) the interpretations of people whose views are more limited than his own.

Li's keen vision, he maintains, sets him apart from contemporaries, whom he repeatedly characterizes as failing to use their eyes. In the excerpt below, composed in 1588, he hints that whereas he boldly dares to trust in his own eyesight and therefore scrutinizes original texts directly, less perspicacious readers rely excessively on the insights of others and comply too readily with received tradition. They timidly and docilely mouth authoritative interpretations that, with each successive generation, stray further and further from the original text and its authorial intent. For this reason, such readers attain only a superficial or skewed understanding of the meaning of the texts at hand. In an essay nominally addressing the incongruous presence of a Confucian statue in a Buddhist monastery, he writes:

> The Confucians of antiquity interpreted Confucius conjecturally; our fathers and teachers recited these conjectures and passed them down, and young children listen to them as if blind and deaf [i.e., incapable of interpreting the texts for themselves]. When ten thousand mouths all utter the same phrase, none can counter what is said; when for a thousand years there is only a single standard, no one can come to understand the world for himself. Nobody says, "I merely chant the *words* of Confucius." Instead they claim, "I understand Confucius himself." . . . So today, although people possess eyes, nobody uses them.[23]

Li asserts that the reason other readers' understanding lags behind his is not that those individuals lack the eyes to discern authorial intentions, but rather that they have been trained not to use this organ. Contrasting himself with these cowards, Li insinuates that whereas they do not examine the source texts for themselves, he boldly pierces through accrued layers of commentary to reveal the pure, true meaning below.

IMPOSING SUBJECTIVE MEANING

The conception of reading as a search for authorial intent clashes with the view, expressed elsewhere in Li's writings, that authors' intentions cannot be known, and therefore that readers should freely establish their own views of the meanings of texts. Perhaps expanding on the notion that incisive reading demands audacity, Li even suggests that commenting on existing texts is as an agonistic enterprise, a contest for control over meaning in which skilled readers struggle to wrest authority away from authors and to assert their own interpretive independence. Casting himself as one such remarkably tactical reader, Li writes, "When ordinary people write, they begin from the outside and attack inwards; when I write, I start from the inside and attack outwards. Having infiltrated the enemy's moat, I eat their grain and command their troops; then, when I level my attack, I leave them utterly devastated."[24] Although this passage avoids explicit mention of the act of reading, it seems nonetheless to illuminate the aggression Li associates with this act. If Mencius encouraged readers to develop empathy for the author's point of view, the theory of reading Li suggests here posits an antagonistic or perhaps parasitic relationship between readers and the texts or authors they take as their subject matter. Opportunistically regarding the words and ideas lodged inside source texts as so much ammunition stored up inside an enemy stronghold, Li describes how he sneaks into these battlements and redeploys the stockpiled resources to serve his own end. Reading of this sort aims to strengthen the individual reader's interpretation at the expense of the original text or its author's intent. It thus resembles what Michel de Certeau describes as "reading as poaching," for it deemphasizes authorial intentions and licenses the reader to manipulate textual meaning at will.[25]

This strategy of reading may be understood in the context of Li's contention, best expressed in his essay "On the Childlike Mind," that the self-styled Confucian readers of his generation had become so mired in uncomprehendingly repeating orthodox interpretations of classical texts that they had lost the ability to think for themselves. Their training in rote memorization, he challenged, "obstructed" (*zhang*) their faculty of moral and aesthetic judgment, their all-important "childlike mind."²⁶ Or, as he declared in his authorial preface to the first section of *A Book to Keep (Hidden)*, ever since Confucianism was established as the state ideology in the Han dynasty, "every single person [had] accepted Confucius' views on right and wrong; so there [had] been no [independent] judgments of right or wrong."²⁷ Li's theory of antagonistic reading may be understood as an attempt to counteract the sclerotic effects of this rigid adherence to orthodoxy and to promote a looser, more pluralistic, and more flexible method of interpretation. At stake here is not the issue of refining one's powers of vision so as to perceive more clearly the singular, correct meaning that resides within a text. Rather, it is a question of releasing readers from the obligation to seek such bounded meaning in the first place. As he states in the same preface, "There is no fixed standard for people's judgments of right and wrong."²⁸

A letter Li wrote in 1584 or 1585 to his intellectual sparring partner, the high-ranking Confucian official Geng Dingxiang, crystallizes the point that readers must do more than simply seek authorial intentions; they must read in a manner consonant with their own nature:

> When heaven produces a person, it has the use value of one person; it is not the case that we must wait and obtain [moral rectitude] from Confucius. If we had to wait and obtain it from Confucius, then a thousand years ago, before the time of Confucius, did people not get the chance to be [ethical]? . . . Confucius never once taught people to study Confucius. If Confucius had taught people to study Confucius, then why, when Yan Hui asked him about benevolence did he say: "To act benevolently is to *follow yourself*" and not "to act benevolently is to follow other people"? Why did he say "the learning of the ancients is: *study for your own edification*"? And why did he also say "The gentleman seeks [the Way] *in himself*"?²⁹

These statements, which resonate strongly with the Neo-Confucian concept of "learning for oneself" (*zide*) and echo Wang Yangming's teaching that each individual has the potential to become a sage, imply that readers need not aim exclusively to reconstruct authorial intentions. Instead Li's remarks illustrate his advocacy of the opinion that readers ought to cultivate the ability to assert their own opinions critically.³⁰

Li not only questioned the desirability of reading with the goal of seeking authorial intentions; he also expressed reservations about the practical feasibility of this endeavor. His essay "On the Childlike Mind" casts doubt on the textual authenticity of the classics and,

Provoking or Persuading Readers?

echoing late Ming concerns about the inauthenticity of book editions, insinuates that in some cases these revered ancient texts may turn out to be forgeries. If so, then even the most careful examination of these writings could yield no insight into the minds of the sages. He writes:

> As for the *Six Classics*, the *Analects*, and the *Mencius*, if they are not words of overdone reverence from official historians, they are phrases of bloated praise from loyal subjects. If not one or the other, then they are what misguided followers and dimwitted disciples wrote down of what they *recall* their teacher said. What they wrote had a beginning, but was missing an ending; or the followers remembered the conclusion, but forgot the introduction. These disciples put down in writing whatever they happened to see. Later scholars did not scrutinize these writings. They simply declared that these words came directly from the mouths of sages and decided to establish them as great classics. Who knows whether more than half these writings are *not* words from the mouths of sages?[31]

Elsewhere too Li cautions against "hastily issuing praise and blame based on [judgments gleaned from] 'authoritative texts.'"[32] Together these statements exhibit Li's severe doubt whether the classics truly provide access to authorial intentions. Corroborating this view, a preface written by his acquaintance Liu Dongxing quotes Li as asserting that the ancients "harbored in their hearts many aspirations we [moderns] can never know."[33] This audacious statement underscores Li's belief in the fundamental alterity of readers and authors.

Acknowledging that reading a text could not necessarily provide any insight into the thought process of its author, Li is reported to have pragmatically announced, "There are many marvelous *uses* to which one may put the writings [of the ancients]."[34] The word "uses" (*zuoyong*) carries particular weight because it accentuates the contrast between Li's view of reading articulated here—namely that readers may creatively appropriate the words of the ancients and bend them to their own ends—and the more traditional view expressed above, namely that readers must strive to uncover the singular correct, though sometimes imperfectly revealed intentions of the author. In a biography of Li, Yuan Zhongdao further remarked upon Li's propensity to twist ancient texts to his own ends: "He particularly loved to read history and had great insight into the marvelous uses [*zuoyong*] to which [historical works could be put]."[35]

Even if the intentions of the ancients could be known, Li asserts, all things change, and so the judgments of the sages may no longer prove relevant in the present: "What was right yesterday is wrong today, and tomorrow it is once again right." So "even if Confucius were to be reborn again in these times, I am not sure what kinds of judgments of right and wrong he would make."[36] These statements, reminiscent of Buddhist notions of impermanence and Daoist ideas of continual flux, accentuate the impossibility of arriving at any lasting judgment anchored in authoritative precedent. Rather, they correspond to the shifting state of signification in the early modern period.

CONTEXTS FOR SUBJECTIVE READING: CHINA AND EUROPE

If Li sporadically championed the view that the meanings of texts, even canonical texts, are not fixed but open-ended, he was certainly not alone in holding this opinion. Across China and throughout early modern Europe, sophisticated readers were attaining higher levels of autonomy and slowly beginning to put forth bold, individualistic and at times radically idiosyncratic interpretations of the texts that captivated their attention. According to European historians Lisa Jardine and Anthony Grafton, "All [students] of early modern culture . . . acknowledge that early modern readers did not passively receive but rather actively reinterpreted their texts."[37] Humanists were known to read "pen in hand, causing the margins of texts . . . to overflow with personal reflections, marks manifesting the reader's personal appropriation."[38] Not infrequently, these remarks took on an adversarial, even pugnacious tone, and consequently, as another Renaissance scholar has remarked, in this period "meaning became a variable corresponding to each individual act of reading, not a fixed message."[39]

This emergent, early modern understanding of the reader's role vis-à-vis the text contrasted with long-standing views of texts as purveyors of timeless wisdom.[40] Citing the medieval European practice of reading aloud rather than silently, Mary J. Carruthers has pointed out the close connection between monastic reading (*lectio*) and meditation (*meditatio*).[41] By pronouncing each word with his own breath (*anima*), religious readers in Europe aspired to reanimate sacred texts and thereby gain access to their divine source of inspiration. In this context, reading required suspending one's subjectivity and entering into spiritual communion with the author, and this quest for authorial intention may be seen to mirror Mencius's idea of "tracing [the meaning of a text] back to what was [originally] in the writer's mind."[42]

However, during the early modern period, as books became more readily available and the practice of reading more widespread in both Europe and China, readers began to approach texts more critically. Growing numbers of European readers, no longer content to restrict their comments to summaries, cross-references, synopses, or glosses—notes intended to elucidate the text's "original" meaning—adopted an increasingly adversarial tone toward texts. Some even vigorously defended their subjective and appropriative habits of reading.[43] Montaigne, for instance, affirmed that "an able reader often discovers in other men's writings perfections beyond those that the author put in or perceived, and lends them richer meanings and aspects."[44] Like Li, Montaigne immodestly applauded his own prodigious powers of interpretation, proclaiming, "I have discovered in Livy a hundred things that another man has not read in him . . . and perhaps which the author never put there."[45] These remarks echo Li's invocation of the "many marvelous uses" to which he put the classical texts of his own tradition. Both men's comments resonate with those of Jin Shengtan, who, in his notes on the popular drama *The Romance of the Western Chamber* (Xixiang ji), remarked, "The text of *The Western Chamber* bearing my commentary is my text; it is no longer the old *Western Chamber*." Jin continued, "*The Western Chamber* is not a work written by an individual named Wang Shifu alone; when I read it carefully, it becomes a work of my own creation."[46] These comments evince the tendency of avant-garde early modern readers to co-create the texts they read.[47]

The notion that the most adept readers would press beyond authorial intentions and bring their own experiences to bear upon the texts they read received corroboration from Li's contemporary Xu Wei. In his "Preface on Poetry" (Shuo shi xu), Xu praised readers who interpreted texts in ways that directly contradicted the author's intentions. He even explicitly granted readers permission to deviate from orthodox interpretations and implied that doing so would yield results superior to those that could be achieved by cleaving to authorized interpretations. Anchoring his ideas in his own personal reading experience, Xu wrote, "I once read Cao Cao's explication of Sunzi's *Art of War* in thirteen chapters, as well as Li Jing and Tang Taizong's discussions of [the same text]. Many of their interpretations did not accord with Sunzi's original intentions. In discussing military strategy, the two men based their interpretations on their own daily experience, which they [then] applied to offensive and defensive strategies.

These readers' accomplishments surpassed those of Sunzi. From this we can tell that not everything written in books can be known to us, and [consequently] that one need not interpret texts in the orthodox manner."[48] Xu's emphasis on readers' ability to *make* sense of texts for themselves supports Montaigne's, Li's, and Jin's view that readers should deploy texts to their own creative ends.

A similar technique is recommended, although in jest, in Cervantes's authorial preface to *Don Quixote*. This work features a conversation between the fictitious authorial persona and his trusted friend, who advises him to embellish the novel with quotations collected from assorted authoritative, classical texts. By suggesting that the quotations be used ornamentally without regard for their original context or their authors' intentions, the friend legitimates the practice of readers-turned-writers appropriating whatever snippets of existing texts assist *them* in bolstering their own arguments. "With a pinch of Latin here and a pinch of Latin there," the friend nudges, "[readers] might even think you're a scholar, which isn't a bad reputation."[49] Montaigne is known to have practiced similar techniques. He delighted in mischievously quoting out of context and even deliberately cutting and splicing passages, twisting them to carry meanings in his text contrary to those they had conveyed in their original contexts.[50]

A raft of analogous techniques began appearing at the turn of the seventeenth century in lowbrow genres of Chinese literature such as drama, vernacular fiction, joke books, and drinking manuals. As Shang Wei and He Yuming have analyzed, authors of texts in these unofficial genres undertook increasingly wild experiments in "hucksterish" (*baifan*) modes of reading that included extracting well-known phrases from canonical or other texts and juxtaposing them with vulgar material so as to generate new and often deeply subversive meanings.[51] For instance the satirical novel *The Plum in the Golden Vase* several times quotes an excerpt from the opening line of the Confucian *Analects*: "To study and often review, there is no greater pleasure than this!" The phrase "there is no greater pleasure than this," wrenched from its original context and inserted into the pages of this erotic novel, takes on a series of hilariously ironic new meanings. In one unforgettable passage it describes the voyeuristic frisson that lascivious Buddhist monks experience when they overhear the sounds of adulterous fornication.[52] By dislodging this ultra-canonical line from its original context, the anonymous author of the vernacular novel exhibited his utter disregard for authorial intentions and exemplified a radical and new, freewheeling attitude toward classical texts. As Li recommended, he treated the canonical text merely as raw material to be *used* in the manner that pleased him.

Thus in early modern Europe and China there was a growing understanding, especially among the cognoscenti, that meaning did not inhere in texts themselves, nor did it reside in some elusive concept of authorial intention. It was plural and malleable, not singular or rigid. And each reader had the right—perhaps even the responsibility—to amplify the meaning of the texts he encountered by bringing his own ideas, experiences, and judgments to bear upon them. In China personal expression of this nature was confined to unofficial genres such as those in which Li wrote, since official genres, including examination essays, still demanded strict adherence to canonical interpretations of the classics. Li's commentaries, however, unbound by such dictates, freely voiced his own idiosyncratic interpretations and arguably even encouraged readers to develop their own critical faculties.

LI ZHI'S INTERPRETATIONS: PENETRATING TO THE CORE OR IMPOSING SUBJECTIVE MEANING?

Many of Li's comments studied below seem to illustrate the centrifugal conception of textual meaning developing in this period and to affirm the proposition that the reader is free to impose or create significance at will. The examples presented here concern three types of unconventional readings evident in *A Book to Keep (Hidden)*, *Commentaries on the Four Books* (Sishu ping), and *Outline of History with Critical Comments* (Shigang pingyao), texts on which contemporary readers recorded their views.[53] In these volumes Li recasts the meanings of individual words, reevaluates the status of entire genres, and reappraises the ethical character of historical personages. In examining his responses to what he read, I inquire whether the interpretive strategies he deploys emphasize his creativity as a reader and provoke readers to sharpen their own powers of personal judgment or accentuate Li's putatively penetrating vision and therefore compel readers to assent to his ready-made judgments.

As a commentator, Li was known for investing familiar words and phrases with unexpected meanings. For example, his interpretation of the well-known line from the poet Tao Qian's (365–427) autobiographical sketch "Mr. Five Willows" (Wu liu xiansheng zhuan) provides an eccentric gloss on the phrase "I do not seek to understand deeply" (bu qiu shen jie). This phrase had historically been interpreted as a self-effacing remark made by the erudite poet, who claimed neither to have sought nor to have attained deep understanding. But Li virtuosically turned the established interpretation on its head: "Since antiquity, one of the people who have most excelled at studying is Tao [Qian]. Why is this? It's because he 'loved to study but did not seek to understand deeply.' Now in studying, 'understanding' is fine. And there's not even anything wrong with 'understanding deeply,' but one must not '*seek* to understand deeply.'"[54] By emphasizing the word "seek" (qiu) and insisting that one may indeed *attain* deep understanding without deliberately *seeking* it, Li creatively endowed the phrase with an unexpected meaning. This strategy is reminiscent of the technique, discussed in chapter four, of revaluing the term "worthies" (xianzhe); in each case Li disrupts the reader's conventional, unreflective understanding of a word.

Readings like this reveal Li's indebtedness to the political radical He Xinyin, who notoriously reinterpreted the following line from the *Analects*: "The Master condemned four attitudes: he condemned having personal opinions, he condemned insisting on certainty, he condemned being stubborn, and he condemned being egotistical."[55] Unlike any reader before him, He deviously construed the passage to mean "The Master condemned four attitudes: *not* having personal opinions, *not* insisting on certainty, *not* being stubborn, and *not* being egotistical."[56] In slanting the passage this way, He cleverly justified his own methodology of asserting an individual opinion and set a powerful precedent for the irreverent interpretations for which Li Zhi would later become famous.

Yet unconventional as both Li's and He's interpretations were, and much as they may have shocked conservative contemporaries, both readings conformed to classical Chinese grammar. They could be considered wrong only insofar as they violated exegetical convention. And the grammatical plausibility of these readings is the source of their power. For one may construe these interpretations either as exemplifying the readers' playful, opportunistic (centrifugal) appropriation of the text—Li's and He's deliberate imposition of meaning upon it—or as expressing the readers' sincere belief that they have discovered a deep substratum of meaning that, although obscured by layers of traditional interpretation, nevertheless resides within the text. The former appears the more convincing interpretation by far. Nevertheless, a sizable number of early modern readers expressed concern that their contemporaries would unreflectingly adopt the latter position and accept Li's judgments as true.

In addition to reinterpreting the meanings of individual words like "seek" (*qiu*), Li also reappraised the value of entire genres. During the late Ming, the proliferation of books resulted in what book historian Kai-wing Chow has described as an erosion of the authority of the Confucian classics. Classical texts came to vie for consumers' attention with fiction, drama, joke books, travel guides, and handbooks on prognostication.[57] During this period some Chinese intellectuals even began to view vernacular fiction and drama, genres previously scorned as the lowest forms of literature, as acceptable substitutes for the classics. While certainly not the sole advocate of the radical view that leveled the hierarchy of genres, Li lustily supported it.[58] In one essay, he writes, "Poetry need not be sought in the ancient *Classic of Poetry* and *Anthology*; prose need not be modeled on the age before the empire arose. The artistic mind broke out in the Six Dynasties to create recent-style verse; it broke out again in Tang tales of the fantastic; again in the Yuan to make libretti and *zaju* opera; again in our time to make the *Romance of the Western Chamber* and the *Outlaws of the Marsh*, and the masters of the essay form.... What need do I have of the Six Classics, Confucius and Mencius?"[59] Here and elsewhere in his writings, Li extolled the ethical value of popular literature, placing it on a par with the greatest Confucian classics. He claimed that the Yuan dynasty opera *The Pavilion for Worshiping the Moon* (Bai yue ting ji) "should awaken in [readers'] minds thoughts of righteous [Confucian] relationships among brothers, sisters, husbands and wives." And he insisted that although the protagonists of this opera violate Confucian ritual propriety—they elope—the play nonetheless exemplified the "acme of chastity and rectitude."[60] He further lauded the contemporary novel *Outlaws of the Marsh* on the grounds that it promoted loyalty and justice, even though its heroes were bandits. So compelling was the moral message Li imputed to this latter work that he declared that rulers who aspired to govern justly "[could] not afford *not* to read it."[61] Perhaps most striking of all, Li praised the contemporary drama *The Story of Red Duster* (Hong fu zhuan), a tale of illicit romance and elopement. Drawing on Confucius's pronouncement that the *Classic of Poetry* "stirs" readers, inspires them to "make observations," causes them to "join together" in fellowship, and provides them with the means by which to "express grievances," Li proclaimed, "Who says that *chuanqi* [wonder-plays] do not possess the ability to 'stir' people, to inspire them to 'make observations,' to 'join together,' and to 'express grievances'? Amid eating and drinking, banquets and entertainments, we are often moved by feelings of righteousness. Contemporary entertainments are just like those of antiquity; I hope we may regard them no differently!"[62] By equating vulgar contemporary entertainment to the most revered texts of the Confucian canon, Li toppled the classics from their pedestal and called into question the system of values undergirding the traditional hierarchy of genres. Yet again, one may imagine readers struggling to ascertain whether his interpretations reflect his genuine conviction that he has unveiled the true essence of these genres or exemplify his impish delight in reversing accepted interpretations simply to prod readers to do the same.

More than any other technique, the strategy of oppositional reading in Li's repertoire that perplexed contemporary readers was his method of analyzing history. An enthusiastic reader of history, Li was by some accounts "one of the finest historians of the Ming."[63] The fifth fascicle of *A Book to Burn*, the third fascicle of *Another Book to Burn*, and the entirety of *A Book to Keep (Hidden)*, *Another Book to Keep (Hidden)*, and *An Outline of History with Critical Commentary* record Li's unconventional opinions on the lives and careers of historical personages. The boldness with which Li attacked accepted judgments and the originality of his opinions was not lost on contemporary readers. In a preface to *A Book to Keep (Hidden)*, Mei Guozhen remarked, "He judged everything on the basis of his own opinions, regardless of whether they accorded with the received judgments of Confucian scholars."[64] And in a preface to Li's *Outline of History with Critical Commentary*, Wu Congxian (Ming, n.d.) observed, "In expressing whatever was on his mind, he did not flee from [those who wielded] the halberds of power, and he certainly was not [intimidated by] old books! Indeed, he maintained that agreeing with [the authors of antiquity] in what was right did not prevent him from having his own views on what was wrong, and agreeing with them on what was wrong did not prevent him from having his own views on what was right."[65] The question of how Li's audacious interpretations of history conditioned readers' interactions with his own writings is the subject of the following section.

DOCTRINAL VERSUS METHODOLOGICAL INTERPRETATIONS AMONG LI'S FIRST READERS

Whatever their position, contemporary readers responded vehemently to Li's writings, especially his comments on history. The imperial censor Zhang Wenda, whose 1602 memorial denouncing Li prompted the emperor to order the destruction of Li's entire literary corpus, feared that readers, trained since their youth to read docilely, would unquestioningly espouse Li's unorthodox beliefs and even imitate his uncouth behavior. Zhang worried lest readers model themselves on Li and take his interpretations as doctrinal truth. These concerns, while undoubtedly exaggerated, did have some basis in fact. However, what Zhang's memorial did not take into account was another, more sophisticated class of readers who focused not on the veracity of Li's individual judgments per se but rather on their subjective, centrifugal tenor. Inspired by Li's style of interpretation, these readers appropriated his critical methods and exposed his writings to critiques as disruptive and irreverent as those he had leveled at the works he analyzed.

Zhang condemned Li for perpetrating "outrageous and transgressive judgments" that threatened to contaminate unsuspecting readers. His memorial of impeachment cites a litany of historical figures censured by the Confucian historiographic traditional whom Li intrepidly reinterpreted in a positive light. Zhang writes, "In [his] books, [Li] considers Lü Buwei and Li Yuan wise counselors, Li Si shrewd, and Feng Dao an official who possessed the moral fiber of a recluse; he estimates that Zhuo Wenjun excelled in choosing an outstanding mate and finds laughable Sima Guang's assertion that Sang Hongyang deceived Emperor Wu of Han; he deems Qin Shihuang the greatest emperor of all time, and he maintains that Confucius' judgments need not be considered standard.[66] Such outrageous and transgressive judgments are too numerous to count. The majority of them violate norms of propriety, so the books must be destroyed."[67] Zhang's account of Li's judgments is factually accurate: Li did indeed praise the individuals Zhang claims he did. But more relevant for our purposes are the conclusions Zhang draws concerning the potential effects of reading Li's writings or witnessing his eccentric behavior. Zhang suspects that significant numbers of readers may lack the discrimination necessary to view Li's writings in a critical light. As evidence, his memorial cites "young men [who] took delight in [Li's] unrestrained wildness and goaded one another to follow suit. They knew no shame and behaved like beasts, openly stealing money and violating other people's wives and daughters. Recently gentry officials have been clasping talismans and reciting the name of the Buddha; they prostrate themselves before monks and hold rosaries in their hands, all in an attempt to abide by the [Buddhist] prohibitions. Such people, who know not how to respect Confucian household instructions but instead indulge their obsession with Buddhist teachings and monks, are becoming increasingly numerous."[68] Apart from illustrating Zhang's pejorative views toward popular Buddhism, these remarks demonstrate that he envisioned a population of trusting and gullible readers much like the "dimwitted disciples" whom Li so harshly rebuked. Such readers, whose critical faculties had presumably been irremediably "obstructed" (*zhang*) by too much rote memorization, Zhang implies, would be inclined to believe and repeat whatever they read. Certainly, as the examples below demonstrate, more than one reader did indeed assent unquestioningly to Li's unconventional judgments, just as Zhang had predicted. Yet whether significant numbers of readers fell into this camp remains uncertain.

The synopsis of *The Collected Writings of Li Wenling* [i.e., *Li Zhi*] preserved in the catalogue of the massive Qing dynasty *Four Treasuries* compendium (Siku quanshu zongmu) asserts that Li's writings "dazzled" (*ying*) those who encountered them and that "petty Confucian scholars in local schools respected and pliantly placed their trust in [his words]."[69] However, Li's close friend Jiao Hong opposed claims that readers docilely assented to Li's judgments. Jiao opined that "many people considered [Li's] statements far-fetched" because "people do not generally trust words they're unaccustomed to hearing."[70] A synopsis of *Upon Arrival at the Lake* (Chutanji) included in the catalogue of the *Four Treasuries* lends credence to Jiao's view. It characterizes Li's opinions as "bizarre and perverse" and claims that "even people of limited literacy knew that his ideas were absurd."[71]

The view that late Ming readers were more likely to believe than to doubt what they read—an opinion that, remarkably, Zhang and Li shared—ironically finds stronger corroboration in contemporaries' reactions to Zhang's own writings than in their responses to any text by Li. As soon as Zhang's memorial of impeachment began to circulate widely, several literati reiterated his accusations verbatim. The insouciance with which contemporary writers echoed Zhang's words attests to the malleability of texts in this period and the fact that ideas of intellectual property were still at an embryonic stage of development. One who loudly denounced Li Zhi in phrases lifted almost directly from Zhang's memorial was Jiang Yihua. He wrote:

> [Li] specialized in converting bad into good and black into white. By temperament, he did not follow other people's estimations of beauty and ugliness, and his judgments were more than adequate to convey this view. He wrote *A Book to Keep (Hidden)*, a work in thirty fascicles, in which he wantonly and wildly meted out praise and blame. For example, he regarded Lü Buwei as a wise counselor, Li Si as shrewd, and Qin Shihuang as the greatest emperor of all time. He considered Feng Dao a court recluse insofar as he served successive dynasties; he maintained that by eloping, Zhuo Wenjun found her rightful place; and he held that Zhao Bao and Wang Ling were matricides. More importantly, he believed that Confucius' judgments did not need to be followed. As soon as this book was published, a great many people fond of heretical ideas marveled at it.[72]

Along with several other contemporary readers, Jiang borrowed freely from Zhang's diction to pile condemnations on Li and to excoriate him for his unorthodox judgments. They claimed he was "behaving eccentrically and deceiving the multitudes" and fretted that his "heretical ideas" might infect either themselves or others.[73] Noting the way people "madly flocked around [Li]," Gu Xiancheng sighed with resignation, "I don't know how many people he has [already] misled."[74] Meanwhile Jiang, jealously guarding his own ideological purity, opted not to acquire a copy of Li's writings lest they "contaminate [his] bookshelf!"[75] These authors all shared the concern that by uncritically accepting Li's judgments as valid, readers might defile their minds.

One reader whose reaction to Li's writings would likely have confirmed these scholars' worst suspicions is Wang Benke, whose editorial preface to *Another Book to Burn* was introduced in the previous chapter. Wang's preface contains the following effusive and thoroughly uncritical approbation of Li's writings:

> Simply by pointing his finger [Li] leveled criticism powerful enough to guide the judgment of ten thousand generations; indeed, his every grunt bore a connection to the ethical teachings of ten thousand generations. Whether conveying derisive laughter or angry rebukes, each work of his was a masterpiece. His language was exceedingly truthful, and his diction astonished the heavens and shook the earth;[76] it could make the deaf hear, the blind see, the dreaming wake, the drunk sober, the sick arise, the dead revive, the fidgety calm, and the

noisy settle down; it could make those with icy innards hot and those with inflamed organs cold; it could make those who were "hemmed in by pickets and pegs"[77] tear out those "pickets and pegs," and make those who were stubbornly unyielding bow their heads in admiration and respect.[78]

In his preface Wang presents himself as a discriminating reader and expresses concern that other readers may lack his perspicacity—his ability to differentiate between authentic and spurious editions of Li's writings. However, Wang's unreserved, indeed virtually fanatical endorsement of Li's every judgment—his every grunt!—testifies to the remarkably uncritical manner in which he consumed Li's ideas. That Wang chose to repeat Li's metaphor of vision underscores this point. Wang's assertion that Li's writings "could make . . . the blind see" calls to mind Li's own boastful claim to possess powerfully acute eyesight. It seems that Wang accepted this statement as fact and concluded that, since Li's keen vision enabled him to discover the core meaning of texts, his judgments deserved to be trusted and absolutely affirmed.

While Wang's praise for Li's writings is by far the most flamboyant I have encountered, the metaphors he used appear frequently in other late Ming and early Qing comments on Li's books. Many readers avowed that Li's texts opened their eyes, hearts, minds, and in some cases also their mouths. Some said that they admired Li on account of his daringly original judgments.[79] Yet it is often difficult to tell whether these readers approved of Li's bold conclusions in the same superficial, "blind," or gullible manner in which they might have assented to orthodox readings of canonical texts or, on the contrary, recognized in Li a model of how to cultivate their own independent judgments.

Perhaps the reader who expressed the most intense interest in the reactions Li's texts were likely to generate both in his own day and in the future was the author's close friend Jiao Hong, who supervised the printing of *A Book to Keep (Hidden)*.[80] As noted earlier, unlike the imperial censor Zhang Wenda, who claimed that Li's texts were already attracting a cult following, Jiao maintained that contemporaries resisted assenting to Li's views and considered them too peculiar to be appealing. Yet all the same, Jiao worried that in time, as Li's writings became more widely available and the novelty of his odd judgments wore off, readers would eventually accept them. This, he pronounced, would be a travesty. In his preface to *A Book to Keep*

(Hidden), Jiao wrote, "I know that the gentleman's works will certainly be transmitted. And in time scholars will become accustomed to his writings. Moreover, they will use them as mirrors [for reflecting right and wrong], as [scales for] weighing [good and bad], and as millfoil and turtle shells [for prognosticating about the future]. What's more, I know that scholars of future generations will not doubt [Li's judgments]. But this is not what the gentleman wanted."[81] Jiao agreed with Zhang insofar as he noted the inadvisability of uncritically imbibing Li's judgments, yet the two provided different rationales. Whereas Zhang feared the potentially morally corrupting influence of Li's writings, Jiao objected to assenting to Li's judgments on the basis of authorial intention: "This is not what the gentleman wanted." Echoing Jiao's nonmoralistic concerns, the Hanlin academician Chen Renxi (1581–1636) added the following words of caution: "The readers of the world who take delight in singing [Li's] works out loud, those who have a fondness for Li's [writings], are precisely those who do them a disservice. Indeed, to put one's trust in Li's judgments simply because one loves his writings is as wrong as to seek to suppress his writings simply because one does not endorse his judgments."[82] Jiao's and Chen's analyses exhibit their perception that the kernel of Li's writings lies not in his particular findings but in his method of subjecting all texts to his personal judgment and accepting nothing on authority.[83] And Jiao, for one, was convinced that some readers were capable of understanding this strategy, embracing it, and even deploying it. He affirmed, "There are readers capable of picking through his assertions and completely overturning established views, denying what the gentleman affirmed; Li would have been delighted with such readers and felt as if they had 'appeared with astonishing speed.'"[84]

Jiao's inkling that such readers did indeed exist is corroborated by critical responses recorded in some contemporary essays and prefaces, as well as in the margins of at least one late Ming edition of Li's texts.[85] The flood of oppositional, "Li Zhi–style" commentaries on fiction and drama that would proliferate in the decades following Li's death further confirms this hunch. Just as Li furiously annotated the texts he read, refusing to accept any doctrine—not even the words of Confucius—on the strength of authority alone, so too did the authors of these comments judge Li's statements and those of other writers according to their own subjective criteria. In his preface to Li's *Outline of History with Critical Commentary*, Wu Congxian wrote, "Each person has his own views on right and wrong, and I too have my own views on right and wrong."⁸⁶ And the early Qing scholar Li Zhonghuang (n.d.) judiciously asserted that "*A Book to Keep (Hidden)* was biased in some regards but fair in others."⁸⁷ Even Yuan Zhongdao, who ultimately agreed with Li Zhi's judgments on many matters, granted that "at times he . . . can be unbalanced in his judgments."⁸⁸ Unlike Wang Benke, who indiscriminately lavished praise on every aspect of Li's work, these readers exercised their independent judgment and subjected Li's commentaries to level-headed critique.

Ironically, even the Qing-era literatus Wang Hongzhuan (1622–1702), who scathingly attacked Li's judgments, did so in a manner reminiscent of Li's personal style. Wang wrote, "[Having] investigated [Li's] behavior and critically examined the positions he held, [I have concluded that] he appears to have been an unscrupulous lout."⁸⁹ Wang's vehement censure echoes Li's often emphatic tone, and the words "investigate" (*kao*) and "examine" (*cha*) evince Wang's independent assessment of Li's character. Although investigation and examination, methods of textual analysis that figured prominently in the evidential scholarship (*kaozheng xue*) movement that was gaining ascendancy during Wang's lifetime, are far less radical than the oppositional reading strategies for which Li was famous, Li approved of any interpretive strategy that liberated readers to form their own views. His essay "On the Childlike Mind" accuses contemporary Confucians for *failing* to "critically examine" (*cha*) the writings of antiquity and for blindly trusting in received texts, hearsay, and authority.⁹⁰ By ridiculing readers who lack critical judgment, Li implicitly calls upon readers to develop this skill. And Wang, despite his negative evaluation of Li, arguably heeded this call. Thus Wang Hongzhuan's engagement with Li's writings contrasts starkly with that of Wang Benke, for while the latter assented to all of Li's judgments, but in doing so overlooked his critical methodology, the former found fault with Li's judgments but adopted a critical stance of which Li would likely have been proud.

Perhaps the most striking example of a reader who understood and applied the critical methods Li endorsed was the annotator of a high-quality late Ming printed edition of *A Book to Burn* currently housed in the Library of Congress (Figure 6.01). In this volume Li's original text occupies the main register and the commentator supplies observations and occasionally adversarial critique in the upper register in red ink. More than once the reader comments, "This argument comes

Provoking or Persuading Readers?

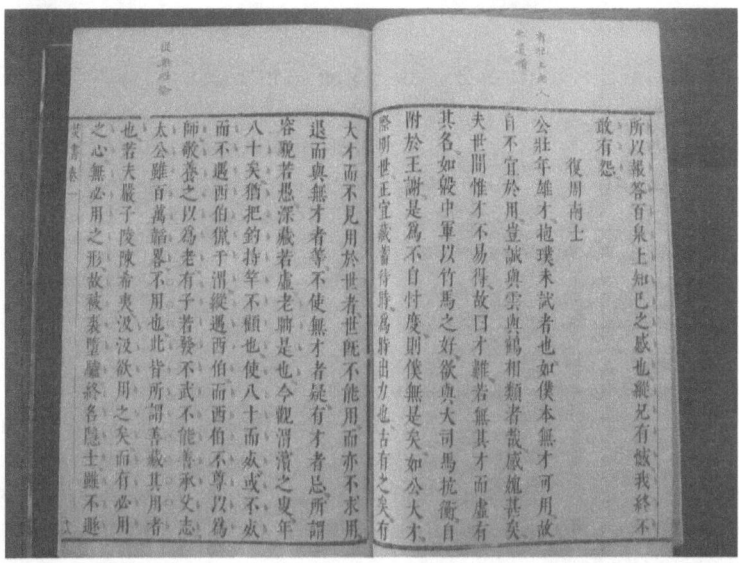

Figure 6.01. Li Zhi, *Fenshu* (A Book to Burn). Ming Wanli woodblock edition with "emphatic punctuation" marks added in red to the right of many words and critical remarks printed in red on the upper register of the page. Library of Congress, Asian Division, Chinese Collection, VK276 L643. Photo by the author.

out of nowhere!" (*cong wu ci lun*).⁹¹ Remarks like this simultaneously exhibit the reader/annotator's admiration for Li's ingenuity as an interpreter and his critical distance from the conclusions Li draws. As such, these comments exhibit the reader's reluctance simply to accept Li's pronouncements on any subject.

In addition to the defiant tone of the commentary, another feature of this edition worthy of notice is the sparseness of the commentary and the comfortable, roomy distance between it and the main text. The spaciousness of the page layout may be construed as inviting readers to make their own comments on this already commented-upon text. Indeed, one could argue that the amount of blank space on the page called out for further commentary: the commentator demonstrated through his remarks how one critically minded reader might reply to the text and left plenty of space in which subsequent readers could continue this task.⁹² Thus the commented-upon edition both responded to Li's initial appeal to readers to engage with his text and also renewed this call, welcoming later generations of readers to do the same.

CONCLUSION

The strategies of bluff everywhere apparent in Li's texts register his embeddedness in the complex and tangled structures of signification in the early modern world. Like so many other signs in this period—sartorial, numismatic, and bibliographical—Li's writings resisted and continue to resist straightforward interpretation. His boast of possessing acute vision shows that to some extent he still clung to a long-standing hermeneutic tradition anchored in the premise of stable, determinate meaning. Meanwhile, his assertion of the impossibility of discerning authorial intentions associates him with the growing early modern awareness of the fluidity and instability of meaning. To the extent that his writings illustrate the unreliability of words and surface appearances, they mirror the material conditions of the day. Merely to survive under such circumstances one needed to develop the ability to judge shifting situations for oneself, independently of past authorities.

Accordingly, discernment becomes not merely a central theme in Li's writings but a real and practical challenge to every reader. For the complicated rhetorical structure of his writings and the copious and irreconcilable contradictions they present offer no clear path for interpretation. Neither Li's practice as a reader and commentator nor his paradoxical statements on the nature of interpretation provide readers with guidance on how to approach his works. Instead they jolt and disconcert readers, unsettling their assumptions and disrupting their ingrained habits of reading. Although it is likely that, whether fans or opponents, some readers remained impervious to these bumps and jolts and continued to approach his writings in the same receptive, author-centered manner they had learned as children, more astute readers put Li's books to *use* as whetstones for honing their personal judgment. By subjecting his works to incisive critiques, these intrepid readers demonstrated their understanding that Li's books were not merely symptoms manifesting the increasingly unreliable state of signification in the early modern world; they were also prescriptions for coping with the contemporary epidemic of semiotic instability.

NOTES

ABBREVIATIONS USED IN NOTES

BBBKH: Li Zhi, *A Book to Burn and Book to Keep (Hidden): Selected Writings*, edited and translated by Rivi Handler-Spitz, Pauline C. Lee, and Haun Saussy. New York: Columbia University Press, 2016.

LZQJZ: Li Zhi, *Li Zhi quanji zhu* 李贽全集注, edited by Zhang Jianye 張建業. 26 vols. Beijing: Shehui kexue wenxian chubanshe, 2010.

LZYJCKZL: *Li Zhi yanjiu cankao ziliao* 李贽研究參考资料, compiled by Xiamen daxue lishi xi. Xiamen: Fujian Renmin chubanshe, 1975.

INTRODUCTION

1. "Un siècle desbordé." Montaigne, "De la Vanité" 3: 9, in *Les Essays*, 946. See also Montaigne, "On Vanity," in *The Complete Essays of Montaigne*, 721.
2. Zhang Dai, "Ziwei muzhiming" 自為墓志銘 (Tomb inscription for myself), in *Zhang Dai shiwen ji*, 5.295.
3. The title of the latter book is a pun, as the word *cang* can be translated either as "to store away for safekeeping" or "to hide."
4. Zhang Wenda, "Shenzong shilu Wanli sanshi nian run er yue yimao like jishizhong Zhang Wenda shu he Li Zhi" 神宗實錄萬曆三十年閏二月乙卯禮科給事中張問達疏劾李贄 (Veritable record of the memorial impeaching Li Zhi, submitted by the supervising censor Zhang Wenda on the *yimao* day of the second intercalary month of the thirtieth year of the reign of emperor Shenzong), in *Ming shilu* 112.369.11.
5. D'Elia, *Fonti Ricciane*, 2.65–69.
6. Zhang Shiyi, "Jidaoxin" 集導辛 (Collected views on bitterness), in *Yuelutang ji* 8.123.
7. The character *ru*, generally translated as "Confucian," is more aptly rendered as "scholar." An increasing number of scholars have opted to use the term "Ru." For example, see Csikszentmihalyi, *Material Virtue*, 15–22.
8. Li Zhi, "Yu yue" 豫約 (Rules agreed upon in advance), in *Fenshu* 4; *LZQJZ* 2:108–120.

9. Gu Yangqian 顧養謙, "Gu Chonglao song xing xu" 顧沖老送行序 (Farewell preface by Gu Chonglao), in Li Zhi, *Fenshu* 2; *LZQJZ* 1:189.

10. Li Zhi, "Ti Kongzi xiang yu Zhifo Yuan" 題孔子像於芝佛院 (An inscription for the image of Confucius in the Cloister of the Flourishing Buddha), in *Xu Fenshu* 4; *LZQJZ* 3:309.

11. Li Zhi, "Yu yue" 豫約 (Rules agreed upon in advance), in *Fenshu* 4; *LZQJZ* 2:108–120.

12. This term is defined in chapter two.

13. In *The Age of Silver*, Ma Ning observes that the boundaries between social classes in this period were more permeable in China than in Europe.

14. Pomeranz, *The Great Divergence*; Frank, *ReOrient*; Wong, *China Transformed*; Wong and Rosenthal, *Before and beyond Divergence*; Goldstone, "Divergence in Cultural Trajectories." Critiques of Pomeranz's work include Philip Huang, "Development or Involution?" On-cho Ng also interrogates the applicability of theories of early modernity to China. Ng, "The Epochal Concept of Early Modernity."

15. The phrase "horizontal continuities" is borrowed from Fletcher, "Integrative History." See also Adshead, *Material Culture in Europe and China*. For a brief introduction to the economic conditions in late imperial China, see Rawski, "Economic and Social Foundations of Late Imperial China," 3–10. For a far more detailed picture, see Brook, *The Confusions of Pleasure*; Brook, *The Trouble Empire*, especially ch. 9.

16. See for instance Vilar, "The Age of Don Quixote"; Niu, *Mingdai houqi*, 82–86.

17. The phrase "epochal concept of early modernity" is On-cho Ng's. See his "Epochal Concept of Early Modernity."

18. For an astute critique of the use of the "early modern" heuristic to the Chinese case, see Struve, *The Qing Formation*, 1–56.

19. Porter, "Sinicizing Early Modernity."

20. Another advantage of focusing on transregional similarities evident within a narrow timeframe is that doing so unsettles triumphalist narratives that trace the roots of European modernity—and Europe's eventual rise to dominance—to putative causes in the sixteenth century. For, as Pomeranz argues, before "the great divergence," roughly the turn of the nineteenth century, fundamentally similar economic conditions prevailed in China and Europe; there was therefore no *necessary* connection between the urbanization and commercialization of the European Renaissance and the subsequent advent of the industrial capitalism.

21. de Bary, "Individualism and Humanitarianism"; Lee, *Li Zhi*; Xu, *Li Zhi sixiang*; Ray Huang, *1587*; Billeter, *Li Chih*; Hok-lam Chan, *Li Chih*; Jin Jiang, "Heresy and Persecution"; Zuo, *Li Zhi yu wanming*; Mizoguchi, *Ri Takugo*.

22. Porter, *Comparative Early Modernities*, 2.

23. Cohen, "Eurasian Literature," 58.

24. Kleutghen, *Imperial Illusions*; Fuchs and Howard, *Made in China*; Cahill, *The Compelling Image*; North, *Artistic and Cultural Exchanges*;

Ellen C. Huang, "From the Imperial Court to the International Art Market"; Odell, "Porcelain, Print Culture and Mercantile Aesthetics."

25. Brook, *Vermeer's Hat*. See also Gerritsen and McDowall, "Global China."

26. The metaphor is borrowed from Brook, *Vermeer's Hat*, 22.

27. Aldridge, *Comparative Literature*, 3. Zhang Longxi, *Unexpected Affinities*.

28. Plaks, "The Aesthetics of Irony."

29. Vinograd, "Cultural Spaces," 353.

30. Pauline Yu, "Alienation Effects"; Eoyang, "Polar Paradigms"; Owen, *Readings in Chinese Literary Thought*, 37–48.

31. For a discussion of Li Zhi's metaphors of illness, see Lee, *Li Zhi*, 62–64.

32. On the concept of family resemblances, see Wittgenstein, *Philosophical Investigations*. For an application of this concept to the writings of Li Zhi, see Lee, *Li Zhi*, 69.

33. Brinker-Gabler, *Encountering the Other(s)*, 1.

34. Struve, *The Qing Formation*, 1–56.

35. Porter, "Global Satire."

36. Needham, *Science and Civilisation in China*, 4.

37. Moraru, "The Worlding of Nations," 193.

38. Collingwood, *The Idea of History*, 217–218.

39. Ibid., 215. Emphasis mine.

40. Claude Lévi-Strauss, "La place de la culture japonaise dans le monde," *Revue d'esthetique* 18 (1990), cited in Waldenfels, "Response to the Other," 41.

41. Palumbo-Liu, "The Utopias of Discourse," 36.

42. *Analects* 14.38.

43. Hans-Georg Gadamer, *Truth and Method*, cited in Waldenfels, "Response to the Other," 39. Emphasis mine.

44. Zhang Longxi, "The Challenge of East-West Comparative Literature," 34.

45. Palumbo-Liu, "The Utopias of Discourse," 36.

46. Fish, "Literature in the Reader," 75.

47. Liszka, *A General Introduction to the Semeiotic of Charles Sanders Peirce*.

48. He Yuming, *Home and the World*, especially the introduction and chapter one.

49. Ibid., 19.

50. For a more complete description of the content of this work and its disorderly presentation, as well as English translations of many essays and poems included within it, see *BBBKH*, especially the introduction.

51. Huang Lin, "*Fenshu* yuanben de jige wenti." See also Wu Guoping, "Ye tan *Fenshu* yuanben de wenti." The introduction to the 1961 Zhonghua shuju (China Press) edition of *Fenshu* also contains notes on the publication history of this book.

52. Although most scholarship (e.g., the editors of the 1961 and 1975 Zhonghua shuju editions) has dated the original publication of *A Book to Burn* (Fenshu) to 1590, Torao Suzuki and Huang Lin argue that a likelier date of first publication is 1592. Huang, "*Fenshu* yuanben de jige wenti," 93; Suzuki, "Ri Takugo nenpu, jō," 45. For a defense of the 1590 publication date, see Wu Guoping, "Ye tan *Fenshu* yuanben de wenti." Even if *A Book to Burn* was not printed until 1592, it was clearly in circulation prior to that point, since in 1591 Cai Yizhong, an angry supporter of Li Zhi's sometime friend and later adversary Geng Dingxiang, penned a rebuttal titled *Fenshu bian* 焚書辯 (Disputing *A Book to Burn*). Lin Haiquan, *Li Zhi nianpu*, 235.

53. For a list of extant editions, see Hok-lam Chan, *Li Chih*, 155–182.

54. Li Zhi, "Yu Wang Dingfu" 與汪鼎甫 (To Wang Dingfu), in *Xu Fenshu* 2; *LZQJZ* 3: 140–141.

55. On the relationships among these texts, see Li Defeng, "Li Zhi *Cangshu* yu Tang Shunzhi"; Qian Maowei, *Mingdai shixue*, 336–341.

56. Qian Maowei, *Mingdai shixue*, 337.

57. Texts also very frequently circulated in manuscript prior to publication. Many of Li Zhi's letters mention sending manuscripts to friends and seeking their comments and suggestions. See for instance Li Zhi, "You yu Jiao Moling" 又與焦秋陵 (Another letter to Jiao Moling [Jiao Hong]), in *Li Wenling ji* 李温陵集 4.11a.

58. This type of additive editorial process continued far beyond the Ming. Modern scholars Deng Changfeng, Song Kyong-ae, and Allan Barr have argued that the Qing literatus Zhang Chao's *Yuchu xinzhi* 虞初新志 (New record of Yuchu), an anthology assembling works by several contemporary authors, was compiled, expanded, and reprinted in successive editions. The first edition, which contained six fascicles, appeared in 1684. It was followed by a second edition of twelve fascicles, published in 1700, and finally by a third edition of twenty fascicles, which was produced in 1700. Son, "Writing for Print," 179.

CHAPTER 1

1. See, for example, the following, all by Li Zhi: "Tongxin shuo" 童心說 (On the childlike mind), in *Fenshu* 3; *LZQJZ* 1:276–279; "Zan Liu Xie" 贊劉諧 (An appraisal of Liu Xie), in *Fenshu* 3; *LZQJZ* 1:358–359; "On He Xinyin" 何心隱論 (He Xinyin lun), in *Fenshu* 3; *LZQJZ* 1.245–251; "Shiji zonglun" 世紀總論 (An overview of all times), in *Cangshu* 1; *LZQJZ* 4.1.

2. Zuo, *Li Zhi yu wanming*, 39. Members of the Return to Antiquity Movement did not regard themselves as conservative; this label was applied to them pejoratively by proponents of the more progressive Gong'an school (Gong'an pai). Members of the Return to Antiquity Movement considered their aesthetic program a welcome respite from the stultifying poetic style favored at court.

3. Xiong, *Ming Qing sanwen*, 257. See also Handler-Spitz, "Provocative Texts," 131.

4. Li Mengyang, "Shiji zixu" 詩集自序 (Authorial preface to my poetry collection), in Guo Shaoyu, *Zhongguo lidai wenlun* 2.283.

5. Xu Wei, "Ye Zisu shixu" 葉子肅詩序 (Preface to the poetry of Ye Zisu) in *Xu Wei ji* 2.19.519–520. An early reference to the analogy of birds mimicking human speech may be found in *Liji* ch. 1, "Qu li shang" 曲禮上, translated by Legge as "Khu Lî" in *The Lî Kî* 27.64. This comparison was also prevalent in European writings from the Renaissance and appears in the epistolary exchange between Angelo Poliziano (1454–1494) and Paolo Cortesi (1465–1510). DellaNeva, *Ciceronian Controversies*, 3.

6. Jiao, "Yu youren lun shu" 與友人論書 (Discussing books with a friend), in *Danyuanji* 1.93. See also Guo Shaoyu, *Zhongguo lidai wenlun* 3.131.

7. Zuo Qiuming was believed to have authored the *Zuozhuan*. Sima Qian composed the *Shiji*.

8. Yuan Zongdao, "Lunwen xia" 論文下 (On literature, part 2) in *Bai Suzhai leiji* 20.285–286. For a sanitized English translation of this passage, see Hung, *The Romantic Vision*, 127.

9. Jiao, "Yu youren lun shu" 與友人論書 (Discussing books with a friend), in *Danyuanji* 1.93. See also Guo Shaoyu, *Zhongguo lidai wenlun* 3.131.

10. Wang Shizhen, *Yiyuan zhiyan* 藝苑卮言 (Drunken words in the garden of art), 4.66.

11. Jiang Yingke, *Xuetao xiaoshu* 雪濤小書, 12. Translation in Chaves, "The Panoply of Images," 347. For further discussion of Jiang Yingke's poetics, see Barr, "Jiang Yingke's Place," 45.

12. Their complete correspondence is translated in DellaNeva, *Ciceronian Controversies*.

13. Erasmus, *The Ciceronian*, 369, 399, 440.

14. Ibid., 387, 368. Pico expresses similar concerns and asks rhetorically, "Do you think, Bembo, that any men of our time will be similar to Cicero in speech, unless they will also be like him in understanding? Augustine surely does not approve of people who admire only Cicero's tongue and not his heart, for he knew very well that learned and ornate language could develop only from the images in a cultivated heart." Pico, "Pico to Bembo," in DellaNeva, *Ciceronian Controversies*, 113.

15. Discussing the interplay between vernacular and literary Chinese in this period, Patrick Hanan asserts that "classical [Chinese] aspired to a standard of good taste not unlike the *elegantia* or *urbanitas* of Classical Latin." Hanan, *The Chinese Vernacular Story*, 16. For an examination of the interactions between vernacular and classical Chinese, as well as a brief contrastive analysis of the relationship between these languages and European classical and vernacular languages, see Mair, "Language and Script" in *The Columbia History*, 19–35. See also Plaks, "Full-Length *Hsiao-shuo*," 167–168.

16. Du Bellay, *La défense et illustration*.

17. On this subject, see Ng, "The Epochal Concept of Early Modernity."

18. On Li's criticisms of the examination system, see Epstein, *Competing Discourses*, 70.

19. Elman, *A Cultural History*, 383. On the civil examination system, see also Gong, *Mingdai baguwen*; Plaks, "The Prose of Our Time." Kai-wing Chow demonstrates that, in contrast to many of his contemporaries, Li Zhi took a certain pleasure in composing eight-legged essays. Chow, "An Avatar."

20. Ho Wai-kam, "Late Ming Literati," 28.

21. Chow, "Writing for Success," esp. 126–127.

22. Li Zhi, "Zhuowu lunlue Dianzhong zuo" 卓吾論略：滇中作 (A sketch of Zhuowu: Written in Yunnan), in *Fenshu* 3; *LZQJZ* 1.233. Pauline C. Lee provides a complete translation of this essay in *BBBKH*, 75–83.

23. Li Zhi, "*Chutanji* xu" 初潭集序 (Preface to *Upon Arrival at the Lake*), in *Chutanji*, *LZQJZ* 12.1. See also Li Zhi, "*Xianxinglu* xu, dai zuo" 先行錄序代作 (Preface to *Record of Acting First*, written upon request), in *Fenshu* 3; *LZQJZ* 1.322–324.

24. For interpretations of this essay, see Lee, *Li Zhi*, ch. 3; Zuo, *Li Zhi yu wanming*, 160–185; Xu, *Li Zhi sixiang*, 269–330; Song and Han, *Xinxue yu wenxue*, 156–185.

25. Li Zhi, "Tongxin shuo" 童心說 (On the childlike mind), in *Fenshu* 3; *LZQJZ* 1.276. Translation modified slightly from that of Haun Saussy in *BBBKH*, 111–113.

26. For instance, Wang Ji (1497–1582) cautions, "Authors who exhibit their true colors and are fully rid of hackneyed phrases do not get stuck [rigidly] adhering to formal rules. . . . But anyone who does not put his faith in his own innate gifts, and cares only about what other people think, who imitates them and schemes underhandedly, is like an actor imitating [the heroic] Sun-shu Ao. [Such a play-actor may] change his appearance, but does not alter his true essence. Thus even if he were to pass the imperial examination, he would be only a mediocrity repeating standard phrases. Those with true aspirations would not behave like this." Wang Ji, "Tianxin tibi" 天心題壁 (Inscribing a jade disk with the heart of heaven), in *Longxi Wang xiansheng quanji* 8.25b.

27. At one point, Bulephorus states, "Any speech that does not come from the heart is cold and dead." Erasmus, *The Ciceronian*, 396.

28. Ibid., 440.

29. Ibid., 366.

30. Historian Ho Ping-ti cautions that this already high number should be taken merely as a low estimate of the total number of individuals purchasing academic degrees, since it is likely that many of the people who did so did not immediately enroll in the academy. Ho, *Ladder of Success*, 33. See also Wu Renshu, *Pinwei shehua*, 60–61.

31. This situation is obliquely satirized in the vernacular novel *Xiyouji* 西遊記 (The journey to the west), wherein the protagonist, Sun Wukong, is several times awarded official titles that he does not merit and that exist in name only.

32. Li Zhi, "Fu Jiao Ruohou" 復焦弱侯 (Another letter to Jiao Ruohou [i.e., Jiao Hong]), in *Fenshu* 2; *LZQJZ* 1.110.

33. Li Zhi, "Wei Huang'an er shangren san shou" 為黃安二上人三首 (Three essays for two monks of Huang'an), in *Fenshu* 2; *LZQJZ* 1.199.

34. Li Zhi, "Da Zhou Liutang" 答周柳塘 (A response to Zhou Liutang), in *Fenshu* 2; *LZQJZ* 1.220. Li was not unusual in expressing his low estimation of contemporary Confucians and their motivations. The early Qing scholar Huang Zongxi concurred that "literati . . . are not concerned with the truth of the sages and worthies. They [study] . . . books for social advancement. . . . Today there is no literatus who is not preoccupied with profit." Huang Zongxi, *Ming wen hai* 明文海, 994–995, cited and translated in Chow, "An Avatar."

35. Celio Calcagnini, "On Imitation," in DellaNeva, *Ciceronian Controversies*, 151.

36. Jiao, "Yu youren lunshu" 與友人論書 (Discussing books with a friend), in *Danyuanji* 1.93.

37. Li Zhi, "Za shuo" 雜說 (On Miscellaneous matters), in *Fenshu* 3; *LZQJZ* 1.272. Translation modified from that of Pauline C. Lee in *BBBKH*, 104. Emphasis mine.

38. Li Zhi, "Shixue ruchen: Sima Tan, Sima Qian" 史學儒臣, 司馬談、司馬遷 (Biographies of Confucian historians: Sima Tan and Sima Qian), in *Cangshu* 49; *LZQJZ* 7.329.

39. Li Zhi, "Zhongyi Shuihuzhuan xu" 忠義水滸傳序 (Preface to *The Loyal and Righteous Outlaws of the Marsh*), in *Fenshu* 3; *LZQJZ* 1.301–304. Emphasis mine. The remark by Sima Qian to which Li Zhi alludes here appears in Sima Qian's authorial preface to *Shiji*, ch. 130, as well as in "Bao Ren Shaoqing shu" 報任少卿書 (Letter to Ren Shaoqing), included in Ban, *Hanshu*, ch. 62, "Sima Qian zhuan" 司馬遷傳 (Biography of Sima Qian). For an alternative translation of Li's preface, see that of Huiying Chen and Drew Dixon in *BBBKH*, 125–28.

40. "Da xu" 大序 (Great preface), cited and translated in Owen, *Readings in Chinese Literary Thought*, 41.

41. Peirce, "Prolegomena," 251.

42. Pauline Yu, "Alienation Effects." See also Owen, *Readings in Chinese Literary Thought*, 20–21.

43. Zhang Longxi opposes such dichotomous views of Chinese and Western literature, and Lu Mingjun argues powerfully against the idea that Chinese and Western poetics spring from irreconcilably different sources. Lu Mingjun, "Natural Inspiration"; Zhang Longxi, *Mighty Opposites*.

44. On contemporary visual artists' condemnations of excessive imitation and concomitant advocacy of "natural" self-expression, see Burnett, "A Discourse of Originality"; Barnhardt, "The 'Wild and Heterodox' School"; Bentley, *The Figurative Works*. On Ming authors' opposition to the culture of literary imitation, see Chou, *Yüan Hung-tao*, esp. ch. 1. See also Chaves, "The Panoply of Images"; Martin Huang, *Desire and Fictional Narrative*, 39–45.

45. Li Zhi, "Za shuo" 雜說 (On miscellaneous matters), in *Fenshu* 3; *LZQJZ* 1.272–276. Translation by Pauline C. Lee in *BBBKH*, 103.

46. Vinograd, "Cultural Spaces," 349; Park, *Art by the Book*, 211.

47. Tang, "Tiaoxiang'an ji xu" 雕象菴集序 (Preface to *Collection from the Studio for Training Elephants*), in *Tang Xianzu ji* 2.30.1038.

48. Tang, "Heqi xu" 合奇序 (Preface on collecting anomalies), in *Tang Xianzu ji* 2.32.1077–1078.

49. Yuan Hongdao, "Xu Xiaoxiu shi" 序小修詩 (Preface to poetry by Xiaoxiu [a.k.a. Yuan Zhongdao]), in *Yuan Hongdao ji jianjiao* 1.4.187. My translation silently modifies James J. Y. Liu's in *Chinese Theories of Literature*, 80. For more examples of Yuan Hongdao's analogies of literary creation to flowing water, see Hung, *The Romantic Vision*, 101, 123.

50. Jin Shengtan, "Yuting wenguan" 魚庭聞貫 (Instructions from my father) in *Jin Shengtan quanji* 4.39. Translation altered from that of Ge, "Authorial Intention," 6.

51. European romantics, including Byron, Shelley, Coleridge, Wordsworth, and Mill, expressed similar views on artistic expression. Mill described poetry as "the thoughts and words in which emotion spontaneously embodies itself," and Byron compared the creative act to a volcanic eruption. Mill, "Ninth Discourse," in *Literary Works* 2.4, cited in Abrams, *The Mirror and the Lamp*, 49.

52. For further instances of Li Zhi's views on literature, see his "Za shuo" 雜說 (On miscellaneous matters), in *Fenshu* 3; *LZQJZ* 1.272–276. On the late Ming conceit of emotion as a guarantor of authenticity in literature, see Wai-yee Li, "The Rhetoric of Spontaneity," 40; Yuan Zongdao, "Lunwen shang xia" 論文上、下 (On literature, parts 1 and 2), in *Bai Suzhai leiji* 20.283–285.

53. Li Zhi, "Geng Chukong xiansheng zhuan" 耿楚倥先生傳 (Record of Master Geng Chukong), in *Fenshu* 4; *LZQJZ* 2.21.

54. Li Zhi, "Da Deng Shiyang" 答鄧石陽 (Reply to Deng Shiyang), in *Fenshu* 1; *LZQJZ* 1.8.

55. On the putative connection between an artist's brushwork, his innate character, and his integrity, see Burnett, "A Discourse of Originality."

56. Jiang Yingke, "Ci huang" 雌黃 (Utter nonsense), in *Jiang Yingke ji* 811.

57. Wang Benke, "Xu ke Li shi shu xu" 續刻李氏書序 (Preface to another printed edition of Mr. Li [Zhi's] writings), in Li Zhi, *Xu fenshu*; *LZQJZ* 3.421–422.

58. Yuan Zhongdao, "Li Wenling zhuan" 李溫陵傳 (Biography of Li Wenling), in *Kexuezhai ji* 2.17.719–725. Translation by Haun Saussy in *BBBKH*, 325–333. Wu Yinghui notes that Li Zhi's emotional intensity was a hallmark of his writing style. The "Li Zhuowu" fiction and drama commentaries, composed in imitation of Li Zhi, often featured dramatic and emotional outbursts reminiscent of the volatile personality of the historical Li Zhi. Wu Yinghui, "Books in Pairs," ch. 1.

59. Wang Chong, "Gu xiang pian" 骨相篇 (On anthroposcopy) in *Lunheng* 1.3.82, cited and translated in Bottéro, "Cang Jie," 145.

60. Xu Shen 許慎, ed. *Shuowen jiezi* 說文解字 (Explaining graphs and analyzing characters), cited and translated in Bottéro, "Cang Jie," 149.

61. Ibid., 149.

62. The eclectic Han philosopher Wang Chong, for instance, asserted that in creating the written language, Cang Jie had undertaken the same

task as heaven and earth. Wang Chong, "Ganxu pian" 感虛篇 (Fictitious influences), in *Lunheng* 論衡 1.5.170. And the medieval literary critic Liu Xie (465–522) declared that written language (*wen* 文) was "born together with heaven and earth." James R. Y. Liu, *Chinese Theories of Literature*, 8. Wang was so deeply convinced that Chinese characters manifested reality that when he observed that the character used to write the name of a hero from antiquity did not graphically illustrate the legend narrating this hero's birth, Wang doubted whether the story was true, not whether the Chinese character had been transmitted accurately. Wang Chong, "Qiguai pian" 奇怪篇 (Miracles), in *Lunheng* 論衡 1.3.114, cited in Bottéro, "Cang Jie," 145. For an English translation of the entire passage, see Forke, *Lun-Hêng, Part I*, 322–323.

63. Li Zhi, "Da Liu Xianzhang" 答劉憲長 (A reply to District Chief Liu), in *Fenshu* 1; *LZQJZ* 1.61.

64. Shang, "The Making of the Everyday World," 75–76. Shang further notes that the protagonist of the erotic novel *The Plum in the Golden Vase* (Jin ping mei) 金瓶梅 frequently applies kinship terms such as "father" and "daughter" to people with whom he has only temporary associations grounded in self-interest rather than lifelong commitments anchored in familial love and obligation.

65. Li Zhi, "You yu Zhou Youshan" 又與周友山 (Another letter to Zhou Youshan), in *Fenshu* 2; *LZQJZ* 1.168.

66. Li Zhi, "Yu yue xiao yin" 豫約小引 (Minor preface to "Rules agreed upon in advance"), in *Fenshu* 4; *LZQJZ* 2.96–97. Francis Bacon expresses similar views in his essay "Of Friends and Followers," in *The Essays*.

67. Rusk highlights the efforts of the Ming scholar Wei Jiao (1483–1543) to recover the original Chinese script, which had been largely destroyed in the bibliocaust perpetrated by the first Qin emperor. Rusk further compares the "rupture" between the lost written language and what remained to the biblical account of the Tower of Babel, discussed below. Rusk, "Old Scripts," 84–86.

68. Ricci, *Xiguo jifa* 西國記法 (Mnemonic Techniques of the West) 11a, cited in Rusk "Old Scripts," 78.

69. Ricci, *Jiaoyou lun* 交友論, translated as *On Friendship*, 104–105.

70. Qian Jibo, *Mingdai wenxue*, 23.

71. Xu Wei, "Xiao Fu shi xu" 肖甫詩序 (Preface to poetry by Xiao Fu), in *Xu Wei ji* 2.19.534.

72. Jin Shengtan, "Xu yi yue 'tongku guren'" 序一曰慟哭古人 (First preface titled "Grieving for the ancients"), in *Jin Shengtan quanji* 3.1.7, cited and translated in Ge, "Authorial Intention," 13.

73. *Analects* 12.11, translation in Lau, 114. For an excellent discussion of the rectification of names in late imperial times, see Epstein, *Competing Discourses*, 21–28.

74. Anthony C. Yu, "Cratylus and Xunzi on Names," 240–241.

75. *Analects* 13.3, translation in Lau, 118.

76. Ibid.

77. Xunzi, "Zheng ming" 正名 (Rectifying names), ch. 22 of *Xunzi jicheng*, 284; Xunzi, *Hsün Tzu: Basic Writings*, 140. Compare Knoblock's translation, "On the Correct Use of Names" in *Xunzi*, 3.128.

78. *Analects* 6.24, translation modified from Lau, 84.

79. Mao Qiling 毛奇齡, *Lunyu jiqiu pian* 論語稽求篇 (Seeking to investigate the *Analects*) 3.8a–8b, cited and translated in Makeham, *Name and Actuality*, 42.

80. Ibid., 43.

81. Thoroughly self-contradictory, Li did not consistently maintain his position in favor of *zhengming*. In one letter he mouths the opinion that "Daoist, Buddhist, and Confucian are all just names." Li Zhi, "Da Geng sikou" 答耿司寇 (Reply to Justice Minister Geng), in *Fenshu* 1; *LZQJZ* 1.74. Elsewhere he adopts the Buddhist view that words are simply vacuous. Li Zhi, "*Xin jing* tigang" 心經提綱 (The hub of the *Heart Sūtra*), in *Fenshu* 3; *LZQJZ* 1.280–284.

82. Plato's dialogue *Cratylus* provides an alternative account of the origins of human language, which also links language closely to the natural world.

83. Foucault, *The Order of Things*, 36.

84. For a discussion of this passage, see Eco, *The Search for the Perfect Language*, 8.

85. Browne, *Religio Medici*, 1.16.15. This type of correlative thinking was also popular among the Jesuits. For more examples of this type of imagery, see Curtius, *European Literature*, 343–345; Robinson, "The Book of Nature"; Huppert, "Divinatio et Eruditio"; Cave, *The Cornucopian Text*, 21.

86. Genesis 11:1–9.

87. The number seventy-two was arrived at by adding up the total number of Noah's descendants as attested in Genesis 10. Ham had thirty descendants, Shem had twenty-seven, and Japheth had fifteen. Thus while it was already well known by the end of the sixteenth century that the number of languages currently being spoken far exceeded this number, the number seventy-two still appears in some Renaissance texts.

88. Donald Lach estimates that during the sixteenth century roughly a hundred words of Asian origin were added to the permanent vocabularies of European languages. Many more foreign words made a brief appearance in European vocabularies before drifting out of circulation. For a list of such terms, see Lach, *Asia in the Making of Europe*, 2.3.530–539, 544–553.

89. Shakespeare, *Romeo and Juliet*, II, ii, 37.

90. "Il y a le nom et la chose: le nom, c'est une voix qui remerque et signifie la chose; le nom, ce n'est pas une partie de la chose ny de la substance, c'est une piece estrangere joincte à la chose, et hors d'elle." Montaigne, "De la gloire" 2: 16 in *Les Essays*, 618. See also Montaigne, "Of Glory," in *The Complete Essays of Montaigne*, 468. For analysis of Montaigne's nominalism, see Compagnon, *Nous, Michel de Montaigne*.

91. "Nostre contestation est verbale. Je demande que c'est que nature, volupté, cercle, et substitution. La question est de parolles, et se paye de

mesme. Une pierre c'est un corps. Mais qui preseroit: Et corps qu'est-ce?—Substance—Et substance quoy? ainsi de suitte." Montaigne, "De l'experience" 3: 13 in *Les Essays*, 1069. See also Montaigne, "Of Experience," in *The Complete Essays of Montaigne*, 818–819.

92. For a useful introduction to this work, see Bowen, "Geofroy Tory's 'Champ Fleury.'"

93. Tory, *Champ Fleury*, xxi.

94. Ibid., xxii.

95. Foucault, *Les Mots et les choses*, 51–52; Foucault, *The Order of Things*, 36–37. I have modified the translation slightly.

96. Eco, *The Search for the Perfect Language*, 18–19. See also Porter, *Ideographia*, 16; Lach, *Asia in the Making of Europe*, 2.3.519.

97. Postel wrote *Linguarum duodecim characteribus differentium alphabetum introductio* (Paris, 1538). Gesner wrote *Mithrades Gesneri, experimens differentias linguarum tum veterum, tum quae hodie, per totum terrarium orbem, in usu sunt* (1555). Bibliander wrote *De ratione communi* (1548). Lach, *Asia in the Making of Europe*, 2.3.515.

98. Gaspar da Cruz, "Treatise in which the things of China are related," in Boxer, *South China*, 161–162.

99. Lach, *Asia in the Making of Europe*, 2.3.514.

100. Juan González de Mendoza, *History of the Great and Mighty Kingdom of China and the Situation Thereof*, 1.121–122, cited in Porter, *Ideographia*, 35.

101. Bacon, *The Advancement of Learning*, bk. 2, sect. 16.2, p. 137.

102. Porter, *Ideographia*, 38.

103. Blaise de Vigenère, *Traicté des chiffres*, cited in Rusk, "Old Scripts," 69. On Webb's *Historical Essay*, see Porter, *Ideographia*, 43–45. Bacon coins the term "characters real" in *Advancement of Learning*, bk. 2, sect. 16.2, p. 137.

104. Bacon, *Advancement of Learning*, bk. 2, sect. 16.2, p. 137.

CHAPTER 2

1. Admittedly, the very broad scope of this term also opens it up to criticism. In a review of Bowen's book, François Rigolot faulted Bowen for attempting to discuss diverse rhetorical phenomena under a single rubric, since doing so, he charged, risked sacrificing precision. Rigolot, "Review of Barbara Bowen's *The Age of Bluff*," 365.

2. On the meaning of the term "heretic" (*yiduan*), literally "another strand," in this period, see Ch'ien, *Chiao Hung*, 73–77.

3. Li Zhi, "Fu Zhou Nanshi" 復周南士 (Reply to Zhou Nanshi), in *Fenshu* 1; *LZQJZ* 1.34. Elsewhere he alludes to Confucius as "our sage" and overtly avers, "I'm a Confucian." Li Zhi, "*Jingang jing* shuo" 金剛經說 (On *The Diamond Sūtra*), in *Xu Fenshu* 2; *LZQJZ* 3.214–217; Li Zhi, "Shu Xiaoxiu shoujuan hou" 書小修手卷後 (Written at the end of Xiaoxiu's [a.k.a. Yuan Zhongdao's] hand scroll), in *Xu Fenshu* 2; *LZQJZ* 3.201–203.

4. Li Zhi, "Yu Zeng Jiquan" 與曾繼泉 (To Zeng Jiquan), in *Xu Fenshu* 1; *LZQJZ* 3.149. Zeng Jiquan studied Buddhism with Li Zhi at the Cloister of the Flourishing Buddha.

5. Li Zhi, "Da Jiao Yiyuan" 答焦漪園 (Reply to Jiao Yiyuan), in *Fenshu* 1; *LZQJZ* 1.18.

6. Li Zhi, "Yu Zeng Jiquan" 與曾繼泉 (To Zeng Jiquan), in *Xu Fenshu* 1; *LZQJZ* 3.149. In a third letter, written to Deng Lincai in 1585, he affirms, "I am a heretic, unworthy of mention." The litotes lurking in the phrase "unworthy of mention" constitutes a subtle example of bluff. Li Zhi, "Da Deng Shiyang" 答鄧石陽 (Reply to Deng Shiyang), in *Fenshu* 1; *LZQJZ* 1.26.

7. On Li Zhi's role as a father and husband, see Epstein, "Li Zhi's Self-Fashioning."

8. On the reputation of the Geng family in Macheng, see Rowe, *Crimson Rain*, 90–94. On the public circulation of letters in the Ming dynasty, especially Li Zhi's letters to Geng Dingxiang, see Brook, "The Public of Letters."

9. Xu Jianping provides a contrasting view. He argues that Li's period of "wildness" (*kuang*) peaked between the years 1586 and 1595, and that in his later years, as Li succumbed to illness and became increasingly fascinated with Buddhism, his personality mellowed. Xu Jianping, "'Kuangguai' he 'yu shi wu zheng.'"

10. For a more detailed discussion of Li's appearance, see chapter three.

11. Bowen, *The Age of Bluff*, 6. Bowen's use of this term has been criticized on the grounds that it is uncorroborated by dictionary definitions. One reviewer even dismissively compared Bowen to the giant talking egg, Humpty Dumpty, who arrogantly declared, "When I use a word . . . it means just what I choose it to mean, neither more nor less." The criticism is excessively harsh, for literary critics often redefine words—or coin new words—to suit their own analytic purposes. Carroll, *Through the Looking Glass*, 113; Rigolot, "Review of Barbara Bowen's *The Age of Bluff*," 364; Frame, "Review of Barbara Bowen's *The Age of Bluff*," 342.

12. Bowen, *The Age of Bluff*, 6.

13. Plaks, "Aesthetics of Irony," 487–500; Porter, "Global Satire."

14. Aristotle, *Posterior Analytics*, 1.2.72a.

15. *Han Feizi xinyi* 36.547.

16. For further discussion of irony in a Chinese context, see Porter, "Global Satire."

17. Lanling Xiaoxiaosheng, *Jin Ping Mei cihua* 1.3. Translation slightly altered from that of Roy in *The Plum in the Golden Vase*, vol. 1, *The Gathering*, 7.

18. The German scholar Otto Franke is reported to have stated, "Li Zhi['s] opinions are essentially negative. He proposes no new cognitive thought or abstract perspective; yet he aims to clear things away." Feng Junpei, "Ping Fulange jiaoshou de Li Zhi yanjiu zhaiyao" 評福蘭閣教授的李贄研究摘要 (Outline of a critical assessment of Franke's study on Li Zhi), in *LZYJCKZL* 2.227. De Bary concurs when he calls Li Zhi's thought "negative individualism . . . incapable of establishing itself in any framework of laws or institutions." de Bary, "Individualism and Humanitarianism," 224.

19. On the history of the word "irony," see Muecke, *Irony and the Ironic*.

20. Aristotle, *Posterior Analytics*, 1.72a.

21. Booth, *A Rhetoric of Irony*, 240; Pomel, "La Fonction critique de l'ironie," 79–80.

22. Literary scholar Wayne Booth distinguishes between stable irony and unstable irony. The type of irony discussed here is unstable. Stable irony refers to clear-cut situations in which an author states precisely the opposite of what he means. The fourteenth-century philosopher Nicolas Oremse summarizes: "Irony is when one *says* one thing, but *means* the contrary" (cited in Pomel, "La Fonction critique de l'ironie," 86). The meaning of such irony, according to Booth, is "firm as a rock" (*A Rhetoric of Irony*, 235). To be sure, ironies of this kind appear in the writings of Li Zhi. However, because their meaning is not open to dispute, they do not constitute examples of bluff. The term "bluff" is reserved to describe ambiguities that provoke conflicting interpretations. A statement by Montaigne illustrates the difference between these two sorts of irony: "If a lie, like truth, had only one face . . . [it] certainty would be the reverse of what the liar said. But the reverse side of truth has a hundred thousand shapes and no defined limits" (Si, comme la vérité, le mensonge n'avoit qu'un visage . . . nous prenderions pour certain l'opposé de ce que diroit le menteur. Mais le revers de la verité a cent mille figures et un champ indefiny). Montaigne, "Des Menteurs" 1: 9, in *Les Essays*, 37. See also Montaigne, "Of Liars," in *The Complete Essays of Montaigne*. This indeterminacy is the essence of bluff.

23. On Buddhist paradox, see Wright, "The Significance of Paradoxical Language"; Foulk, "The Form and Function of Koan Literature."

24. This phrase appears in a letter to Sir Henry Wotton, likely composed in 1600. Simpson, *A Study of the Prose Works of John Donne*, 298. I have updated Donne's spelling. Donne insists that paradoxes are *not* the revelation of truth but simply prods that nudge the reader to uncover the truth for himself.

25. However, the English word "alarm" also conveys another meaning not present in the Chinese case. Derived from the French *à l'arme*, it refers to a call to arms, and by extension a call to action. Chan paradoxes, by contrast, do not typically function as calls to action.

26. Li Zhi, "Da Liu Xianzhang" 答劉憲長 (Reply to District Chief Liu), in *Fenshu* 1; *LZQJZ* 1.61.

27. The incident involving the monk's enlightenment is recorded in a biography of the monk Wunian Shenyou (1544–1627), cited and translated in Wu Jiang, *Enlightenment in Dispute*, 68–70. One essay in which Li Zhi sternly instructs monks is "Yu yue" 豫約 (Rules agreed upon in advance), in *Fenshu* 4; *LZQJZ* 2.120. See also "Jie zhong seng" 戒眾僧 (Disciplining the sangha), *Fenshu* 4; *LZQJZ* 2.73–75. The latter essay is translated by Jennifer Eichman in *BBBKH*, 181–184.

28. Wai-yee Li, "The Problem of Genuineness."

29. For the story of the virtuous Bo Yi and Shu Qi, see Sima Qian, *Shiji* 史記 [Records of the grand historian], ch. 61.

30. For the story of the wicked man of Qi, see *Mengzi* 孟子 (Mencius), 4B33.

31. Mengzi describes Yi Yin as a virtuous man who refused to give anything away or take anything that did not rightfully belong to him. Ibid., 5A7.

32. According to Mencius, Yang Zhu was so stingy that he would not pluck a single hair from his head, even if doing so could benefit the entire world. Ibid., 3B9.

33. Zigong, a disciple of Confucius, asked: "When the people in the village all hate a person, how's that?"

The master said "That is not sufficient."

"When the people in the village all hate a person, how's that?"

"That is not sufficient. It would be better that the good villagers like him and the bad dislike him." *Analects* 13.23.

34. Li Zhi, "Zi zan" 自贊 (Self-appraisal), in *Fenshu* 3; *LZQJZ* 1.356–358.

35. In a letter written to Liu Jincheng in 1595, Li Zhi repeats the claim that he would willingly suffer hunger for the sake of righteousness. Li Zhi, "Yu Chenglao" 與城老 (To Chenglao), in *Xu Fenshu* 1; *LZQJZ* 3.62–65.

36. "Si vous dictes: Je ments, et que vous dissiez vray, vous mentez donc." Montaigne, "Apologie de Raimond Sebond" (Apology for Raymond Sebond) 2: 12, in *Les Essays*, 527. Compare Frame's translation in Montaigne, *The Complete Essays of Montaigne*, 392.

37. Zuo, *Li Zhi yu wanming*, 66.

38. Wai-yee Li, "The Problem of Genuineness." In a similar vein, James Cahill and Richard Vinograd have pointed out the exaggerated and at times indecorous ways in which some painters of the period depicted themselves. Cahill, *Fantasics and Eccentrics*, 28; Vinograd, *Boundaries of the Self*, 31–33.

39. The full passage may be found in Xu Wei, "Zi wei muzhiming" 自為墓志銘 (Self tomb inscription) in *Xu Wei ji* 2.26.638. My translation modifies that of Kafalas in "Weighty Matters," 61–62.

40. Wu Cheng'en, *Xiyou ji* 西遊記 (Journey to the West), ch. 58. For an analysis of this scene, see He Yuming, *Home and the World*, 207.

41. On this subject see Volpp, *The Worldly Stage*, esp. ch. 1.

42. Xu Wei, *Ci Mulan* 雌木蘭 (The female Mulan), in Lu Jiye, *Ming zaju xuan*, 37; Kwa and Idema, *Mulan*, 25.

43. Shakespeare, *As You Like It*, II, vii, 42. Shakespeare's Antonio in *The Merchant of Venice* echoes this sentiment, stating, "I hold the world . . . a stage where every man must play a part" (I, i, 4).

44. Tang, *Mudan ting*, sc. 55, 263, 264; Tang, *Peony Pavilion*, 329.

45. For further discussion of doubled or mistaken identity in this period, see Tina Lu, *Persons, Roles, and Minds*; Kwa, *Strange Eventful Histories*.

46. Bentley points out that Chen's portrait of Du Fu also shares these features and that they may therefore be regarded as a "type." Bentley, "Authenticity and the Expanding Market," 178.

47. Ibid., 177–178.

48. Vinograd, "Hiding in Plane Sight," 149; Vinograd, "Cultural Spaces." On Min Qiji and metapictures, see Wu Hung, *The Double Screen*, 243–259; Hsiao, *The Eternal Present*, 217–227.

49. Steinberg, "Velazquez' *Las Meninas*." I am particularly grateful to Stephen Whiteman for discussing these ideas with me.

50. Cervantes, *Don Quijote*, 51–53.

51. This word also carries a third meaning (and a different pronunciation, *zang*), which refers to Buddhist and Daoist scriptures. This meaning, however, does not appear relevant to the title of Li's book.

52. Li Zhi, "Cangshu shiji liezhuan zongmu qianlun" 藏書世紀列傳總目前論 (Preface to the Combined "Dynastic Records" and "Biographies" Sections of *A Book to Keep [Hidden]*), in *Cangshu*; *LZQJZ* 4.1. For an alternative translation of this preface, see that of Pauline C. Lee in *BBBKH*, 317–319.

53. Liu Dongxing, "Liu Dongxing xu" 劉東星序 (Preface by Liu Dongxing), in Li Zhi, *Cangshu*; *LZQJZ* 8.697.

54. Mei Guozhen, "Mei Guozhen xu" 梅國楨序 (Preface by Mei Guozhen), in Li Zhi, *Cangshu*; *LZQJZ* 8.698.

55. The first printed edition did not appear until 1599. Qian Maowei, *Mingdai shixue*, 337.

56. Li Zhi, "Yu Jiao Yiyuan" 與焦漪園 (To Jiao Yiyuan), in *Fenshu* 1; *LZQJZ* 1.17.

57. Lin Haiquan, *Li Zhi nianpu*, 363.

58. Li Zhi, "Yu Geng Zijian" 與耿子健 (To Geng Zijian), in *Xu Fenshu* 1; *LZQJZ* 3.135.

59. The Buddhist term "eyes of flesh" (*rou yan*; Sanskrit: *māmsa-caksus*) refers to the most mundane form of vision, which an utterly unenlightened person might possess. It represents the lowest of five levels. "Eyes of flesh" are followed by "eyes of heaven" (*tian yan*; Skt: *dibbacakkhu*), a kind of vision attainable through study and Chan meditation; "eyes of wisdom" (*hui yan*; Skt: *prajña-caksus*), the perception that all phenomena are empty; "dharma eyes" (*fa yan*; Skt: *dharmacaksus*), the insight possessed by bodhisattvas; and finally "Buddha eyes" (*Fo yan*; Skt: *buddha-caksus*), the complete understanding of a Buddha. Wu Rujun, *Fojiao da cidian*, 119.

60. Ziyun is the courtesy name of the philosopher Yang Xiong (53 BCE–ca.18 CE). Li Zhi, "Zi xu" 自序 (Author's preface), in *Fenshu*; *LZQJZ* 1.1.

61. "Bao Ren Shaoqing shu" 報任少卿書 (Letter to Ren Shaoqing), in "Sima Qian zhuan" 司馬遷傳 (Biography of Sima Qian), ch. 62, in Ban, *Hanshu*, 3.62.1892.

62. Li Zhi, "Zhongyi Shuihuzhuan xu" 忠義水滸傳序 (Preface to *The Loyal and Righteous Outlaws of the Marsh*), in *Fenshu* 3; *LZQJZ* 1:301–304.

63. The close filiation between *A Book to Keep (Hidden)* and *The Left Scribe's Records* was not lost upon late Ming and early Qing scholars like Gu Dashao (b. 1576), who remarked that Li relied heavily on Tang's text but added and deleted passages at will. On Li Zhi's debt to Tang Shunzhi, see Li Defeng, "Li Zhi *Cang shu* yu Tang Shunzhi"; Qian Maowei, *Mingdai shixue*, 336–341.

64. Li Zhi, "Zi xu" 自序 (Author's preface), in *Fenshu*; *LZQJZ* 1.1. On the authenticity of the "author's preface," see Huang Lin, "*Fenshu* yuanben de jige wenti"; Wu Guoping, "Ye tan *Fenshu* yuanben de wenti," 46.

65. Zhang Wenda, "Shenzong shilu Wanli sanshi nian run er yue yimao like jishizhong Zhang Wenda shu he Li Zhi" 神宗實錄萬曆三十年閏二月乙卯

禮科給事中張問達疏劾李贄 (Veritable record of the memorial impeaching Li Zhi, submitted by the supervising censor Zhang Wenda on the *yimao* day of the second intercalary month of the thirtieth year of the reign of emperor Shenzong), in *Ming shilu* 112.369.11.

66. Li Zhi, "Zi xu" 自序 (Author's preface), in *Fenshu* 1; *LZQJZ* 1.1.
67. Ibid.
68. Lejeune, *Le pacte autobiographique*.
69. "Buveurs très illustres," "vérolés." Rabelais, *Oeuvres complètes*, 38–41. See also Rabelais, *Gargantua and Pantagruel*, 7.
70. "Rompre l'os et sugcer la sustantificque mouelle." Rabelais, *Oeuvres complètes*, 39. See also Rabelais, *Gargantua and Pantagruel*, 8.
71. "Belles billes vezées," "cerveau caséiforme." Rabelais, *Oeuvres complètes*, 41. See also Rabelais, *Gargantua and Pantagruel*, 9. For further discussion of Rabelais's prefaces, see Gray, "Ambiguity and Point of View"; Coleman, "The Prologues of Rabelais."
72. "Parens et amis: a ce que [l]'ayant perdu . . . ils y puissant retrouver aucuns traits de [ses] conditions et humeurs." Montaigne, "Au lecteur," in *Les Essays*, 3. See also Montaigne, "To the Reader," in *The Complete Essays of Montaigne*, 2. On Montaigne's participation in the process of publication, see Hoffmann, *Montaigne's Career*, 94. On his relationship with his printer, Simon Millanges, see Hoffmann, "Wagering on Publication," ch. 2 of *Montaigne's Career*.
73. "Ce n'est pas raison que tu employes ton loisir en un subject si frivole et si vain." Montaigne, "Au lecteur," in *Les Essays*, 3. See also Montaigne, "To the Reader," in *The Complete Essays of Montaigne*, 2. This passage is followed by a slightly misleading date. On the modification of this date in successive editions, as well as the questions this unreliable dating raises, see Delègue, *Montaigne et la mauvaise foi*, 29–30.

CHAPTER 3

1. Li's head was shaved for the first time in the summer of 1588. That same summer, in the seventh month, Li learned of his wife's death in far-off Fujian. However, I have not been able to determine whether the news reached him before or after he shaved his head. Ray Huang speculates that perhaps Li shaved his head first and that his wife's shock on learning of his action may have hastened her demise. However, this chronology seems implausible, given the slow speed with which information traveled and the fact that Li's wife died during the intercalary sixth month. *LZQJZ* 2.260n1, 12.2n3; Lin Haiquan, *Li Zhi nianpu*, 185–186, 194; Huang, *1587*, 192.

The identity of the person who shaved Li is unknown. For the sake of simplicity, I speak of Li as shaving his own head. However, it was customary for senior monks to shave the heads of junior monks, so it is plausible that Li enlisted a member of the monastic community to shave him.

2. In many premodern societies, both East and West, sumptuary laws were deployed to maintain the social hierarchy. Hunt, *Governance of the Consuming*

Passions, 140–141. Violations of these rules were often recorded—and parodied—in the literature of the period. Kwa, *Strange Eventful Histories*.

3. One notable exception is the eccentric literatus and member of the Taizhou branch of Wang Yangming's School of the Mind, Deng Huoqu (1489–1578), for whom Li Zhi had the utmost respect. Wu Jiang, *Enlightenment in Dispute*, 100. Li mentions Deng frequently in *A Book to Burn*. For example, see "Wei Huang'an er shangren sanshou" 為黃安二上人三首 (Three essays for two monks of Huang'an), in *Fenshu* 2; *LZQJZ* 1.194–200, and "Gao jie shuo" 高潔說 (On loftiness and cleanliness), in *Fenshu* 3; *LZQJZ* 1.294–297.

4. On Li's self-presentation and the difficulties of interpretation it raised, see Zhang Ying, "Li Zhi's Image Trouble."

5. On the rampant infractions of Renaissance sumptuary laws, especially in Elizabethan England, see Garber, *Vested Interests*, 25–40. Garber's discussion focuses primarily on gender transvestitism.

6. "Wang zhi" 王制 (Royal regulations), in *Liji* 禮記 (Book of Rites) 5.170, 189; Legge, *The Lî Kî*, 27.217, 237.

7. "Xigong ershisi nian" 僖公二十四年 (Twenty-fourth year of Duke Xi), in *Zuozhuan* 1.280.

8. Xunzi, "Yuelun" 樂論 (On music), in *Xunzi jicheng* 20.264. My translation slightly modifies Knoblock's in *Xunzi*, 3.87.

9. The *Book of Changes* (Yijing) also analogizes suitable raiment to orderly governance and states that in high antiquity, when the Yellow Emperor and the sage kings Yao and Shun "draped their upper and lower garments ... heaven and earth were put in order." "Xici xia" 繫辭下 (Appended phrases, part 2), in *Zhouyi dazhuan jinzhu*, 562. For a complete translation of this passage, see Wilhelm, *I Ching*, 356. Also cited and translated in Ko, "Bondage in Time," 204. My translation differs slightly from Ko's.

10. Jia, "Fu yi" 服疑 (Discourse on dress), in *Xin shu*, 44. Translation by Yuan Zujie in "Dressing for Power," 185.

11. Rickett, *Guanzi*, 108–109. This passage also appears in the *Spring and Autumn Annals* (Chunqiu); Queen and Major, *Luxuriant Gems*, 268. Additionally, the Han historian Ban Gu (32–92 CE) stated, "The ancients used clothing to distinguish between the noble and the common and to illustrate virtue so as to encourage the imitation of good example." Ban, "Yishang" 衣裳 (Garments), in *Baihutong* 2.18. Translation modified from Vollmer's in *Silks for Thrones and Altars*, 8.

12. Yuan Zujie, "Dressing for Power," 185.

13. Ibid., 186–187.

14. Jiang Yonglin, *The Great Ming Code*; Liu Xiaoyi, "Clothing, Food, and Travel," 91.

15. Zhang Lu 張鹵, *Huang Ming zhi shu* 皇明制書 (The system of the august Ming), 1:52, cited and translated in Yuan Zujie, "Dressing for Power," 187n20. On the role and purpose of sumptuary laws, also see Berry, *The Idea of Luxury*, 31.

16. D'Elia, *Fonti Ricciane*, 1:65–66, cited and translated in Peterson, "What to Wear?," 404–405.

17. Yuan Zujie, "Dressing the State," 201–203. See also McDermott, *State and Court Ritual*, 312. Craig Clunas exaggerates when he pronounces, "Sumptuary laws received no updating precisely at the time they were being most openly and consistently ignored," during the late Ming period. Clunas, "The Art of Social Climbing," 371. Additional laws were enacted up until the final years of the dynasty. For a complete list of these laws, see Lin Liyue, "Mingdai jinsheling chutan," 76–84. See also *Da Ming huidian* 2.60–61.1017–1072.

Across Europe, infringements of sumptuary laws were also rising throughout the sixteenth century and laws struggled to catch up. In France, sumptuary legislation reached a climax between 1560 and 1580, with more than fifteen sumptuary statutes passed during this period. Laws regulating luxury goods also increased in the German states, England, and Switzerland. But these laws exerted little influence; clergy and merchants continued to dress gaudily in silks and other luxury fabrics nominally limited to the nobility. Moyer, "Sumptuary Laws," 61–62.

18. Yuan Gun 袁袞, "Shihui" 世諱 (Taboos of the times), cited in Wu Cuncun, *Ming Qing shehui*, 72–73. See also Yuan Zujie, "Dressing for Power," 201–202.

19. Wu Renshu, "Mingdai pingmin fushi," 84, 73.

20. Admittedly, this phrase is meant to be taken figuratively. Li's point is that contemporary Confucians, because they do not behave ethically, deserve neither to bear the title of Confucian officials nor to wear the corresponding uniforms. Li is not implying that actual outlaws dress up as Confucian officials. Li Zhi, "Luo Jinxi xiansheng gaowen" 羅近溪先生告文 (In memoriam Master Luo Jinxi), in *Fenshu* 3; *LZQJZ* 1.340. This phrase seems to riff on the idiom "beasts wearing clothes" (*yi guan qin shou*), which refers to uncouth, unmannered individuals. See also Yuan Zujie, "Dressing the State," 201–202.

21. On the licit and illicit giving and receiving of robes bearing the restricted python insignia, both in the fictional narrative of *The Plum in the Golden Vase* (Jin ping mei) 金瓶梅 and in the world outside this novel, see Volpp, "The Gift of a Python Robe." Volpp cites Shen Li (1531–1615) as writing, "Nowadays, no one pays attention to rank or status. Python robes and jade belts gleam on the steps to the throne room, and the flying-fish robe is everywhere on the streets." *Yiyutang gao* 亦玉堂稿 (Manuscript from Jade-like Hall), translated in Volpp, "The Gift of a Python Robe," 133. Elsewhere in this article, she mentions that the eunuch Liu Ruoyu (b. 1584?) accused the notorious eunuch Wei Zhongxian (1568–1627) of corruption and claimed that in his day even low-ranking officials wore python robes (157). On this subject, see also Yuan Zujie, "Dressing the State," 97. Another example of contravening sumptuary laws, culled from contemporary fiction, may be found in Feng Menglong's story "Song xiao guan tuanyuan po zhan li" 宋小官團圓破氈笠 (Young Mr. Song reunites with his family by means of a tattered felt hat), in *Jingshi tongyan* 警世通言 (Stories to caution the world).

22. Wang Yi, a scholar in the Han Imperial Library, is thought to have compiled the *Chu ci* 楚辭 (Songs of the South), one of the earliest anthologies

of Chinese poetry. Although the exact nature of Wang's editorial role is a matter of debate, he undoubtedly commented upon many of the poems in the collection and even added some poems of his own. Hawkes, *Ch'u Tz'u*, 2.

23. In ancient times it was customary for people to wear different types of jade ornaments, which marked their profession or status in society. A *xi* is a carved ornamental hook made of horn or bone. The sharp end could be used for untying knots. A *jue* is a flat doughnut-shaped jade disc, often with a narrow slit in the top. The round shape may have symbolized the resolution of doubt. "Nei ze" 內則 (Pattern of the family), in *Liji* 禮記 (Book of Rites), ch. 12.

24. Li Zhi, "Wu suo bu pei" 無所不佩 (Adorned with every mark of dignity), in *Fenshu* 5; *LZQJZ* 2.208–209. Elsewhere Li criticizes civil officials so ignorant and ineffectual that all they know of Confucianism is how to bow to one another politely: "When there is a crisis, they look at each other pale and speechless, [and] try to shift the blame." Li Zhi, "Yin ji wang shi" 因記往事 (Written in commemoration of past events), in *Fenshu* 4; *LZQJZ* 2.52–53. Translation by de Bary in "Individualism and Humanitarianism," 223.

25. Wang Chong, "Shujie pian" 書解篇 (On literary work), in *Lunheng* 論衡 2.28.890. For an alternative translation of this passage, see Forke, *Lun-Hêng, Part II*, 229.

26. Ibid. I have silently modified Forke's romanization.

27. Wang Gen was not entirely alone in desiring to wear ancient-style dress. Others, in some cases spurred by enthusiasm for the Return to Antiquity Movement, displayed similar enthusiasm. On the trend of wearing ancient-style clothing in this period, see Wu Renshu, "Mingdai pingmin fushi," 70. See also his *Pinwei shehua*, ch. 3.

28. Huang Zongxi, "Chu shi Wang Xinzhai xiansheng Gen" 處士王心齋先生艮 (Biography of Wang Gen), in *Mingru xue'an* 32, 2: 709. Translation by Ching in Huang Tsung-hsi, *The Records of Ming Scholars*, 174.

29. Li Zhi, "Zan Liu Xie" 贊劉諧 (Appraisal of Liu Xie), in *Fenshu* 3; *LZQJZ* 1:358–359. Translation by Pauline C. Lee in *BBBKH*, 140.

30. Li Le, *Jianwen zaji* 1.2.13. Another contemporary, Zhang Han (ca. 1511–ca.1593), bemoaned that "the customs of the present age have reached an extreme of extravagance." Zhang Han, "Ji fengsu" 風俗紀 (Record of customs), in *Songchuang mengyu* 7, 122. Translation in Clunas, "The Art of Social Climbing," 370.

31. Fan Lian 范濂, "Ji Fengsu" 記風俗 (Recording customs), in *Yunjian jumu chao* 雲間據目抄 (Record of observations made in Yunjian) 2 [1593], in *Biji xiaoshuo daguan* 13:110–111. Translation modified from Ko's in "Bondage in Time," 204.

32. Hong Wenke 洪文科, "Dai jin zhi lan" 戴巾之濫 (Excesses of apparel), in *Yu kui jin gu* 語窺今古 (Glimpses of the past and present), cited in Wu Renshu, "Mingdai pingmin fushi," 87. In Europe, this scheme was more than a mere pipedream. In France actual "investigations into nobility" (*recherches de noblesse*) were occasionally conducted, in which officials required families to prove their noble status before being allowed to partake of luxury

items restricted by sumptuary laws. In Italy municipalities appointed prosecutors to press charges against people who offended against sumptuary laws. Moyer, "Sumptuary Laws," 68; Hughes, "Sumptuary Law," 96.

33. Li Zhi, "*Zhongyi Shuihu zhuan* xu" 忠義水滸傳序 (Preface to *The Loyal and Righteous Outlaws of the Marsh*), in *Fenshu* 3; *LZQJZ* 1:301–304. Compare Huiying Chen and Drew Dixon's translation in *BBBKH*, 126.

34. *Xingshi yinyuan zhuan* 1.26.277–283, translated in Liu Xiaoyi, "Clothing, Food, and Travel," 108–109.

35. Hunt, *Governance of the Consuming Passions*, 121.

36. "Il est malaisé de distinguer les nobles, d'autant que toute façon de gens portent leurs bonnets de velours, et tous des épées au côté." Montaigne, *Journal de Voyage*, 125.

37. Stefano Guazzo, *Civil Conversation* (1586), cited and translated in Clunas, *Superfluous Things*, 50–51.

38. Stubbes, *The Anatomie of Abuses*, 71. Other instances of the difficulty of determining who is who in Renaissance Europe are recorded in Groebner, "Describing the Person," and Davis, *The Return of Martin Guerre*.

39. de Santa María, *República y policía christiana*, 200. See also de Santa María, *Policie Unveiled*, 364–365.

40. "L'habit ne faict poinct le moine." Rabelais, *Gargantua*, in *Oeuvres completes*, 39. Similarly, Shakespeare's Queen Katherine in *The Life of King Henry the Eighth* comments that "all Hoods make not Monks" (III, i, 57).

41. For a discussion of soldiers' costumes in this period, see Yuan Zujie, "Dressing for Power," 198.

42. Wilson, *The World in Venice*, 102.

43. Jones and Stallybrass, *Renaissance Clothing*, 2.

44. Jonson, *Timber*, in *The Works of Ben Jonson*, 8.593.

45. Correspondences between verbal and sartorial signs have also been explored by modern, Western critics. See for instance, Lurie, *The Language of Clothes*; Barthes, *Système de la mode*; Hollander, *Seeing through Clothes*.

46. Li Zhi, "Yu Yang Dingjian" 與楊定見 (To Yang Dingjian), in *Fenshu* 2, *LZQJZ* 1.157–158. Liu Tong and Yu Yizheng, "Li Zhuowu mu" 李卓吾墓 (Li Zhuowu's grave), in *Dijing jingwulue*, 367. During the Ming dynasty, this square headdress was worn by Confucian scholars who had not yet attained the rank of *jinshi*.

47. Bai Yinchang 白胤昌, "Li Zhuowu" 李卓吾, in *Rong'anzhai sutan* 容安齋酥譚 (Relaxed chats at Rong'an Studio), 10, cited in *LZYJCKZL* 2.171.

Although the majority of biographies of Li Zhi that I have examined agree that Li habitually clad himself in Confucian robes, some sources shed doubt on these claims. Yuan Zhongdao, for instance, reports that "those who spread malicious rumors contend[ed] that [Li Zhi], after shaving off his hair . . . , still wore the official cap." He concludes by asking rhetorically, "Is this possible?" Yuan Zhongdao, "Li Wenling zhuan" 李溫陵傳 (Biography of Li Wenling), in *Kexuezhai ji* 17, 2:725. Translation by Haun Saussy in *BBBKH*, 333.

Additionally, the Qing scholar Peng Shaosheng (1740–1796) avowed that Li "cut his hair and abandoned the Confucian hat and garb." However, Peng adds that when visitors came to the monastery and accused Li of "acting eccentrically and misleading the masses," Li replied, "I am indeed an eccentric, so it is permissible for me to wear a Confucian hat!" This account is corroborated almost verbatim by Wu Yu (1872–1949), who noted that after shaving his head Li "immediately donned his former robes." Peng Shaosheng, "Li Zhuowu zhuan" 李卓吾傳 (Biography of Li Zhuowu), in *Jushi zhuan* 2:43; Wu Yu, "Ming Li Zhuowu biezhuan" 明李卓吾別傳 (Unofficial biography of Li Zhuowu of the Ming dynasty), in *Wu Yu wenlu* 2:25. Even if Li Zhi occasionally wore garments or headgear other than those appropriate for Confucian officials, it seems likely that much of the time he presented himself in Confucian attire.

48. He Jiaoyuan, "Chu de shang" 畜德上 (Accumulating virtue, part 1), in *Min shu* 152, cited in *LZYJCKZL* 1.23. He Jiaoyuan's text seems to be unstable; the *Siku quanshu* edition replaces this cited phrase with the words "he shaved his hair and lived beyond the bounds of civilization, covering his bald head with a cornered hat [typically worn by recluses]." He Jiaoyuan, "Chu de shang" 畜德上 (Accumulating virtue, part 1), in *Minshu* 152.30a, in *Siku quanshu cunmu congshu* 207.737.

49. Wang Keshou, "Zhuowu laozi mubei" 卓吾老子墓碑 (Old Man Zhuowu's grave stele), in *Jifu tongzhi* 166.25ab.

50. "Xiao jing" 孝經 (The book of filial piety), ch. 1.

51. Weikun Cheng, "Politics of the Queue," 126–127. On the significance of hair in imperial China, see also Godley, "The End of the Queue."

52. Billeter, *Li Chih*, 202.

53. Martín de Rada, "The Relation of Fr. Martín de Rada," in Boxer, *South China*, 282. On a similar theme, see the remarks of Fr. Gaspar da Cruz, O.P., translated in Boxer, *South China*, 138. For analysis of these passages, see Godley, "The End of the Queue," 55.

54. Olivelle, "Hair"; Obeyesekere, *Medusa's Hair*, 39.

55. Li Zhi, "*Jingangjing* shuo" 金剛經說 (On *The Diamond Sūtra*), in *Xu Fenshu* 2; *LZQJZ* 3.214–217. Translation altered very slightly from Jennifer Eichman's in *BBBKH*, 273–75.

56. Even some Chinese Buddhist texts, mimicking Confucian discourse, referred to head shaving in derogatory terms. For example, the verse chanted when the final tuft of hair was removed from a novice monk's head during the initiation ceremony was referred to as *hui xing jie* 毀形偈 (The verse of disfigurement).

57. Li Zhi, "Da Zhou Erlu" 答周二魯 (Reply to Zhou Erlu), in *Fenshu* 2; *LZQJZ* 1.214.

58. Wang Keshou, "Zhuowu laozi mubei" 卓吾老子墓碑 (Old Man Zhuowu's grave stele), in *Jifu tongzhi* 166.25a–b.

59. Geng's presumption that Li Zhi was wearing Buddhist robes is recorded in a letter from Li Zhi to Geng. Li Zhi, "Da Geng Sikou" 答耿司寇 (Reply to Justice Minister Geng), in *Fenshu* 1; *LZQJZ* 1.74.

60. On the late Ming trend of literati "escaping into Chan," see Wu Jiang, *Enlightenment in Dispute*, 100–101.

61. Geng, "You yu Zhou Liutang" 又與周柳塘 (Another letter to Zhou Liutang), letter 20, in *Geng Tiantai xiansheng wenji* 1.3.363.

62. Li Zhi, "Gankai pingsheng" 感慨平生 (Reflections on my life), in *Fenshu* 4; *LZQJZ* 2.108–120. In this letter, Li Zhi refers to Deng Yingqi by his sobriquet, Dingshi. For a partial translation of this essay see that of Martin Huang in *BBBKH*, 185–189.

63. Wang Keshou, "Zhuowu laozi mubei" 卓吾老子墓碑 (Old Man Zhuowu's grave stele), in *Jifu tongzhi*, 166.25a–b. Emphasis mine.

64. Xu Jianping provides a contrasting analysis of this scene. He argues that by the time this encounter between Wang and Li took place, Li had already renounced his "wild," anti-authoritarian lifestyle and wholeheartedly embraced Confucianism. Xu's interpretation, however, overlooks the fact that Li's head remained shaved at the time. Xu Jianping, "'Kuangguai' he 'yu shi wu zheng,'" 28.

65. One passage in which Li refers to himself as a monk appears in Li Zhi, "Lisong Yaoshi gaowen" 禮誦藥師告文 (A petition of worship and recitation to the Medicine Buddha), in *Fenshu* 4; *LZQJZ* 2.38–39. Several other sources repeat the claim that Li Zhi "cut his hair and became a monk." Wu Yu attributes this remark to Xie Zhaozhe in "Ming Li Zhuowu biezhuan" 明李卓吾別傳 (Unofficial biography of Li Zhuowu of the Ming dynasty), in *Wu Yu wenlu* 2, 36. Tang Xianzu also refers to Li as both a "bald monk" and a "bald bodhisattva." Tang Xianzu, "Li Shi quanshu zongxu" 李氏全書總序 (Preface to Mr. Li's complete works), cited in *LZYJCKZL* 2.109. See also Wu Yuancui (fl. 1595), *Lin ju manlu*, unpaginated edition. Qian Qianyi (1582–1664) refers to Li Zhi as "the bald gentleman" in "Song Ying heshang baoenshi caoxu" 松影和尚報恩詩草序 (Preface to the Monk Song Ying's poem on repaying kindness), in *Muzhai youxueji* 2.21.884. Even Matteo Ricci remarked in his diary upon Li Zhi's peculiar baldness. D'Elia, *Fonti Ricciane*, 2.66–67.

66. Ray Huang, *1587*, 194, 197, 218. Additionally, Li's behavior was sternly criticized by the eminent monk Zhuhong (1535–1616) in "Li Zhuowu er" 李卓吾二 (Li Zhuowu, second essay), in *Zhuchuang sanbi* 竹窗三筆 (Jottings by a bamboo window, third volume), cited in *BBBKH*, 181n2.

67. Ray Huang, *1587*, 197. For discussions of Li Zhi's vegetarianism, see Li Zhi, "Lisong *Yaoshi jing* bi gaowen" 禮誦藥師經畢告文 (A petition upon completion of worshipful recitation of *The Medicine Master Sūtra*), in *Fenshu* 4; *LZQJZ* 2:41–42, and "Shu Xiaoxiu shoujuan hou" 書小修手卷後 (Written at the end of Xiaoxiu's [a.k.a. Yuan Zhongdao's] hand scroll), in *Fenshu* 2; *LZQJZ* 3:201–203. Both texts are translated by Jennifer Eichman in *BBBKH*, 175–177 and 267–269.

68. I borrow the phrase "Confucian monk" from Cheng Pei-kai, "Reality and Imagination," 205.

Over a century after Li's death, another of his biographers, Peng Shaosheng, wrote, "The fact that the recluse [Li Zhi] left home and did not abide by [Buddhist] prohibitions is not especially peculiar; but that, on the contrary, he would dress in a Confucian hat and robe [did strike me as odd]. Was this some kind of a joke?! Surely something must have motivated him to act this way. But if so, I lack the insight to know what it was." Peng Shaosheng, "Li Zhuowu zhuan" 李卓吾傳 (Biography of Li Zhuowu), in *Jushi zhuan* 2.43.

69. "Li Zhi zhuan" 李贄傳 (Biography of Li Zhi), in *Quanzhoufu zhi* 3.54.44.

70. He Jiaoyuan, "Chu de shang" 畜德上 (Accumulating virtue, part 1), in *Min shu* 152.30a.

71. "Wang zhi" 王制 (Royal regulations), in *Liji* 禮記 (Book of Rites) 5.

72. Li Zhi, "Yu Zhou Youshan shu" 與周友山書 (To Zhou Youshan), in *Fenshu* 2; *LZQJZ* 1.133.

73. In the letter, Li claims, "My willingness to correct my errors truly comes from the depths of my heart. In the past, I unwittingly went astray because of my craving to become a Buddha. I did not knowingly transgress. Since my misdeeds were committed inadvertently, in principle, I ought to be forgiven. And since I'm willing to correct my errors right away, I even deserve to be provided with a gift of food, not *merely* pardoned" (emphasis mine). The flagrant hyperbole signals that this passage should be read ironically. Ibid., *LZQJZ* 1.133.

74. It is not certain whether or not Li actually let his hair grow on this occasion. In a poem composed in 1596 he proclaims that there is "no hair upon my head" and another, written two years later, confirms, "For years now I have let my hair fall to the shaving razor," yet a text from 1601 refers to the author's "white hair." See Li Zhi, "Du shu le" 讀書樂 (The pleasure of reading, with a prologue) (1596), in *Fenshu* 6; *LZQJZ* 2.241; "Yuan ri Jilesi dayuxue" 元日極樂寺大雨雪 (Heavy rain and snow at the Temple of Paradise on New Year's Day) (1598), in *Fenshu* 6; *LZQJZ* 2.330; "Mituo si" 彌陀寺 (Amitabha Temple), in *Xu Fenshu* 5; *LZQJZ* 3.355. Timothy Billings and Yan Zinan's translations of these poems appear in *BBBKH*, 211–214, 228, and 298.

75. Yuan Zhongdao, "Li Wenling zhuan" 李溫陵傳 (Biography of Li Wenling), in *Kexuezhai ji* 2.17.721.

76. "Li Zhi zhuan" 李贄傳 (Biography of Li Zhi), in *Quanzhoufu zhi* 3.54.44. This narrative is repeated almost verbatim in a Jiaqing-era (1796–1820) record of the Li family history. *LZYJCKZL* 1.180.

77. Liu Tong and Yu Yizheng, *Dijing jingwulue*, 367.

78. Wang Keshou, "Zhuowu laozi mubei" 卓吾老子墓碑 (Old Man Zhuowu's grave stele), in *Jifu tongzhi* 166.25a–b.

79. Li Zhi, "Gankai pingsheng" 感慨平生 (Reflections on my life), in *Fenshu* 4; *LZQJZ* 2.110.

80. Ibid. In another letter, written to Liu Dongxing in 1590, Li reiterates that "shaving one's head is not easy." Li Zhi, "Da Liu Xianzhang" 答劉憲長 (Reply to District Chief Liu), in *Fenshu* 1; *LZQJZ* 1.61.

81. Li Zhi, "Gankai pingsheng" 感慨平生 (Reflections on my life), in *Fenshu* 4; *LZQJZ* 2.110.

82. Li Zhi's aspiration to free himself from social responsibilities is especially evident in his decision to present himself to Zhou Yi, the magistrate of Macheng, as a "sojourner-traveler," the understanding being that "sojourners" incurred no social obligations. Ibid., 109. In a separate letter to Zhou Yi, Li describes the dispute between himself and Geng Dingxiang, saying, "I resolved to shave my hair [because] by fleeing to the depths of the mountains, I wanted to avoid competing with people of the world. . . . How could several

strands of hair suffice to prevent me from meeting with the disapprobation of the masses?" Li Zhi, "Da Zhou Erlu" 答周二魯 (Reply to Zhou Erlu), in *Fenshu* 2; *LZQJZ* 1.214.

83. Li Zhi, "Yu Zeng Jiquan" 與曾繼泉 (To Zeng Jiquan), in *Xu Fenshu* 1; *LZQJZ* 3.149.

84. Ray Huang estimates that when Li returned to his home district to mourn his father's death in the 1550s, he was obliged to take care of and feed over thirty relatives, even though he lacked the financial resources to do so. Huang, *1587*, 192.

85. Li Zhi, "Ti fa" 薙髮 (On shaving my head), in *Fenshu* 6; *LZQJZ* 2.260. See also "Chutanji xu" 初潭集序 (Preface to *Upon Arrival at the Lake*), in *Chutanji*; *LZQJZ* 12.1.

CHAPTER 4

1. In invoking the comparison with Europe, one must proceed with caution, for each European country faced unique economic challenges. Economic and numismatic conditions even varied within countries due to imperfect channels of communication and transportation. Thus even the economic landscapes of the most highly developed coastal cities in China and Europe never perfectly mirrored one another.

2. The same source claims that Li may have been responsible for some of his own financial woes, since although he "took seriously every coin he earned, he also gave away vast sums as if they were grass." Jiao, "Hongfu shu gaoshang ce hou" 宏甫書高尚冊後 (Written at the end of Li Zhi's composition on loftiness), in *Jiao shi bisheng* 2.29b.

3. Li Zhi, "Zhuowu lunlue Dianzhong zuo" 卓吾論略, 滇中作 (A sketch of Zhuowu, written in Yunnan), in *Fenshu* 3; *LZQJZ* 1.233–242.

4. Li Zhi, "Ziyou jie Lao xu" 子由解老序 (Preface to Su Che's explication of Laozi), in *Fenshu* 3; *LZQJZ* 1.305–307.

5. Hawkes, "Exchange Value and Empiricism," 79.

6. Fischer, *Econolingua*, 28.

7. For examples, see Fiero, "When the Coin Is Madness"; Wenzel, *Changing Notions*; Carey, "Donne and Coins"; Desan, *Les Commerces de Montaigne*; Woodbridge, *Money and the Age of Shakespeare*.

8. Doty, "Money" 42.

9. The theoretical literature on the correspondence between the semiotic systems of money and language is extensive. See, among other sources, Gray, "Buying into Signs"; Marx, *Capital*; Shell, *The Economy of Literature*; Heinzelman, *The Economics of Imagination*; Goux, *Freud, Marx*; Woodmansee and Osteen, *The New Economic Criticism*; Derrida, "White Mythology"; Hoey, "The Name on the Coin." Earlier Western authors who have commented upon this analogy include Quintilian, Ovid, Nietzsche, Lessing, and Leibniz, among many others.

10. Braudel, *The Wheels of Commerce*, 196. For extensive information on the varieties of money circulating in early sixteenth-century Europe, see Munro, "Money and Coinage." On the situation in France, see also Desan,

Notes to Chapter 4

L'Imaginaire économique, 40–52. On the situation in England, see Fischer, *Econolingua*, 23.

11. Wenzel, *Changing Notions*, 40.

12. Abbé Tollemer, *Journal Manuscrit d'un Sire de Gouberville et du Mesnil-au-Val Gentilhomme campagnard, au Cotentin, de 1553 à 1562* (1897), republished as *Analyse par l'abbé Tollemer du Journal Manuscrit d'un Sire de Gouberville*, 45–46. On Shakespeare's familiarity with foreign coins, see Sternlicht, "Shakespeare and Renaissance Coinage." Like Shakespeare's poetry, John Donne's abounds in evidence of his familiarity with many varieties of coins. Carey, "Donne and Coins." The accounts Montaigne kept during his travels likewise record his fluency with large numbers of foreign coins. Nakam, *Les Essais de Montaigne*, 50.

13. Ray Huang, *Taxation and Governmental Finance*.

14. Peng Xinwei, *Zhongguo huobishi*, 660–661. Primary sources that attest to this include Ye Mengzhu 葉夢珠 (b. ca. 1623), "Qianfa" 錢法 (Monetary laws), in *Congshu jicheng xubian* 50.537–538.

15. Dong, "Ban'er" 板儿 (Boards), in *Bili zacun* 碧裡雜存 1.58.

16. Hamilton, "American Treasure," 35. See also Braudel, *The Structures of Everyday Life*, 459–460; Bodin, *Response to Paradoxes*, 16.

17. Von Glahn, *Fountain of Fortune*, 88, 99; Peng Xinwei, *Zhongguo huobishi*, 678–679.

18. Gu Yanwu, "Qianfa zhi bian" 錢法之變 (Changes to monetary laws) in *Rizhi lu* 2.11.664.

19. On the origins of international commerce in this period, see Von Glahn, *Fountain of Fortune*; Geiss, "Peking under the Ming"; Flynn and Giráldez, "Born with a 'Silver Spoon.'"

20. Brook, *Vermeer's Hat*, 160. On the types of foreign coins circulating in China in this period, see Peng Xinwei, *Zhongguo huobishi*, 661–663.

21. In England Henry VIII carried out the Great Debasement in the 1550s; in France, Henri III debased the national currency in 1577; and in Spain, Philip III debased the currency in 1602. The Spanish debasement was so radical that, in the words of one scholar, it removed "the last vestiges of intrinsic value" from the currency. Fiero, "When the Coin Is Madness," 95–96. See also Glassman and Redish, "Currency Depreciation"; Potter, "Images of Majesty."

22. Boyer-Xambeu et al., *Private Money*, 58–62. In France, the "naturalization" of foreign currencies ended with the major monetary reforms of 1577. Levasseur, *Histoire du commerce*, 225–226.

23. For a discussion of this image in the context of the expanding world trade in this period, see Brook's chapter on "weighing silver" in *Vermeer's Hat*. Other examples of early modern European pictorial representations of economic transactions or weighing money include *Moneylender and His Wife* by Quentin Metsys (1466–1530), *The Money Changer and His Wife* by Marinus van Reymerswaele (1490–1546), *The Moneylender* by Gerrit Dou (1613–1675), and *Interior with a Woman Weighing Gold Coin* by Pieter de Hooch (1629–1684).

24. P. de las Cortes, *Relación del viaje naufragio y captiverio . . .* (1621–1626), mentioned in Braudel, *The Structures of Everyday Life*, 454.

25. References to weighing silver abound in Chinese literature of the period. Some examples are *Xingshi yinyuan zhuan* ch. 1. A relevant passage from this chapter is translated into English in Von Glahn, *Fountain of Fortune*, 170. Feng Menglong's "Maiyoulang du zhan huakui" 賣油郎獨占花魁, in *Xingshi hengyan* 3, which appears in *Yushi mingyan, jingshi tongyan, xingshi hengyan*, 18–42, translated by Shuhui Yang and Yunqin Yang as "The Oil-Peddler Wins the Queen of Flowers" in Feng, *Stories to Awaken the World*, 38–77. See also Feng Menglong, "Du Shiniang nuchen baibaoxiang" 杜十娘怒沉百寶箱, in *Jingshi tongyan* 32, in *Yushi mingyan, jingshi tongyan, xingshi hengyan*, 278–288, translated by Shuihui Yang and Yunqin Yang as "Du Shiniang Sinks Her Jewel Box in Anger," in Feng, *Stories to Caution the World*, 547–565. See also Li Yu's 李玉 opera *Wan li yuan* 萬里圓 (Thousand-mile reunion), in which silver is not only measured out as payment, but its quality is also tested by biting. *Li yu xiqu ji*, 3.1623. I am thankful to Paize Keulemans for bringing this reference to my attention. For analysis of the role of silver in Chinese literature of this period, see Ma Ning, *The Age of Silver*.

26. This analysis accords with the etymology of the Greek word for money, *nomisma*, from the root *nomos*, meaning "law": in a smoothly functioning economy, the value of money is regulated by law. McKeon, *Introduction to Aristotle*, 409. Other European monetary theorists who elaborated on this idea are Girolamo Butigella (1470–15151), François Hotman (1524–1590), René Budel (1530–1591), Jakob Bornitz (1560–1625), and Geminiano Montanari (1633–1687).

27. Jin Xueyan, "Jin Shao zai zoushu" 靳少宰奏疏 (Memorial submitted by Governor Jin Shao), in *Ming jingshi wenbian* 299, cited in Xiao, *Gudai huobi sixiangshi*, 267.

28. Von Glahn, *Fountain of Fortune*, 110–111, 149–151.

29. Gao Gong, "Muzong" 穆宗, in *Ming shilu* 44.6b–7b, cited and translated in Von Glahn, *Fountain of Fortune*, 112.

30. Liu Yingqiu 劉應秋 (1547–1620), "Yu da situ Shi Dongquan shu" 與大司徒石東泉書 (Letter to the grand minister of education, Shi Dongquan), in Chen Zilong, ed., *Liu Wenjie gong ji* 劉文節公集, in [*Huang*] *Ming jingshi wenbian* 6.4716. Translation modified from Von Glahn, *Fountain of Fortune*, 153–154.

31. On the Price Revolution, see Fisher, "The Price Revolution."

32. Ye Mengzhu (b. ca.1623), "Shihuo yi" 食貨一 (Food and commodities, part 1), in *Congshu jicheng xubian* 50.530.

33. Gu Yanwu, "She xian fengtu lun" 歙縣風土論 (On the local customs of She county), in *Tianxia junguo libingshu* 2.9.712. Translation modified from Peterson, *The Bitter Gourd*, 70. Accounts from contemporary France outline similar misfortunes after the monetary debasement of 1577. Families went bankrupt; some starved. Nakam, *Les Essais de Montaigne*, 32–33.

34. Li Zhi, "Fu Deng Dingshi" 復鄧鼎石 (Reply to Deng Dingshi), in *Fenshu* 2; *LZQJZ* 1.123.

35. Li Zhi, "Zhuowu lunlue Dianzhong zuo" 卓吾論略滇中作 (A Sketch of Zhuowu, written in Yunnan), in *Fenshu* 3; *LZQJZ* 1:234. Translation

by Pauline C. Lee in *BBBKH*, 79. In another essay, Li singles out for praise a merchant who "does not vary the price of oil [based on the customer to whom he is selling]." That Li deemed such behavior worthy of comment indicates how prevalent price gouging had become. Li Zhi, "Li sheng shi jiao wen" 李生十交文 (Mr. Li's Ten Kinds of Association), in *Fenshu* 3; *LZQJZ* 1.354.

36. Li Zhi, "Shu Jin Chuan Weng shoujuan hou" 書晉川翁壽卷後 (Written to Old Mr. Jin Chuan at the end of the volume in honor of his birthday), in *Fenshu* 2; *LZQJZ* 1:180.

37. Li Zhi, "Fuguo mingchen zonglun" 富國名臣總論 (Preface to "Famous ministers who enriched the country"), in *Cangshu* 17; *LZQJZ* 5.386.

38. Li Zhi, "Liu Yan, miao ren" 劉晏, 妙人 (Liu Yan, extraordinary individual), in *Cangshu* 17; *LZQJZ* 5.396.

39. Several decades later, as economic woes continued unabated, Gu Yanwu spoke in similar terms, nostalgically describing a mythic, prehistoric society in which wealth was measured in staple goods like grain and cloth, commodities whose value, Gu naïvely asserted, was immune to fluctuation. Gu Yanwu, "Qian liang lun shang" 錢糧論上 (Discourse on money and grain, part 1), in *Gu Yanwu shiwen xuanyi*, 181.

40. Li Zhi, "Da Liu Fangbo shu" 答劉方伯書 (A letter in reply to Provincial Officer Liu), in *Fenshu* 2; *LZQJZ* 1.131. The letter, composed in 1591, is addressed to Liu Dongxing, an imperial censor whose biography is recorded in the Ming dynastic history. A close friend of Li's, and the recipient of several pieces included in *A Book to Burn*, Liu Dongxing composed prefaces for Li's *Book to Keep (Hidden)* and *Dao gu lu* 道古錄 (Record of the antiquity of the Dao), also known as *Ming deng dao gulu* 明燈道古錄 (Record of the bright lamp of the antiquity of the Dao).

41. Verbal sleights of hand like this abound in Li's writings. A similar example may be found in Li's ironic use of the term *renzhe* 仁者, "benevolent people," in his letter "Da Geng zhongcheng" 答耿中丞 (Reply to Censor Geng), in *Fenshu* 1; *LZQJZ* 1.41.

42. Li Zhi, "Yu Jiao Ruohou" 與焦弱侯 (To Jiao Ruohou), in *Fenshu* 2, *LZQJZ* 1.152–153. Similar observations about the instability of personal identity over time may be found in the writings of the painter and playwright Xu Wei, who inscribed the following statement on a portrait of himself: "I was born fat but by the time I was capped I had become so emaciated that I could no longer bear the weight of the clothes I was dressed in. By the age of thirty, I had again gradually grown fat. I had already passed my fiftieth year by the time the idiotic figure you see depicted here was drawn. Yet who can say that this idiotic figure of the present will not again become as emaciated as before, like the drying up of a mountain marsh? To seek me out by means of this portrait would be akin to marking the side of the boat at the place where the sword fell into the stream." Campbell, "Madman or Genius," 206.

43. Li Zhi, "*Chutanji* xu" 初潭集序 (Preface to *Upon Arrival at the Lake*), in *Chutanji*; *LZQJZ* 12.1. Emphasis mine.

44. Xu Jianping makes a similar point in his "'Kuangguai' he 'yu shi wu zheng,'" 27.

45. Potter, "Images of Majesty," 70.

46. "Plusieurs personnes indifféremment prennent et allouent les monnayes d'or et d'argent, tant du coing de France qu'estrangères." *Cri des monnaies* of 1554, cited in Levasseur, *Histoire du commerce*, 223.

47. Counterfeiting was officially prohibited in England in 1615 and 1618, and even the importation of counterfeit money was outlawed in 1625. Sargent and Velde, *The Big Problem*, 265.

48. Bruce Rusk's study of the shape of silver taels provides an insightful analysis of techniques used for assaying silver in the late Ming. Rusk, "Silver, Liquid and Solid."

49. Xie Zhaozhe, "Wubu si" 物部四 (Objects, part 4), in *Wuzazu* 2.357.

50. Counterfeiting of identity, social class, and gender all pervade late Ming fiction and drama. Analyses of the subject of monetary counterfeiting in early seventeenth-century British literature include Forman, "Material Dispossession" and Nugent, "Usury and Counterfeiting."

51. The penalty for counterfeiting paper currency was beheading. For privately casting copper coins, the punishment was strangulation. Clipping or grinding copper coins as well as counterfeiting silver or gold coins was punishable by beating. Jiang Yonglin, articles 382–383 of *The Great Ming Code*, 210–212.

52. Von Glahn, *Fountain of Fortune*, 97.

53. Ibid., 86. Albert Chan, *The Glory and Fall*, 283. A similar situation is known to have arisen in 1561, when Eloi Mestrell, who had previously worked at a mint in Paris, moved to England, where he manufactured counterfeit money for eleven years before he was hanged for his crime. Carey, "Donne and Coins" 152n4.

54. Li Zhi, "Pengyou pian" 朋友篇 (On friendship), in *Fenshu* 5; *LZQJZ* 2.227–228.

55. Ibid., *LZQJZ* 2.227.

56. Li Zhi, "Yu Jiao Ruohou" 與焦弱候 (To Jiao Ruohou), in *Fenshu* 2; *LZQJZ* 1.153.

57. Li Zhi, "Pengyou pian" 朋友篇 (On friendship), in *Fenshu* 5; *LZQJZ* 2.227; *Mengzi* (Mencius), 1A1.

58. Student Huang has been identified as Huang Kehui (1524–1590). Li's decision to suppress Huang's given name and accentuate instead his status as a self-proclaimed student supports the idea that Li regarded Huang as representative of the phony Confucian "scholars" so numerous in his day. *LZQJZ* 1.121n9; Chen Cunguang, "Li Zhi feiyi 'shanren,'" 315; Lin Haiquan, *Li Zhi nianpu*, 217–218.

59. Li Zhi, "You yu Jiao Ruohou" 又與焦弱候 (Another letter to Jiao Ruohou), in *Fenshu* 2; *LZQJZ* 1.119. For an alternative translation of this passage, see de Bary, "Individualism and Humanitarianism," 205.

60. Ray Huang, *1587*, 194; Chow, "An Avatar." Jiao Hong explicitly denies this claim, stating that "throughout his life, Li Zhi was never willing to borrow from others." However, this assertion seems to have been motivated more by Jiao's desire to defend Li's reputation than by strict adherence to facts. Jiao, "Hongfu shu gaoshang ce hou" 宏甫書高尚冊後 (Written at the end of Li Zhi's composition on loftiness), in *Jiao shi bisheng* 2.29a–b.

61. *Analects* 8.13.

62. For discussions of the late-Ming discourse on "mountain men" see Chen Wanyi, *Wanming xiaopin*, 43–59, 88; Hung, *The Romantic Vision*, 62; de Bary, "Individualism and Humanitarianism," 205; Cahill, *The Compelling Image*, 137; Wai-yee Li, "The Collector," 284; Park, *Art by the Book*, 22–24; Chen Cunguang, "Li Zhi fei yi 'shanren'"; Luo, "From Imperial City to Cosmopolitan Metropolis," 109–110.

63. Shen Defu's *Wanli yehuo bian* devotes several chapters to mountain men 23.584–587).

64. Li Zhi, "You yu Jiao Ruohou" 又與焦弱侯 (Another letter to Jiao Ruohou), in *Fenshu* 2; *LZQJZ* 1.119.

65. Ibid., emphasis mine.

66. Li Zhi, "Gao jie shuo" 高潔說 (On loftiness and cleanliness), in *Fenshu* 3; *LZQJZ* 1.294–295; Li Zhi, "Ji jing you shu" 寄京友書 (Letter to a friend in the capital), in *Fenshu* 2; *LZQJZ* 1.171.

67. Li Zhi, "Da youren shu" 答友人書 (Reply to a friend's letter), in *Fenshu* 2, *LZQJZ* 1.143.

68. Doty, "Money" 42.

69. Li Zhi, "Gao jie shuo" 高潔說 (On loftiness and cleanliness), in *Fenshu* 3, *LZQJZ* 1.295.

70. This is an allusion to Zhuangzi's comments on men exiled to the far southern region of Yue: "A few days after they have left their homelands, they are delighted if they come across an old acquaintance. When a few weeks or a month have passed, they are delighted if they come across someone they had known by sight when they were at home. By the time a year has passed, they are delighted if they come across someone who even looks as though he might be a countryman." Zhuangzi, "Xu wu gui" 徐無鬼, in *Zhuangzi duben* 24; Zhuangzi, *The Complete Works of Chuang Tzu*, 262.

71. Li Zhi, "Gao jie shuo" 高潔說 (On loftiness and cleanliness), in *Fenshu*, 3; *LZQJZ* 1.294–295.

72. Li Zhi, "Li xiansheng shi jiao wen" 李先生十交文 (On Mr. Li's ten kinds of association), in *Fenshu* 3; *LZQJZ* 1.355.

73. Li Zhi, "Gao jie shuo" 高潔說 (On loftiness and cleanliness), in *Fenshu* 3; *LZQJZ* 1.294.

74. Ibid.

75. Li Zhi, "Li sheng shi jiao wen" 李先生十交文 (On Mr. Li's ten kinds of association), in *Fenshu* 3; *LZQJZ* 1.354.

76. Li Zhi, "Wu si pian" 五死篇 (On five types of death), in *Fenshu* 4; *LZQJZ* 2.69. For more detailed analysis of this passage, see Martin Huang, "The Perils of Friendship."

CHAPTER 5

1. Chia, "Three Mountains Street," 112. For more explicit comparisons of European and Chinese print culture see Brokaw, "On the History of the Book"; Blair, *Too Much to Know*. On printing practices in this period and their influence in Europe, see Eisenstein, *The Printing Press as an Agent of*

Change; Febvre, *L'Apparition du livre*; Chartier, *L'Ordre des livres*; Pallier, *Recherches sur l'imprimerie*; Martin, *Livre, pouvoirs et société*.

2. Xiuranzi 修髯子, "*Sanguozhi tongsu yanyi* (jielu)" 三國志通俗演義 (節錄) (The romance of the three kingdoms [excerpts]) (1522), cited and translated in McLaren, "Constructing New Reading Publics," 159.

3. Erasmus, "Festina lente/Make haste slowly," in *The Adages* II, i.1, 145.

4. Sanchez, *Quod nihil scitur*, cited and translated in Blair, *Too Much to Know*, 57.

5. Yang Yucheng, "Qimeng yu baoli," 911.

6. Roughly speaking, Gournay's prefaces may be divided into two kinds: the long preface, which extends over fifty pages and which appeared in the editions of 1595, 1625, and 1635, and the short preface, a mere half-page in length, which replaced the longer preface in the editions of 1598, 1600, 1602, 1604, and 1611. Since discrepancies exist among the various versions of the long preface, I concentrate on the first (1595) edition, in which Gournay, as a woman and a first-time editor, had the most at stake in establishing the reliability of her text. This version makes the strongest bid for the book's authenticity. Gournay, *Oeuvres*, 1.273. On the history and interpretation of Gournay's preface, see Desan, *Montaigne dans tous ses états*, 193–216; Bauschatz, "Marie de Gournay's 'Préface'"; Boase, *The Fortunes of Montaigne*, 52.

7. The Jesuit missionary Matteo Ricci remarked in his diary upon "the exceedingly large numbers of books in circulation [in China] and the ridiculously low prices at which they are sold," as well as upon the differences in techniques of book printing in China and Europe. Ricci, *China in the Sixteenth Century*, 21. Some books could be obtained for the price of several winter melons. Greenbaum, *Chen Jiru*, 64. This calculation is based on appendices 3 and 4 in Chow, *Publishing, Culture and Power*, 260–263. For more detailed information on book prices in this period, see Dennis, *Writing, Publishing, and Reading*, ch. 5.

8. Cynthia Brokaw has argued that the reading public expanded more quickly in China than in Europe. One reason for this was that Chinese parents, eager for their sons to succeed on the examinations, were willing to invest in their education; this phenomenon had no direct corollary in Europe. Brokaw, "On the History of the Book," 11. On the expanding readership in China in this period, see McLaren, "Constructing New Reading Publics." On the growth of reading publics in Europe in this period, see Chartier, "Publishing Strategies," 149–159.

9. Ye Sheng, "Xiaoshuo xiwen" 小說戲文 (Novels and plays), in *Shuidong riji* 21.21a–b.

10. Meskill, *Ch'oe Pu's Diary*, 155.

11. McLaren, "Constructing New Reading Publics," 160.

12. Erasmus, *Paraclesis*, in Olin, *Christian Humanism*, 96–97.

13. Grendler, "Printing and Censorship," 25–26.

14. Rosenthal and Jones, *The Clothing of the Renaissance World*, 11.

15. Grendler, "Printing and Censorship," 28.

16. Ming printing is often classified in three types: official printing (*guan ke*), commercial printing (*fang ke*), and private printing (*si ke* or *jia ke*). Chia, *Printing for Profit*.

17. K. T. Wu, "Ming Printing and Printers," 229.

18. Ling Mengchu, Feng Menglong, and other notable literati also cited errors in slipshod editions of musical and dramatic texts. Zeitlin, "Between Performance, Manuscript, and Print," 274. However, the phenomenon of printers' mistakes was not unique to the Ming. Plenty of Song dynasty scholars also expressed frustration about typographical errors. For examples, see Cherniack, "Book Culture," 47–51; Wagner, "Twice Removed from the Truth," 36–37.

19. Xie Zhaozhe, "Shibu yi" 事部一 (Matters, part 1), in *Wuzazu*, 1.381. On the Jianyang printing business, see Chia, *Printing for Profit*.

20. Shen Zijin, "Ouzuo: Qiexiao cike sha fengjing shi" 偶作: 竊笑詞客煞風景事 (An occasional piece: Laughing at a poet's overkill), in *Shen Zijin ji* 203. For a complete translation of the lyric in which this line appears, see Zeitlin, "Between Performance, Manuscript, and Print," 264.

21. Lu Xinyuan 陸心源, "Yigutang tiba" 儀顧堂題跋 (Colophon on the Hall for Gazing Appropriately), cited and translated in He Yuming, *Home and the World*, 2n2.

22. "Tu excuseras les fautes de l'Imprimeur: car tous les yeux d'Argus ny verroient assez clair." Ronsard, *Les Quatre Premiers Livres de la Franciade*, cited in Hoffmann, *Montaigne's Career*, 87–88n10. See also Rigolot, "The Renaissance Fascination with Error."

23. "Autant qu'il y aura d'ancre et de papier au monde." Montaigne, "De la Vanité" 3: 9, in *Les Essays*, 946. See also Montaigne, "On Vanity" in *The Complete Essays of Montaigne*, 721. Although Montaigne stated that he only added to his essays and never deleted from them, this was not, in fact, the case.

24. Bacon, *The Essays*, 55.

25. "Cinquiesme edition augmentée d'un troisieme liure et de six cens additions aux deux premiers." Desan, *Montaigne in Print*, 41.

26. "Edition nouvellement prise sur l'exemplaire trouué apres le deceds de l'Autheur, reueu & augmenté d'un tiers outre les precedentes impreßions." Ibid., 51.

27. According to the Qing literatus Zhang Fang, "In the mid-Ming, the regulations were clear and enforced; the official style was unified; most books were printed and circulated by the Bureau of Rites." *Huike Tang Song miben shu lunlüe* 徽刻唐宋秘本書論略 (Overview of Tang and Song dynasty rare books printed in Huizhou), cited in Miao Yonghe, *Mingdai chubanshi*, 401.

28. Brokaw, "On the History of the Book," 18; Alford, *To Steal a Book*, 13–19; Chow, "Writing for Success," 135; Hok-lam Chan, *Control of Publishing*, 23.

29. Son, "Writing for Print." See also Brook, *The Confusions of Pleasure*, 170.

30. Li Zhi, "Da Jiao Yiyuan" 答焦漪園 (Reply to Jiao Yiyuan), in *Fenshu* 1; *LZQJZ* 1.17.

31. Li Zhi, "Shizi xu zhi xu" 釋子須知序 (Preface on what a Buddhist ought to know), in *Xu Fenshu* 2; *LZQJZ* 3.168. These comments were repeated nearly verbatim by the literatus Zhang Dafu (1554–1630), who

affirmed that Li's "brush was always moist and his ink stone always wet." Zhang Dafu, "Bu ke yi" 不可已 (Unstoppable), in *Meihua caotang ji* 10.12.

32. Li Zhi, "Laoren xing xu" 老人行序 (Preface to *The Actions of an Old Man*), in *Xu Fenshu* 2; *LZQJZ* 3.177. From the perspective of hindsight, the word *jin* 禁 takes on an ironic meaning since it means "stop" but also "ban." Li Zhi's books were banned in 1602 and again in 1625.

33. Many of Li Zhi's letters mention sending manuscripts to friends and seeking their comments and suggestions. On the widespread practice of circulating manuscript letters in late Ming China, see Brook, "The Public of Letters."

34. He Yuming, *Home and the World*, 7; Brokaw, "On the History of the Book," 19.

35. Ma Jinglun, "Yu Li Linye dujian zhuan shang Xiao sikou" 與李麟野都諫轉上蕭司寇 (To Minister of Justice Xiao, care of Capital Censor Li Linye), in *Li Wenling waiji* 281–282.

36. Zhang Chao, *Chidu oucun* 尺牘偶存 (Letters that happen to have been preserved), 11.12b, cited and translated in Son, "Between Writing and Publishing Letters," 889–890. Additionally, some contemporary artists are reported to have viewed the unauthorized reproduction of their paintings with equanimity. When someone informed the popular painter Shen Zhou (1427–1509) that his works were being widely forged, Shen allegedly replied, "If my poems and paintings, which are only small efforts to me, should prove to be of some aid to the forgers, why should I hold a grudge?" Zhu Yunming 祝允明, *Ji Shitian xiansheng hua* 記石田先生畫 (A record of the paintings of the Gentleman of the Stony Field), 8r, cited in Fong, "The Problem of Forgeries," 100. I have slightly altered Fong's translation.

37. Jardine, *Worldly Goods*, 155–156. He did, however grouse about pervasive typos. Hoffmann, *Montaigne's Career*, 85.

38. See the instructions for the printer in the *Edition de Bordeaux*. Philippe Desan, private communication, April 30, 2009.

39. Lang Ying, "Shuce" 書冊 (Volumes), in *Qixiu leigao* 45.664–665. My translation here differs only slightly from Ding Naifei's in *Obscene Things*, 53.

40. Zhang Nai, "Du Zhuowu laozi shu shu" 讀卓吾老子書述 (Upon reading Old Zhuowu's writings), in Li Zhi, *Xu Fenshu*; *LZQJZ* 3.420.

41. Yuan Zhongdao, "Da Yuan Wuyai" 答袁無涯 (Response to Yuan Wuyai), in *Kexuezhai ji* 3.24.1041.

42. Similar acts of literary piracy, albeit using different forms of technology, can be traced as far back as ancient Rome. White, "Bookshops."

43. Jardine, *Worldly Goods*, 158; Head, *The English Rogue*, ch. 23, 205. See also Johns, *The Nature of the Book*, ch. 2.

44. Yuan Zhongdao, "Da Yuan Wuyai" 答袁無涯 (Reply to Yuan Wuya), in *Kexuezhai ji* 3.24.1041.

45. Ding, *Obscene Things*, 55. On the fiction and drama commentaries attributed to Li Zhi, see Rolston, *Traditional Chinese Fiction*, 31–33; Rolston, *How to Read*, 356–363; Plaks, *Four Masterworks*, 513–517; Lin Yaling, "Ye Zhou xiaoshuo pingdian xilun"; Guo Lixuan, "Lun Liu Xingxi

Notes to Chapter 5

kanben 'Li Zhuowu xiansheng piping *Xixiangji*.'" Wu Yinghui's manuscript in progress "Books in Pairs" and Robert Hegel's essay "Performing Li Zhi" provide compelling interpretations of these forged commentaries.

46. On the forgeries of the "Li Zhi" commentaries on *Shuihu zhuan* 水滸傳 (Outlaws of the marsh), see Irwin, *The Evolution of a Chinese Novel*, 79–80.

47. Chow, *Publishing, Culture, and Power*, 139–142.

48. Within a decade, Yu Xiangdou sold the book *Gujin lishi dafang jian bu* 古今歷史大方鑒補 (Mirror and supplement to general principles of ancient and modern history) under the names of Li Tingji, Ji Cheng, and Yuan Huang. Ironically, however, Yu complained bitterly when his own writings were "[re]printed by people hunting for profit." Wu Yuantai 吳原泰, *Dongyouji, baxian zhuan yin* 東遊記、八仙傳引 (Preface to *Journey to the East* and *Biography of Eight Immortals*), cited in Miao Yonghe, *Mingdai chubanshi*, 404.

49. Greenbaum, *Chen Jiru*, 203.

50. Rusk, "The Rogue Classicist," 34, 271. See also Wang Fansen, "Mingdai houqi de weizao"; Rusk, "Artifacts of Authentication," 180–181.

51. Yang Chenbin, "Tan Mingdai shuhua zuowei"; Yang Xin, "Shangpin jingji"; Laing, "*Suzhou Pian* and Other Dubious Paintings"; Fong, "The Problem of Forgeries."

52. Bentley, "Authenticity in a New Key," 40.

53. Clunas, *Pictures and Visuality*, 33. Elsewhere Clunas avers, however, that books clearly "formed part of the cocoon of material possessions which were one of the defining marks of élite status." Clunas, "Books and Things," 136.

54. Egan, "On the Circulation of Books," 10. Timothy Brook estimates that the largest private library in the mid-Ming may have belonged to Ge Jian, who owned ten thousand *titles*, not ten thousand fascicles. Brook, *The Confusions of Pleasure*, 169. See also Wu Han, *Jiang Zhe cangshujia*, 205.

55. Li Zhi, "Da Zhi dui yu" 大智對雨 (Watching the rain with Da Zhi), in *Xu Fenshu* 5; LZQJZ 3.398.

56. Martin, *The French Book*, 57–58. Peraita, "Marginalizing Quevedo," 39.

57. Hu Yinglin, "Jingji huitong" 經籍會通 (Classics condensed), in *Shaoshi shanfang bicong* 4.46. For further discussion of late-Ming book collecting, see Rusk, "The Rogue Classicist," 117–128.

58. Chen Baoliang and Wang Xi, *Zhongguo fengsu tongshi*, 482.

59. "Multitudo voluminum facilitatem inveniendi aufert . . . his inspice quos libros tibi emere habeas; Bibliopola, quam listam empturo dare, quo sub ordine imprimere libros atque compaginare." Nevizzano, *Inventarium librorum in utroque iure hactenus impressorum* (1522), cited and translated in Balsamo, *Bibliography*, 31. On the care with which early modern European readers assembled their personal libraries, see De Smet, *Les Humanistes et leur bibliothèque*.

60. Wu hu laoren, "*Zhongyi Shuihu quan zhuan* xu" 忠義水滸全傳序 (Preface to *The Complete Loyal and Righteous Outlaws of the Marsh*), in Ma Tiji, *Shuihu ziliao huibian*, 9. Translation modified from that of Ding in *Obscene Things*, 62.

61. Grafton, *Forgers and Critics*, 31.

62. "Non enim eruditis solum sed quibuslibet hunc Indicem collegimus, ut etiam rudes inde tamquam a praeceptore muto de authoritate utilitateque singulorum librorum, et contra, admoneantur." Gesner, *Bibliotheca universalis, sive Catalogus omnium scriptorum locupletissimus, in tribus linguis, Latina, Graeca et Hebraica: extantium et non extantium, veterum et recentiorum in hunc usque diem, doctorum et indoctorum, publicatorum et in Bibliothecis latentium . . .* (1545), cited and translated in Balsamo, *Bibliography*, 36. Of course, despite Gesner's rhetoric concerning the usefulness of his book to readers of all kinds, his massive compilation and the ones mentioned below were probably priced well beyond the means of all but the wealthiest bibliophiles.

63. "Plusieurs usurpent & s'attribuent le labeur d'autruy, & ce livre les descouvrira." "Je [les] déteste, & abhorre autant qu'autre qui vive de mon siècle." La Croix du Maine, "Préface," in *Les Bibliothèque Françoise*, xxij, lxv. B 1857 509, vols. 1–2, Houghton Library.

64. "Je ne me suis pas contenté d'avoir mis en icelles Bibliothèques Latine & Françoise, le catalogue des oeuvres, ou escrits de chacun autheur: mais outre celà j'y ay compris chez qui ils font imprimez, en quelle marge ou grandeur, en quelle année, combien ils contiennent de feuilles, & sur-tout le nom de ceux ou celles ausquels ils ont esté dediez, sans y obmettre toutes leurs qualitez entieres: Et outre celà j'ay mis le commencement ou premiere ligne de leur ouvrage & composition, & en quel temps les autheurs d'iceux vivoient, & plusieurs autres menues recherches, que je ne raconte pas icy, lesquelles toutefois j'ai observées in iceux Catalogues." Ibid., lviij.

65. "Il a écrit un nombre infini d'Almanachs & Prognostications, lesquelles étoient tellement reçus, & se vendoient si bien, que plusieurs en ont fait à son imitation, & ont emprunté le nom dudit Nostredamus, pour qu'elles eussent plus grand vogue et reputation." La Croix du Maine, "Michel de Nostre Dame," in *Les Bibliothèques Françoises*, vol. 2: 133–134.

66. Dai, "China's Bibliographic Tradition," 11, 29–30.

67. Shen Defu, "Jimo guwan" 籍沒古玩 (Registering and confiscating antiques), in *Wanli yehuo bian* 1.8.211.

68. Hu Yinglin, "Jingji huitong" 經籍會通 (Classics condensed), in *Shaoshi shanfang bicong* 4.47.

69. Qian Xiyan, "Yan shu" 贋書 (False books), in *Xi xia* 3.32b. On Ye Zhou's impersonation of Li Zhi, see Hegel, "Performing Li Zhi."

70. Qian Xiyan, "Yan shu" 贋書 (False books), in *Xi xia* 3.32b.

71. Little is known about Zhang Nai, but Wang Benke hailed from Xin'an district in Anhui and in 1594 moved to Dragon Lake to study with Li Zhi. In *Another Book to Burn* Li addresses letters to Wang under his sobriquet Dingfu 鼎甫. *Xu Fenshu* 1; *LZQJZ* 3.21, 137, 140–141.

72. Desan, *Montaigne dans tous ses états*, 196. Desan describes the exact manner in which the texts were altered.

73. Ken Keffer points out that Gournay's efforts to establish a single edition of the *Essays* as definitive actually violated the spirit of the original work, since Montaigne was committed to augmenting and expanding his work indefinitely. Keffer, "La Textomachie," 140.

74. Jiao Hong, "Li shi *Xufenshu* xu" 李氏續焚書序 (Preface to Mr. Li's *Another Book to Burn*), in Li Zhi, *Xu Fenshu*; *LZQJZ* 3.419.

75. Wang Benke, "Xu ke Li shi shu xu" 續刻李氏書序 (On reprinting Mr. Li's writings), in Li Zhi, *Xu Fenshu*; *LZQJZ* 3.421.

76. This phrase alludes to a story involving the monk Zhang Sengyou 張僧繇 of the Liang dynasty (sixth century). Upon the wall of the Anle Temple in Jinling, he painted a dragon. As soon as he painted the pupils of the dragon's eyes, the dragon soared into the sky and flew away. This story is recounted in Zhang Yanyuan, *Lidai minghua ji* 7.148.

77. This common adage derives from an anecdote told in the *Lü Buwei Chunqiu* 呂不韋春秋 (Annals of Lü Buwei): When paddling a boat, a dim-witted man from the state of Chu accidentally dropped his oar into the water. Oblivious to the fact that his boat was moving, he made a notch in the gunwale, saying, "This is to mark the spot where the oar sank."

78. Zhang Nai, "Du Zhuowu laozi shu shu" 讀卓吾老子書述 (On reading the works of Old Man Zhuowu), in Li Zhi, *Xu Fenshu*; *LZQJZ* 3.420. The following chapter discusses eyes as organs of discernment.

79. Ibid.

80. Jiao Hong, "Li shi *Xufenshu* xu" 李氏續焚書序 (Preface to Mr. Li's *Another Book to Burn*), in Li Zhi, *Xu Fenshu*; *LZQJZ* 3.419. The phrase I have translated as "not worthy of discussion" occurs in the sentence "[Li Zhi's] genuine books are important, but fakes are not worthy of discussion" (*zhen shu zhong er yan shu keyi wu bian*) 真書重而贗書可以無辨. Since the character *bian* 辨 literally means "to distinguish," it would be tempting to translate this sentence as "[Li Zhi's] genuine books are important, but it's *not necessary to distinguish* between [genuine and] fake editions." However, this reading directly contradicts Zhang Nai's opinions expressed elsewhere in the preface. More likely, the character 辨 is a misprint for its homophone *bian* 辯, meaning "to discuss." A nearly identical phrase—with the character 辯 used (correctly) instead of 辨—occurs in Li Zhi's letter "Da Zhou Liutang" 答周柳塘 (A Response to Zhou Liutang), in *Fenshu* 2; *LZQJZ* 1.220. Needless to say, it is ironic that this sort of misprint would have crept into a preface that lauds Wang Benke for his meticulous editorial work!

81. Wang Benke, "Xu ke Li shi shu xu" 續刻李氏書序 (On reprinting Mr. Li's writings), in Li Zhi, *Xu Fenshu*; *LZQJZ* 3.421.

82. The legend is recorded in "Tang wen" 湯問 (The Questions of Tang), in *Liezi* 列子 5.

83. In the 1595 version Gournay writes, "I am not myself except insofar as I am his daughter" (Je ne suis moy-mesme que par où je suis sa fille). Gournay, *Oeuvres*, 1.281.

84. "C'est à moy d'en parler [de sa religion], car moy seule avois la parfaicte cognoissance de cette grande ame [celle de Montaigne], et c'est à moy d'en estre creue de bonne foy." Gournay, *Oeuvres*, 1.303. This sentence, appearing in the 1595 edition, was struck from later editions, but the sentiments it conveys were not. In the 1635 edition Gournay boasts of the "unique acquaintance that I have with this work" (connaissance toute particuliere, que j'ay de cét Ouvrage). Gournay, *Oeuvres*, 1.340.

85. "Une autre luy-mesme." Gournay, *Oeuvres*, 1.281.

86. Wang Benke, "Xu ke Li shi shu xu" 續刻李氏書序 (On reprinting Mr. Li's Writings), in Li Zhi, *Xu Fenshu*; *LZQJZ* 3.421.

87. Jiao Hong, "Li shi *Xufenshu* xu" 李氏續焚書序 (Preface to Mr. Li's *Another Book to Burn*), in Li Zhi, *Xu Fenshu*; *LZQJZ* 3.419.

88. Zhang Nai, "Du Zhuowu laozi shu shu" 讀卓吾老子書述 (On reading the works of Old Man Zhuowu), in Li Zhi, *Xu Fenshu*; *LZQJZ* 3.420.

89. "Desrobeurs et frippeurs de livres." This phrase was omitted from later editions. Gournay, *Oeuvres*, 1:327. For a discussion of Marie de Gournay's editorial "paranoia," see Desan, *Montaigne dans tous ses états*, 196.

90. "[Son impression] l'a [Montaigne] plus qu'exactement suivy." This phrase was struck from later editions. However, on the same page, Gournay wrote, "In addition to the natural difficulty of correction that presents itself in the *Essays*, the copy [from which I worked] had so many others that it was no small undertaking even to read it. . . . In sum, having said that [the book] needed a worthy guardian, I dare boast that it needed, for its own good, none other than myself. (Outre la naturelle difficulté de correction qui se void aux *Essays*, ceste copie en avoit tant d'autres que ce n'estoit pas legere entreprise que la bien lire. . . . Somme, apres que j'ay dict qu'il [le livre] luy falloit un bon tuteur, j'ose me vanter qu'il ne luy en falloir, pour son bien, nul autre que moy.) Gournay, *Oeuvres*, 1.330.

91. Desan, *Montaigne dans tous ses états*, 195.

92. Johns continues, "The consequences for both authorship and the reading of printed materials were substantial. . . . To modern historians it often appears that the introduction of printing led to an augmentation of certainty, with uniform editions and standardized texts providing the sure fulcrum with which intellectual worlds could be overturned (or protected). To contemporaries, the link between print and knowledge seemed far less secure. . . . In the realm of print, truths became falsehoods with dazzling rapidity, while ridiculous errors were the next day proclaimed as neglected profundities. . . . Far from fixing certainty and truth, print dissolved them." Johns, *The Nature of the Book*, 171–172.

CHAPTER 6

1. Iser, "The Reading Process"; Jauss, *Toward an Aesthetic of Reception*, 23.

2. The phrase is borrowed from Fish, "Literature in the Reader," 75.

3. Ge, "Authorial Intention," 5. See also Martin Huang, *Snakes' Legs*, 25–26.

4. Martin Huang, "Author(ity) and Reader," 62. Sally Church concurs, emphasizing that Jin Shengtan's fiction and drama commentaries aimed to convince readers of the "correctness" of his interpretations. Church, "Beyond the Words," 77. However, Kai-wing Chow points out that book editions that purveyed contrasting commentaries may have encouraged readers to adopt a more "open attitude" toward even such revered texts as the Confucian classics. Chow, "Writing for Success," 138.

5. Scholes, *Protocols of Reading*, 8.

Notes to Chapter 6

6. Li Zhi, "Du shu le, bing yin" 讀書樂并引 ("The pleasure of reading," with a prologue), in *Fenshu* 6; *LZQJZ* 2.240. Translation by Timothy Billings and Yan Zinan in *BBBKH*, 211. Another description of Li's constant reading appears in Li Zhi, "Yu Jiao Ruohou" 與焦弱侯 (To Jiao Ruohou), in *Xu fenshu* 1; *LZQJZ* 3.124.

7. Li Zhi, "Du shu le, bing yin" 讀書樂并引 ("The pleasure of reading," with a prologue), in *Fenshu* 6; *LZQJZ* 2.240. Translated by Timothy Billings and Yan Zinan in *BBBKH*, 214.

8. Liu Dongxing 劉東星, "Liu Dongxing xu" 劉東星序 (Preface by Liu Dongxing), in Li Zhi, *Cangshu*; *LZQJZ* 8.697; Jiang Yihua, "Ji Li Zhuowu" 紀李卓吾 (Record of Li Zhuowu), in *Xitai manji* 2.31a.

9. Jiang Yihua, "Ji Li Zhuowu" 紀李卓吾 (Record of Li Zhuowu), in *Xitai manji* 2.31a.

10. Yuan Zhongdao, "Li Wenling zhuan" 李溫陵傳 (Biography of Li Wenling), in *Kexuezhai ji* 2.17.721. Translation by Haun Saussy in *BBBKH*, 327.

11. Jiang Yihua, "Ji Li Zhuowu" 紀李卓吾 (Record of Li Zhuowu), in *Xitai manji* 2.31a. Li himself avowed, "My hands are a blessing, for even though I am a septuagenarian I can still write commentaries in small print." "Du shu le, bing yin" 讀書樂并引 ("The pleasure of reading," with a prologue), in *Fenshu* 6; *LZQJZ* 2.240. Translation by Timothy Billings and Yan Zinan in *BBBKH*, 211.

12. Yuan Zhongdao, "Li Wenling zhuan" 李溫陵傳 (Biography of Li Wenling), in *Kexuezhai ji* 2.17.721. Translation by Haun Saussy in *BBBKH*, 327.

13. Wu Yinghui's study of the "Li Zhuowu" commentaries spuriously attributed to the historical Li Zhi reveals fascinating parallels between the literary style of the fictional persona of the commentator "Li Zhuowu" and the personality of the historical Li Zhi. Wu Yinghui, "Books in Pairs," ch. 1.

14. Yang Yucheng, "Qimeng yu baoli," 914.

15. Li Zhi, "Cangshu shiji liezhuan zongmu qianlun" 藏書世紀列傳總目前論 (Preface to the combined "Dynastic Records" and "Biographies" sections of *A Book to Keep [Hidden]*), in *Cangshu*; *LZQJZ* 4.1. Compare Pauline C. Lee's translation in *BBBKH*, 317–318.

16. Li Zhi, "Du shu le, bing yin" 讀書樂并引 ("The pleasure of reading," with a prologue), in *Fenshu* 6; *LZQJZ* 2.240. This translation very slightly modifies that of Timothy Billings and Yan Zinan in *BBBKH*, 211–212.

17. *Mengzi* 5A42. Translation by Owen in *Readings in Chinese Literary Thought*, 24.

18. Liu Xie, "Zhi yin" 知音 (An understanding critic), in *Wenxin diaolong* 48,. Translation slightly modifies Shih, *The Literary Mind*, 262, and Ge, "Authorial Intention," 6.

19. "Xi ci zhuan" 系辭傳 (Appended sayings), in *Yijing*. Translation slightly modifies Owen, *Readings in Chinese Literary Thought*, 31.

20. The prominent Song scholar Zhu Xi, among others, urged readers not to be content with surface (skin-deep) meanings but, through careful rereading, to enter as fully as possible into the mind-sets of ancient writers. Gardner, *Learning to Be a Sage*. See also Gardner, "Transmitting the Way," 158–159. Lianbin Dai argues that the methods of reading Zhu Xi

advocated continued to exert a powerful influence well into the Ming period. Dai, "Books, Reading, and Knowledge." See also Yu Li, "A History of Reading," 91.

21. In "Yu Jiao Ruohou" 與焦弱侯 (To Jiao Ruohou) Li Zhi repeats the assertion that through reading he comes face to face with authors from the past. *Xu fenshu* 1; *LZQJZ* 3.124. Similar assertions may be found in the writings of Zhu Xi among other premodern Chinese scholars. Gardner, *Learning to Be a Sage*, 129.

22. Li Zhi, "*Chutanji* xu" 初潭集序 (Preface to *Upon Arrival at the Lake*), in *Chutanji*; *LZQJZ* 12.1.

23. Li Zhi, "Ti Kongzi xiang yu Zhifo yuan" 題孔子像於芝佛院 (An inscription for the image of Confucius in the Cloister of the Flourishing Buddha), in *Xu Fenshu* 4; *LZQJZ* 3.309. Translation by Pauline C. Lee in *BBBKH*, 290.

24. Li Zhi, "Yu youren lun wen" 與友人論文 (Discussing literature with a friend), in *Xu Fenshu* 1; *LZQJZ* 3.21.

25. de Certeau, *The Practice of Everyday Life*, 169. Steven Zwicker articulates clearly the ways in which the experience of reading in early modern Europe both resembles and diverges from the type of reading de Certeau envisions. Zwicker, "What Every Literate Man Once Knew," 84–85.

26. Li Zhi, "Tongxin shuo" 童心說 (On the childlike mind), in *Fenshu* 3; *LZQJZ* 1.276-279.

27. Li Zhi, "Cangshu shiji liezhuan zongmu qianlun" 藏書世紀列傳總目前論 (Preface to the combined "Dynastic Records" and "Biographies" sections of *A Book to Keep [Hidden]*), in *Cangshu*; *LZQJZ* 4.1. Translation by Pauline C. Lee in *BBBKH*, 318.

28. Ibid., *LZQJZ* 4:1; Pauline C. Lee offers an alternative translation in *BBBKH*, 317.

29. Li Zhi, "Da Geng Zhongcheng" 答耿中丞 (Sent in reply to Senior Censor Geng), in *Fenshu* 1; *LZQJZ* 1.40-41. Timothy Brook provides an alternative translation in *BBBKH*, 38.

30. For a discussion of this passage and its context see Lee, *Li Zhi*, 85. For analysis of the concept of "learning for oneself" see de Bary, *Learning for Oneself*, especially 43–70.

31. Li Zhi, "Tongxin shuo" 童心說 (On the childlike mind), in *Fenshu* 3; *LZQJZ* 1.276-279. Translation by Pauline C. Lee and Rivi Handler-Spitz in *BBBKH*, 109.

32. Li Zhi, "Cangshu shiji liezhuan zongmu qianlun" 藏書世紀列傳總目前論 (Preface to the combined "Dynastic Records" and "Biographies: sections of *A Book to Keep [Hidden]*), in *Cangshu*; *LZQJZ* 4.1.

33. Liu Dongxing, "Liu Dongxing xu" 劉東星序 (Preface by Liu Dongxing), in Li Zhi, *Cangshu*; *LZQJZ* 8.697.

34. Ibid.

35. Yuan Zhongdao, "Li Wenling zhuan" 李溫陵傳 (Biography of Li Wenling), in *Kexuezhai ji* 2.17.719-725.

Notes to Chapter 6

36. Li Zhi, "Cangshu shiji liezhuan zongmu qianlun" 藏書世紀列傳總目前論 (Preface to the combined "Dynastic Records" and "Biographies" sections of *A Book to Keep [Hidden]*), in *Cangshu*; *LZQJZ* 4.1.

37. Jardine and Grafton, "Studied for Action," 30.

38. "L'humaniste lit la plume à la main. Il surcharge les marges des ouvrages lus de réflexions personnelles, marques manifestes d'une appropriation personnelle des textes lus." Vernus, *Histoire d'une pratique ordinaire*, 23. See also Cave, "The Mimesis of Reading"; Zwicker, "What Every Literate Man Once Knew," 84.

39. Glidden, "Recouping the Text," 148.

40. To be sure, in both Europe and China the attitude that classical texts conveyed the wisdom of the ancients persisted well into the sixteenth century and beyond. European scholars continued to scour ancient texts for nuggets of wisdom to apply to their daily lives. And in China, the conservative methods of reading advocated by Zhu Xi remained influential throughout the Ming. However, in both regions, more critical modes of reading also gained adherents. Grafton, "The Humanist as Reader," 203; Zwicker, "What Every Literate Man Once Knew," 84–85; Dai, "Books, Reading, and Knowledge," 280; Yu Li, "A History of Reading," 121; Handler-Spitz, "Provocative Texts."

41. Carruthers, *The Book of Memory*, 162.

42. *Mengzi* (Mencius), 5A42. Translated by Owen in *Readings in Chinese Literary Thought*, 24.

43. Ann Blair emphasizes the incremental nature of the shift from reverential reading to more adversarial reading in early modern Europe and insists that most marginalia from this period were simply reading notes intended to facilitate retrieval of specific passages. Blair, *Too Much to Know*, 59, 71; Zwicker, "The Reader Revealed," 14–15.

44. "Un suffisant lecteur descouvre souvant és escrits d'autruy des perfections autres que celles que l'autheur y a mises et apperceues, et y preste des sens et des visages plus riches." Montaigne, "Divers Evenements de Mesme Conseil" 1: 24, in *Les Essays*, 127. See also Montaigne, "Various Outcomes of the Same Plan," in *The Complete Essays of Montaigne*, 93.

45. "J'ay leu en Tite-Live cent choses que tel n'y a pas leu . . . et, à l'aventure, ce que l'auteur y avoit mis." Montaigne, "De l'institution des enfans" 1: 26, in *Les Essays*, 156; translation modified from Frame's "Of the Education of Children," in *The Complete Essays of Montaigne*, 115.

46. Jin Shengtan, "Du diliu caizi shu *Xixiangji* fa" 讀第六才子書西廂記法 (On reading the sixth book of genius, *The Romance of the Western Chamber*), in *Jin Shengtan quanji* 3.19. Translation modified from Martin Huang's in "Author(ity) and Reader," 59.

47. For further examples of early modern European readers responding to texts in idiosyncratic and occasionally humorously aggressive ways, see Grafton, "The Humanist as Reader," 208; Grafton, "John Dee Reads," 35; Jardine and Grafton, "Studied for Action"; Zwicker, "The Reader Revealed," 13; Sharpe, "Uncommonplaces?"

48. Xu Wei, "Shi shuo xu" 詩說序 (Preface on poetry), in *Xu Wei ji* 2.19.521–522.

49. Cervantes, *Don Quijote*, 9.

50. A quotation from Montaigne's essay "Of the Education of Children" (De l'institution des enfans) illustrates this point. To support an argument in favor of skepticism, Montaigne cites a single line from Dante's *Inferno*: "Questioning, no less than knowing, pleases me." In its original context, this line suggests a rather different meaning. In the *Inferno*, Dante speaks these words after having asked Virgil, his guide, about the punishments of Hell. After Virgil replies in detail, Dante responds, "You do content me so when you solve [or answer my questions] / that questioning, no less than knowing, pleases me." In the *Inferno*, this quotation, far from advocating skepticism, rewards the guide for having provided a conclusive answer. Montaigne deliberately disregards this original meaning, preferring to bend the words creatively to his own purpose. Montaigne's deployment of this technique is analyzed in Rendall, "*Mus in Pice*," 70–71.

51. He Yuming and Kathryn Lowry also discuss ways in which the disorderly visual presentation of material on the printed pages of joke books and song books encouraged readers to embark on creative reinterpretations of their own. Shang, "*Jin Ping Mei*," 193; He Yuming, *Home and the World*, 2–3; Lowry, *The Tapestry of Popular Songs*, 66–67.

52. Lanling Xiaoxiaosheng, *Jin Ping Mei cihua* 1.8.89. For an analysis of the way this excerpt functions snatched from its original context and inserted into the novel, see Shang, "*Jin Ping Mei*," 197–198.

53. Given the uncertain attribution of the numerous "Li Zhuowu" commentaries on fiction and drama, the discussion centers on works whose authorship is less disputed. Jiao Hong, in his preface to *Another Book to Keep (Hidden)*, also disputed the authenticity of portions of that work. Jiao Hong, "Xu cangshu xu" 續藏書序 (Preface to *Another Book to Keep (Hidden)*), in Li Zhi, *Xu cangshu*, LZQJZ 11.358.

54. Li Zhi, "Si shu ping xu" 四書評序 (Preface to *Commentary on The Four Books*), in *Si shu ping*, LZQJZ 21.1.

55. *Analects* 9.4. My translation alters that of Lau, 96.

56. He Xinyin, "Da zhanguo zhu gong Kongmen shidi zhi yu zhi bie zai luo yiqi yu bu luo yiqi" 答戰國諸公孔門師弟之與之別在落意氣與不落意氣 (Response to various Warring States Confucian masters and disciples' discussions of losing or sustaining one's spirit), in *He Xinyin ji* 3.54. For analysis of He's interpretation and its influence on Li, see Billeter, *Li Chih*, 150; Anne Cheng, "Les Métamorphoses," 217–218.

57. Chow, "Writing for Success," 142–143.

58. Qu You (1341–1427) also argued in his preface to *Jian deng xin hua* 剪登新話 (New stories to [read while you trim] the lamp) that stories could substitute for the classics. Yuan Fengzi made a similar point in his 1547 preface to *San guo zhi zhuan* 三國志傳 (The narrative of the Three Kingdoms). McLaren, "Constructing New Reading Publics," 157–158. Within a few generations, sentiments of this kind had become quite widespread and were expressed in the writings of Jin Shengtan and later Zhang Zhupo. For

discussion of Jin Shengtan's views, see Church, "Beyond the Words," 9; for discussion of Zhang Zhupo's views, see Shang, "*Jin Ping Mei*," 216.

59. Li Zhi, "Tongxin shuo" 童心說 (On the childlike mind), in *Fenshu* 3; *LZQJZ* 1.277. Translation by Haun Saussy in *BBBKH*, 109.

60. Li Zhi, "Bai yue" 拜月 (The pavilion for worshiping the moon), in *Fenshu* 4; *LZQJZ* 2.132–133. Translation by Huiying Chen, in *BBBKH*, 191.

61. Li Zhi, "*Zhongyi Shuihuzhuan* xu" 忠義水滸傳序 (Preface to *The Loyal and Righteous Outlaws of the Marsh*), in *Fenshu* 3; *LZQJZ* 1.301–304. Emphasis mine.

62. Li Zhi, "Hong fu" 紅拂 (Red duster), in *Fenshu* 4; *LZQJZ* 2:133–134. Translation by Huiying Chen in *BBBKH*, 193. For the comments of Confucius, see *Analects* 17.9.

63. Qian Maowei, *Mingdai shixue*, 336.

64. Mei Guozhen, "Mei Guozhen xu" 梅國楨序 (Preface by Mei Guozhen), in Li Zhi, *Cangshu*; *LZQJZ* 8.698.

65. Wu Congxian, "*Shigang pingyao* xu" 史綱評要序 (Preface to *Outline of History with Critical Comments*), in *Xiao chuang zi ji* 4, 402.

66. Lü Buwei (291?–235 BCE) was chancellor to the first emperor of China. He inveigled his way into the court by arranging for the empress dowager, a lewd old woman, to have an illicit affair with a man whose penis was exceedingly large. Sima Qian, "Lü Buwei liezhuan" 呂不韋列傳 (Biography of Lü Buwei), in *Shiji* 85. Li Yuan (third cent. BCE), in order to advance his own career, ordered that the prime minister of the state of Chu, Chun Shenjun, be assassinated. Sima Qian, "Chun Shenjun liezhuan" 春申君列傳 (Biography of Chun Shenjun), in *Shiji* 78. Li Si (ca. 280–208 BCE) served as prime minister to the notoriously cruel and autocratic first emperor of the Qin dynasty, Qin Shihuang. In an effort to quash opposition from Confucian scholars, this legalist advisor proposed that the first emperor "burn [Confucian] books and bury [Confucian scholars alive]." The emperor implemented this policy, which later garnered harsh criticism from centuries of Confucian scholars, beginning with Sima Qian. Li Zhi borrows the title of *A Book to Burn* from this phrase. Sima Qian, "Li Si liezhuan" 李斯列傳 (Biography of Li Si), in *Shiji* 87. Feng Dao (882–954) was reviled for having served under several dynasties. Zhuo Wenjun (second cent. BCE) eloped with the great poet, musician, and historian Sima Xiangru. Sima Qian, "Sima Xiangru liezhuan" 司馬相如列傳 (Biography of Sima Xiangru), in *Shiji* 117. Sang Hongyang (d. 80 BCE) served under Emperor Wu of Han (156–87 BCE), helped the Han government solidify its monopolies over salt and iron, and so bolstered the economic stability of the empire. He was assassinated when he came under suspicion for having been involved in a plot to overthrow the emperor. Ban, *Hanshu* 38.

67. Zhang Wenda, "Shenzong shilu Wanli sanshi nian run er yue yimao like jishizhong Zhang Wenda shu he Li Zhi" 神宗實錄萬曆三十年閏二月乙卯禮科給事中張問達疏劾李贄 (Veritable record of the memorial impeaching Li Zhi, submitted by the supervising censor Zhang Wenda on the *yimao* day of the second intercalary month of the thirtieth year of the reign of emperor Shenzong), in *Ming shilu* 112.369.11.

68. Ibid.

69. *Li Wenling ji* 李溫陵集 (The Collected Writings of Li Wenling) included in its pages *A Book to Burn, A Book to Keep (Hidden)*, and several other titles. The synopsis continues, "To this day, [Li's writings] have exerted a deleterious effect on both customs and people's minds. For this reason Li Zhi deserved to be executed and his books destroyed." Yong, "*Li Wenling ji*, ershi juan, Jiangsu Zhou Houyu jia cangben" 李溫陵集二十卷江蘇周厚堉家藏本 (The collected works of Li Wenling in twenty fascicles. Edition from the collection of Zhou Houyu of Jiangsu), in *Siku quanshu zongmu* 2.178.1599.

70. Jiao Hong, "Jiao Hong xu" 焦竑序 (Preface by Jiao Hong), in Li Zhi, *Cangshu*; *LZQJZ* 8.696.

71. Yong, "Chutanji, ershi juan, neifu cangben" 初潭集二十卷内府藏本 (*Upon Arrival at the Lake* in twenty fascicles. Edition from the imperial collection), in *Siku quanshu zongmu* 1.131.1120.

72. Jiang Yihua, "Ji Li Zhuowu" 紀李卓吾 (Record of Li Zhuowu), in *Xitai manji* 2.31a. For more examples, see Zhuhong 褚宏, "Li Zhuowu" 李卓吾, in *Zhu chuang suibi* 竹窗隨筆 (Casual jottings by the bamboo window), cited in *LZYJCKZL* 2.161; Zhou Yingbin 周應賓, "Li Zhuowu" 李卓吾, in "Shi xiao pian" 識小篇 (Short essays), cited in *LZYJCKZL* 2.165; Shen Defu, "Huang Shenxuan zhi zhu" 黃慎軒之逐 (The expulsion of Huang Shenxuan), in *Wanli yehuo bian* 1.10.171–171; Wang Fuzhi, "Sao shou wen" 搔首問 (Scratching my head in perplexity), in *Chuanshan yishu* 17.9923; Wang Hongzhuan, "Li Zhi" 李贄, in *Shan zhi* 4.15b; Fang Yizhi, "Ming jiao" 名教 (Confucian teachings), in *Dongxijun*, 129.

73. Li Zhi, "Yu Zhou Youshan shu" 與周友山書 (To Zhou Youshan), in *Fenshu* 2; *LZQJZ* 1.133. This letter recounts Li Zhi's experience being harassed by an angry mob at the Yellow Crane Pavilion in Wuchang in 1591. Li attributes the accusation that he "behaves eccentrically and deceives the multitudes" to the thugs that attacked him.

74. Gu Xiancheng, "Dangxia yi" 當下繹 (Impromptu interpretations), in *Gu Duanwen gong yishu* 顧端文公遺書 (The remaining writings of Mr. Gu Duanwen), 14.

75. Jiang wrote, "For some time now I have had an obsession with books, but I found fault with this imprint [of Li's writings] for repudiating the classics and creating chaos out of order. Fearing that it might pollute my bookshelf, I decided not to add it to my collection." Jiang Yihua, "Ji Li Zhuowu" 紀李卓吾 (Record of Li Zhuowu), in *Xitai manji* 2.31b. Similar accusations continued to be voiced in the early Qing dynasty. For instance, Gu Yanwu decried Li Zhi as a "betrayer of the sages." Gu Yanwu, "Li Zhi" 李贄, in *Rizhi lu* 2.18.1070.

76. Wang is quoting Li's immodest estimation of his own words here. Li Zhi, "Yu Zhou Youshan" 與周友山 (To Zhou Youshan), in *Xu Fenshu* 1; *LZQJZ* 3.47.

77. Refers to Zhuangzi, "Tian di" 天地 (Heaven and Earth), in *Zhuangzi* 12; Zhuangzi, *The Complete Works of Chuang Tzu*, 141.

78. Wang Benke, "Xu ke Li shi shu xu" 續刻李氏書序 (On reprinting Mr. Li's writings), in Li Zhi, *Xu Fenshu*; *LZQJZ* 3.421.

Notes to Chapter 6

79. Qian Qianyi, "Jiashulun juye zashuo" 家塾論舉業雜說 (Random jottings on private school discussions of preparing for exams), in *Muzhai youxueji* 45, 3:1509. Zhang Shiyi, "Jidaoxin" 集導辛 (Collected views on bitterness), in *Yuelutang ji* 8.123.

80. Zhu Shilu, "Zhu Shilu xu" 祝世祿序 (Preface by Zhu Shilu), in Li Zhi, *Cangshu*; *LZQJZ* 8.699.

81. Jiao Hong, "Jiao Hong xu" 焦竑序 (Preface by Jiao Hong), in Li Zhi, *Cangshu*; *LZQJZ* 8.696.

82. Chen Renxi, "Cangshu xu" 藏書序 (Preface to *A Book to Keep [Hidden]*), in *Wumengyuan ji*, section "Ma si" 馬四 (Horses, part 4), unpaginated edition.

83. Confirming this interpretation while slightly restricting its scope, another preface writer to *A Book to Keep (Hidden)* averred that readers should feel free to differ from Li's judgments, provided that their interpretations be grounded in a firm ethical foundation. He wrote, "If [a reader] is capable of governing with benevolence as a genuine Confucian scholar, then even if he says that [Li Zhi's] judgments betray the sages, [Li] would not object." Zhu Shilu, "Zhu Shilu xu" 祝世祿序 (Preface by Zhu Shilu), in Li Zhi, *Cangshu*; *LZQJZ* 8.699.

84. Jiao Hong, "Jiao Hong xu" 焦竑序 (Preface by Jiao Hong), in Li Zhi, *Cangshu*; *LZQJZ* 8.696. The phrase "dan mu yu zhi" 旦暮遇之 alludes to Zhuangzi, "Qi wu lun" 齊物論 (Discussion on making all things equal), in *Zhuangzi* 2. The line in the original is: "After ten thousand generations, a great sage may appear who will know [the meaning of contradictory assertions], and it will still be as though he appeared with astonishing speed." Zhuangzi, *The Complete Works of Chuang Tzu*, 48.

85. I have seen no early editions of Li's writings that contain marginalia written by contemporary hands. However, Yuan Hongdao is reported to have jotted down his responses in the margins of Li's texts. Hung, *The Romantic Vision*, 190.

86. Wu Congxian 吳從先, "*Shigang pingyao* xu" 史綱評要序 (Preface to *Outline of History with Critical Comments*), in *LZYJCKZL* 2.113.

87. Li Zhonghuang 李中黃, "Lun wen" 論文 (On literature), in *Yilou si lun* 逸樓四論 (Four discourses by Li Yilou), cited in *LZYJCKZL* 2.157.

88. Yuan Zhongdao, "Li Wenling zhuan" 李溫陵傳 (Biography of Li Wenling), in *Kexuezhai ji* 2.17.719–725. Translation by Haun Saussy in *BBBKH*, 330.

89. Wang Hongzhuan, "Li Zhi" 李贄 in *Shan zhi* 4.15b.

90. Li Zhi, "Tongxin shuo" 童心說 (On the childlike mind), in *Fenshu* 3; *LZQJZ* 1.276–279.

91. Marginal comment on "Fu Zhou Nan shi" 復周南士 (Reply to Zhou Nanshi). This comment is repeated twice in the letter. Library of Congress's Ming edition of *Fenshu*, 18–19.

92. Chambers, "Commentary in Literary Texts," 327, 335.

GLOSSARY OF CHINESE CHARACTERS

Anhui 安徽
Anle Temple 安樂寺

bagu wen 八股文
Bai Yinzhang 白胤昌 (1584–1658)
Bai yue ting ji 拜月亭記
baifan 稗販
Ban Gu 班固 (32–92 CE)
Bo Ya 伯牙
bu qiu shen jie 不求甚解

Cai Yizhong 蔡毅中 (late Ming, n.d.)
cang 藏
Cang Jie 倉頡
cang zhu ming shan 藏諸名山
Cangshu 藏書
Cao Cao 曹操 (155–220)
cha 察
Changlu 長蘆
Chen Hongshou 陳洪綬 (1598–1652)
Chen Jiru 陳繼儒 (1558–1639)

Chen Renxi 陳仁錫 (1581–1636)
chuanqi 傳奇
Chunqiu 春秋
Chun Shenjun 春申君
ci 刺
cong wu ci lun 從無此論

da maimai 大買賣
Da Ming ling 大明令
Dao gu lu 道古錄
Daoxue chao 道學抄
daoxue xiansheng 道學先生
Deng Huoqu 鄧豁渠 (1489–1578?)
Deng Lincai 鄧林材 (*juren* 1561)
Deng Yingqi 鄧應祁 (*jinshi* 1586)
dizi 弟子
Du Fu 杜甫 (712–770)

fa yan 法眼
fan 反
Fan Li 范蠡 (Spring and Autumn pd., n.d.)

Fan Lian 范濂 (Ming, n.d.)
fandu 反讀
fanfeng 反諷
fang ke 坊刻
Fang Yizhi 方以智 (1611–1671)
feng 諷
Feng Dao 馮道 (882–954)
Feng Fang 豐坊 (1493–1566)
Feng Junpei 馮君培
Feng Menglong 馮夢龍 (1574–1646)
fengci 諷刺
Fenshu 焚書
Fenshu bian 焚書辯
Fo yan 佛眼
Fugu pai 復古派
Fujian 福建

Gao Gong 高拱 (1510–1578)
Ge Jian 葛澗 (Ming, n.d.)
Geng Dingli 耿定理 (d. 1584)
Geng Dingxiang 耿定向 (ca.1524–1597)
gong'an (Jp. kōan) 公案
Gong'an pai 公安派
gu 觚
Gu Dashao 顧大韶 (b. 1576)
Gu Xiancheng 顧憲成 (1550–1612)
Gu Yangqian 顧養謙 (1537–1604)
Gu Yanwu 顧炎武 (1613–1682)
guan 觀

guan ke 官刻
Guanzi 管子 (6th cent. BCE)

Han Feizi 韓非子 (d. 233 BCE)
Hangzhou 杭州
hao 號
haoshizhe 好事者
He Jiaoyuan 何喬遠 (1558–1631)
He Jingming 何景明 (1483–1521)
He Xinyin 何心隱 (1517–1579)
heshang 和尚
Hong fu zhuan 紅拂傳
Hong Wenke 洪文科 (Ming, n.d.)
Hu Yinglin 胡應麟 (1551–1602)
Huang Kehui 黃克晦 (1524–1590)
Huang Yuji 黃虞稷 (1629–1691)
Huang'an 黃安
Hubei 湖北
Huguang 湖廣
hui yan 慧眼
Huizhou 徽州
hun 溷

Ji Cheng 吉澄 (fl. 1633)
jia ke 家刻
Jia Yi 賈誼 (201–169 BCE)
Jiajing reign 嘉靖 (1522–1566)
Jiang Yihua 蔣以化 (fl. Wanli pd., n.d.)

Glossary of Chinese Characters

Jiang Yingke 江盈科 (1553–1605)
Jiangxi 江西
jianshangzhe 鑒賞者
Jianyang 建陽
Jiao Hong 焦竑 (1541–1620)
Jiaoyou lun 交友論
jin 禁
Jin Shengtan 金聖歎 (1608–1661)
Jin Xueyan 靳學顏 (fl. 1570)
Jining 濟寧
Jinling 金陵
jinshi 進士
jinxian 進賢
juan 卷
jue 玦

kao 考
kaozheng xue 考證學
ke 可
kuang 狂

Lang Ying 郎瑛 (1487–1566)
li (transgress) 戾
li (profit) 利
Li Jing 李靖 (571–649)
Li Le 李樂 (*jinshi* 1568)
Li Mengyang 李夢陽 (1475–1531)
Li sao 離騷
Li Si 李斯 (280?–208 BCE)
Li Tingji 李廷機 (Ming, n.d.)

Li Yuan 李園 (third cent. BCE)
Li Zhonghuang 李中黃 (n.d.)
Li Zhuowu 李卓吾
liang 兩
Liangxi 梁溪
Lidai shi ji zuobian 歷代史籍左編
Lin Yuncheng 林雲程 (late Ming, n.d.)
Liu Dongxing 劉東星 (1538–1601)
Liu Jincheng 劉近城 (n.d.)
Liu Ruoyu 劉若愚 (b. 1584?)
Liu Tong 劉侗 (Ming, n.d.)
Liu Xie 劉勰 (ca. 465–ca. 522)
Liu Xie 劉諧 (fl. 1570)
Liu Yan 劉晏 (716–780)
Liu Zongyuan 柳宗元 (773–819)
Longhu 龍湖
Longqing reign 隆慶 (1567–1572)
Longxi ji 龍溪集
Lü Buwei 呂不韋 (291?–235 BCE)

Ma Jinglun 馬經綸 (1562–1605)
Macheng 麻城
Mao Qiling 毛奇齡 (1623–1716)
maodun 矛盾
Mei Guozhen 梅國楨 (1542–1605)
mengdong dizi 懞懂弟子
Mi Fu 米芾 (1051–1107)

Min Qiji 閔齊伋 (1580–after 1661)
ming 名
Mingdeng lu 明燈錄
miu 謬

Nanxun lu 南詢錄

Pao Xi 庖犧
pei 佩
Peng Shaosheng 彭紹升 (1740–1796)
pengyou 朋友
piaoke 嫖客

Qian Qianyi 錢謙益 (1582–1664)
Qian Xiyan 錢希言 (fl. 1612)
qian zhe quan ye 錢者權也
Qianlong reign 乾隆 (1735–1796)
Qin Shihuang 秦始皇 (259–210 BCE)
Qu You 瞿佑 (1341–1427)
Qu Yuan 屈原 (ca. 340–278 BCE)
Quanzhou 泉州

Rongyutang 容與堂
rou yan 肉眼
Ru 儒
Runing 汝寧

Sang Hongyang 桑弘羊 (d. 80 BCE)
Sanjiao pin 三教品

Shaanxi 陝西
shanren 山人
Shanxi 山西
Shen Defu 沈德符 (1578–1642)
Shen Li 沈鯉 (1531–1615)
Shen Zijin 沈自晉 (1583–1665)
si ke 私刻
Sima Guang 司馬光 (1019–1086)
Sima Qian 司馬遷 (145?–86? BCE)
Sima Xiangru 司馬相如 (ca. 180–117 BCE)
su shi 俗士
Su Xun 蘇洵 (1009–1066)
sui 歲
Sun Wukong 孫悟空
Suzhou 蘇州

Taizhou pai 泰州派
Tang Shunzhi 唐順之 (1507–1560)
Tang Xianzu 湯顯祖 (1550–1616)
Tao Qian 陶潛 (365–427)
tian yan 天眼
tongxin 童心
Tongzhou 通州

Wang Anshi 王安石 (1021–1086)
Wang Benke 汪本鈳 (fl. 1594)
Wang Bolun 汪伯倫 (n.d.)
Wang Chong 王充 (27–91)

Glossary of Chinese Characters

Wang Fuzhi 王夫之 (1616–1692)
Wang Gen 王艮 (1483–1540)
Wang Hongzhuan 王宏撰 (1622–1702)
Wang Ji 王畿 (1497–1582)
Wang Keshou 汪可受 (d. 1620)
Wang Ling 王陵 (d. 181 BCE)
Wang Shifu 王實甫 (fl. 1295–1307)
Wang Shizhen 王世貞 (1526–1590)
Wang Yi 王逸 (fl. 130–140)
Wanli reign 萬曆 (1572–1620)
Wanling 宛陵
Wei Jiao 魏校 (1483–1543)
wei shengren li yan 為聖人立言
Wei Zhongxian 魏忠賢 (1568–1627)
Weimo an 維摩庵
wen 文
Wu Congxian 吳從先 (Ming, n.d.)
Wu hu laoren 五湖老人
"Wu liu xiansheng zhuan" 五柳先生傳
Wu Yu 吳虞 (1872–1949)
Wu Yuancui 伍袁萃 (fl. 1595)
Wuchang 武昌
Wunian Shenyou 無念深有 (1544–1627)

xi 觿
Xiamen 廈門
xianzhe 賢者
xiao maimai 小買賣
Xie Lingyun 謝靈運 (385–433)
Xie Zhaozhe 謝肇淛 (1567–1624)
Xiguo jifa 西國記法
xin 信
Xin'an 新安
Xingshi yinyuan zhuan 醒世姻緣傳
Xinxue pai 心學派
Xixiang ji 西廂記
Xu Cangshu 續藏書
Xu Fenshu 續焚書
Xu Wei 徐渭 (1521–1593)
Xunzi 荀子 (313–238 BCE)

Yan Hui 顏回 (521–490 BCE)
Yang Shen 楊慎 (1488–1559)
Yang Xiong 揚雄 (53 BCE–~18 CE)
Yao'an 姚安
Ye Mengde 葉夢德 (1077–1148)
Ye Sheng 葉盛 (1420–1474)
Ye Zhou 葉晝 (fl. 1595–1624)
yi 義
yi guan qin shou 衣冠禽獸
yiduan 異端
Yijing 易經
ying 熒
Yinguo lu 因果錄
Yiyuan zhiyan 藝苑卮言
Yongle reign 永樂 (1402–1424)
Yongping 永平

yu fu yu fu 愚夫愚婦
Yu Xiangdou 餘象門 (fl. 1596)
Yu Yizheng 于奕正 (Ming, n.d.)
Yuan Fengzi 元峰子 (fl. 1547)
Yuan Hongdao 袁宏道 (1568–1610)
Yuan Huang 袁黃 (1533–1606)
Yuan Zhongdao 袁中道 (1570–1623)
Yuan Zongdao 袁宗道 (1560–1600)
Yuchu xinzhi 虞初新志
Yunnan 雲南

zaju 雜劇
Zeng Jiquan 曾繼泉 (fl. 1588)
zhang 障
Zhang Chao 張潮 (1650–ca. 1711)
Zhang Dafu 張大復 (1554–1630)
Zhang Dai 張岱 (1597–1679)
Zhang Fang 張芳 (Qing, n.d.)
Zhang Han 張瀚 (1510–1593)
Zhang Nai 張鼐 (*jinshi* 1604)
Zhang Wenda 張問達 (fl. 1600)
Zhang Zhupo 張竹坡 (1670–1698)
zhanzhuan 輾轉
Zhao Bao 趙苞 (d. 177)

zheng (correct, upright) 正
zheng (to govern) 政
Zhengde reign 正德 (1506–1521)
zhengming 正名
Zhenzong 真宗 (968–1022)
zhi 志
Zhifo yuan 芝佛院
zhiyin 知音
Zhong Xing 鍾惺 (1574–1625)
Zhong You 仲由 (542–480 BCE)
Zhong Ziqi 鐘子期
Zhou Sijing 周思敬 (d. 1597)
Zhou Sijiu 周思久 (*jinshi* 1553)
Zhou Yi 周釴 (n.d., contemporary of Li Zhi)
zhu jun 諸君
Zhu Shilu 祝世祿 (1539–1610)
Zhu Xi 朱熹 (1130–1200)
Zhu Yuanzhang 朱元璋 (1328–1398)
Zhuhong 袾宏 (1535–1615)
Zhuo Wenjun 卓文君 (2nd cent. BCE)
zi 字
zide 自得
Zilu 子路 (542–480 BCE)
Ziyun 子雲 (53 BCE–~18 CE)
Zuo Qiuming 左丘明 (5th cent. BCE)
zuoyong 作用

BIBLIOGRAPHY

Abrams, M. H. *The Mirror and the Lamp: Romantic Theory and the Critical Tradition.* New York: Oxford University Press, 1953.

Adshead, S. A. M. *Material Culture in Europe and China, 1400–1800: The Rise of Consumerism.* New York: St. Martin's Press, 1997.

Aldridge, Alfred Owen. *Comparative Literature: Matter and Method.* Urbana: University of Illinois Press, 1969.

Alford, William P. *To Steal a Book Is an Elegant Offense.* Stanford: Stanford University Press, 1995.

Aristotle. *Posterior Analytics.* In *Introduction to Aristotle*, edited by Richard McKeon. New York: Random House, 1947.

Bacon, Francis. *The Advancement of Learning*, edited by G. W. Kitchin. London: J. M. Dent and Sons, 1973.

———. *The Essays.* London: Penguin Classics, 1985.

Balsamo, Luigi. *Bibliography: History of a Tradition*, translated by William A. Pettas. Berkeley CA: Bernard M. Rosenthal, 1990.

Ban Gu 班固. *Baihutong* 白虎通. 2 vols. Beijing: Beijing tushuguan chubanshe, 2005.

———. *Hanshu xinzhu* 漢書新注, edited by Shi Ding 施丁. 3 vols. Xi'an: Sanqin chubanshe, 1994.

Barnhardt, Richard. "The 'Wild and Heterodox' School of Ming Painting." In *Theories of the Arts in China*, edited by Susan Bush and Christian F. Murck, 365–396. Princeton, NJ: Princeton University Press, 1983.

Barr, Allan H. "Jiang Yingke's Place in the Gong'an School." *Ming Studies* 45–46 (2002): 41–68.

Barthes, Roland. *Système de la mode.* Paris: Éditions du Seuil, 1967.

Bauschatz, Cathleen M. "Marie de Gournay's 'Préface de 1595': A Critical Evaluation." *Bulletin de la Sociéte des Amis de Montaigne*, 7th series, 3–4 (1986): 73–82.

Bentley, Tamara Heimarck. "Authenticity and the Expanding Market in Chen Hongshou's Seventeenth-Century Printed Playing Cards." *Artibus Asiae* 49.1 (2009): 147–188.

———. "Authenticity in a New Key: Chen Hongshou's Figurative Oeuvre, 'Authentic Emotion,' and the Late Ming Market." PhD diss., University of Michigan, 2000.

———. *The Figurative Works of Chen Hongshou (1599–1652): Authentic Voices/Expanding Markets*. Burlington, VT: Ashgate, 2012.

Berry, Christopher. *The Idea of Luxury: A Conceptual and Historical Investigation*. Cambridge, UK: Cambridge University Press, 1994.

Biji xiaoshuo daguan 筆記小說大觀. 35 vols. Yangzhou: Jiangsu guangling guji keyinshe: Yangzhou gujie shujidian faxing, 1984.

Billeter, Jean-François. *Li Chih, philosophe maudit (1527–1602)*. Geneva: Librairie Droz, 1979.

Blair, Ann. *Too Much to Know: Managing Scholarly Information before the Modern Age*. New Haven, CT: Yale University Press, 2010.

Boase, Alan Martin. *The Fortunes of Montaigne: A History of the Essays in France, 1580–1669*. London: Methuen, 1935.

Bodin, Jean. *Response to Paradoxes of Malestroict*, translated by Henry Tutor and R. W. Dyson. Bristol, UK: Thoemmes Press, 1997.

Booth, Wayne C. *A Rhetoric of Irony*. Chicago: University of Chicago Press, 1974.

Bottéro, Françoise. "Cang Jie and the Invention of Writing: Reflections on the Elaboration of a Legend." In *Studies in Chinese Language and Culture: Festschrift in Honour of Christoph Harbsmeier on the Occasion of His Sixtieth Birthday*, edited by Christoph Anderl and Halvor Eifring, 133–155. Oslo: Hermes Academic, 2006.

Bowen, Barbara C. *The Age of Bluff: Paradox and Ambiguity in Rabelais and Montaigne*. Urbana: University of Illinois Press, 1972.

———. "Geofroy Tory's 'Champ Fleury' and Its Major Sources." *Studies in Philology* 76.1 (1979): 13–27.

Boxer, C. R. *South China in the Sixteenth Century*. London: Hakluyt Society, 1953.

Boyer-Xambeu, Marie-Thèse, Ghislain Deleplace, and Lucien Gillard. *Private Money and Public Currencies: The Sixteenth Century Challenge*, translated by Azizeh Azodi. Armonk, NY: M. E. Sharpe, 1994.

Braudel, Fernand. *The Structures of Everyday Life: Civilization and Capitalism 15th–18th Centuries*, translated by Siân Reynolds. New York: Harper & Row, 1979.

———. *The Wheels of Commerce: Civilization and Capitalism 15th–18th Centuries*, translated by Siân Reynolds. New York: Harper & Row, 1982.

Brinker-Gabler, Gisela, ed. *Encountering the Other(s): Studies in Literature, History, and Culture*. Albany: State University of New York Press, 1995.

Brokaw, Cynthia J. "On the History of the Book in China." In *Printing and Book Culture in Late Imperial China*, edited by Cynthia J. Brokaw and Kai-wing Chow, 3–54. Berkeley: University of California Press, 2005.

Brook, Timothy. *The Confusions of Pleasure: Commerce and Culture in Ming China*. Berkeley: University of California Press, 1998.

———. "The Public of Letters: The Correspondence of Li Zhi and Geng Dingxiang." In *The Objectionable Li Zhi: Fiction, Syncretism, and Dissent in Late Ming China*, edited by Pauline C. Lee, Rivi Handler-Spitz, and Haun Saussy. Manuscript in progress.

———. *The Troubled Empire: China in the Yuan and Ming Dynasties*. Cambridge, MA: Belknap Press, 2010.

———. *Vermeer's Hat: The Seventeenth Century and the Dawn of the Global World*. New York: Bloomsbury, 2008.

Browne, Thomas. "Religio Medici." 1643. In *Religio Medici and Other Works*, edited by L. C. Martin, 1–80. Oxford: Clarendon Press, 1964.

Burnett, Katharine P. "A Discourse of Originality in Late Ming Chinese Painting." *Art History* 23.4 (2000): 522–558.

Cahill, James. *The Compelling Image: Nature and Style in Seventeenth Century Chinese Painting*. Cambridge, MA: Harvard University Press, 1982.

———. *Fantastics and Eccentrics in Chinese Painting*. New York: Asia Society, 1967.

Calcagnini, Celio. "On Imitation." In *Ciceronian Controversies*, edited by Joann Dellaneva and translated by Brian Duvick, 144–181. Cambridge, MA: The I Tatti Renaissance Library, Harvard University Press, 2007.

Campbell, Duncan. "Madman or Genius: Yuan Hongdao's 'Biography of Xu Wei.'" In *Asia 2000: Modern China in Transition*, edited by Dov Bing, S. Lim, and M. Lin, 196–220. Hamilton, New Zealand: Outrigger, 1993.

Carey, John. "Donne and Coins." In *English Renaissance Studies: Presented to Dame Helen Gardner in Honour of Her Seventieth Birthday*, edited by John Carey, 151–163. Oxford: Clarendon Press, 1980.

Carroll, Lewis. *Through the Looking Glass and What Alice Found There*. New York: Bloomsbury, 2001.

Carruthers, Mary J. *The Book of Memory: A Study of Memory in Medieval Culture*. Cambridge, UK: Cambridge University Press, 1990.

Cave, Terrence. *The Cornucopian Text: Problems with Writing in the French Renaissance*. Oxford: Clarendon Press, 1979.

———. "The Mimesis of Reading in the Renaissance." In *Montaigne: A Collection of Essays. A Five-Volume Anthology of Scholarly Articles*, edited by Dikka Berven. *Vol. 5: Reading Montaigne*, 125–144. New York: Garland, 1995.

Cervantes, Michel de. *Don Quijote*, translated by Burton Raffel. New York: Norton, 1999.

Chambers, Ross. "Commentary in Literary Texts." *Critical Inquiry* 5 (1978): 323–337.

Chan, Albert. *The Glory and Fall of the Ming Dynasty*. Norman: University of Oklahoma Press, 1982.

Chan, Hok-lam. *Control of Publishing in China, Past and Present*. Canberra: Australian National University Press, 1983.

———. *Li Chih (1527–1502) in Contemporary Chinese Historiography*. White Plains, NY: M. E. Sharpe, 1980.

Chartier, Roger. *L'Ordre des livres*. Paris: Éditions Alinea, 1992.

———. "Publishing Strategies and What the People Read, 1530–1660." In *The Cultural Uses of Print in Early Modern France*, translated by Lydia G. Cochrane, 145–182. Princeton, NJ: Princeton University Press, 1987.

Chaves, Jonathan. "The Panoply of Images: A Reconsideration of the Literary Theory of the Kung-an School." In *Theories of the Arts in China*, edited by Susan Bush and Christian F. Murck, 341–364. Princeton NJ: Princeton University Press, 1983.

Chen Baoliang 陳寶良 and Wang Xi 王熹. *Zhongguo fengsu tongshi: Mingdai juan* 中國風俗通史：明代卷. Shanghai: Shanghai wenyi chubanshe, 2005.

Chen Cunguang 陳存廣. "Li Zhi feiyi 'shanren' yu Huang sheng qi ren—tan Li Zhi sixiang yanjiuzhong yinggai chengqing de yige shifei yu wujie jiaocha wenti" 李贄非議'山人'與黃生其人——談李贄思想研究中應該澄清的一個是非與誤解交叉問題. In *Li Zhi yanjiu* 李贄研究, edited by Xu Zaiquan 許在全 and Zhang jianye 張建業, 313–318. Quanzhoushi shehui kexue lianhehui bian 泉州市社會科學聯合會編. Quanzhou: Guangming ribao chubanshe, 1989.

Chen Qinghui 陳清輝. "Li Zhi Chanxue de guiyi" 李贄禪學的歸依. Guoli Qiaosheng daxue xianxiuban xuebao, 11.

Chen Renxi 陳仁錫. *Wumengyuan chuji* 無夢園初集. Microform. China: Dayao chenya, 1633?

Chen Wanyi 陳萬益. *Wanming xiaopin yu Mingji wenren shenghuo* 晚明小品與明季文人生活. Taipei: Da'an chubanshe, 1988.

Chen Zilong 陳子龍 et al., ed. [*Huang*] *Ming jingshi wenbian* [皇]明經世文編. 1637. Hong Kong: Zhuji shudian, 1964.

Cheng, Anne. "Les Métamorphoses du lecteur des classiques dans la Chine impériale." In *Des Alexandries II: Les métamorphoses du lecteur*, edited by Christian Jacob, 207–220. Paris: Bibliothèque Nationale de France, 2001.

Cheng Pei-kai. "Reality and Imagination: Li Chih and T'ang Hsien-tsu in Search of Authenticity." PhD diss., Yale University, 1980.

Cheng, Weikun. "Politics of the Queue: Agitation and Resistance in the Beginning and End of Qing China." In *Hair: Its Power and Meaning in Asian Cultures*, edited by Alf Hiltebeitel and Barbara D. Miller, 123–142. Albany: State University of New York Press, 1998.

Cherniack, Susan. "Book Culture and Textual Transmission in Sung China." *Harvard Journal of Asiatic Studies* 54.1 (1994): 5–125.

Chia, Lucille. "Of Three Mountains Street: The Commercial Publishers of Ming Nanjing." In *Printing and Book Culture in Late Imperial China*, edited by Cynthia J. Brokaw and Kai-wing Chow, 107–151. Berkeley: University of California Press, 2005.

———. *Printing for Profit: The Commercial Publishers of Jianyang, Fujian (11th–17th Centuries)*. Cambridge, MA: Harvard University Press, 2002.

Ch'ien, Edward T. *Chiao Hung and the Restructuring of Neo-Confucianism in the Late Ming*. New York: Columbia University Press, 1986.

Chou Chih-p'ing. *Yüan Hung-tao and the Kung-an School*. Cambridge, UK: Cambridge University Press, 1988.

Chow Kai-wing. "An Avatar of the Extraordinary (*qi*): Li Zhi as a Shishang Writer and Thinker in the Late Ming Publishing World." In *The Objectionable Li Zhi: Fiction, Syncretism, and Dissent in Late Ming China*, edited by Pauline C. Lee, Rivi Handler-Spitz, and Haun Saussy. Manuscript in progress.

———. *Publishing, Culture, and Power in Early Modern China*. Stanford: Stanford University Press, 2004.

———. "Writing for Success: Printing, Examinations, and Intellectual Change in Late Ming China." *Late Imperial China* 17 (1996): 120–157.

Church, Sally. "Beyond the Words: Jin Shengtan's Perception of Hidden Meanings in *Xixiang ji*." *Harvard Journal of Asiatic Studies* 59.1 (1999): 5–77.

Cipolla, Carlo. "The So-Called 'Price Revolution': Reflections on 'the Italian Situation.'" In *Economy and Society in Early Modern Europe: Essays from Annales*, edited by Peter Burke, 43–46. London: Routledge, 1972.

Clunas, Craig. "The Art of Social Climbing in Sixteenth Century China." *Burlington Magazine*, June 1991, 368–375.

———. "Books and Things: Ming Literary Culture and Material Culture." In *Chinese Studies: Papers Presented at a Colloquium at the School of Oriental and African Studies, University of London, 24–26 August, 1987*, edited by Frances Wood, 136–142. London: British Library, 1988.

———. *Pictures and Visuality in Early Modern China*. London: Reaktion Books, 2009.

———. *Superfluous Things: Material Culture and Social Status in Early Modern China.* Urbana: University of Illinois Press, 1991.

Cohen, Walter. "Eurasian Literature." In *Comparative Early Modernities 1100–1800*, edited by David Porter, 47–72. New York: Palgrave, 2012.

Coleman, Dorothy. "The Prologues of Rabelais." *Modern Language Review* 62 (1967): 407–419.

Collingwood, R. G. *The Idea of History.* Oxford: Clarendon Press, 1956.

Compagnon, Antoine. *Nous, Michel de Montaigne.* Paris: Éditions du Seuil, 1980.

Congshu jicheng xubian 叢書集成續編. 180 vols. Shanghai: Shanghai shudian, 1994.

Csikszentmihalyi, Mark. *Material Virtue: Ethics and the Body in Early China.* Leiden: Brill, 2004.

Curtius, Ernst. *European Literature and the Latin Middle Ages*, translated by Willard R. Trask. Princeton, NJ: Princeton University Press, 1973.

Dai Lianbin. "Books, Reading, and Knowledge in Ming China." PhD diss., University of Oxford, 2012.

———. "China's Bibliographic Tradition and the History of the Book." *Book History* 17 (2014): 1–50.

Da Ming huidian 大明會典, edited by Li Dongyang 李東陽 et al. 5 vols. Taipei: Zhongwen shuju, 1963.

Davis, Natalie Zemon. "Printing and the People." In *Society and Culture in Early Modern France: Eight Essays*, edited by Natalie Zemon Davis, 189–226. Stanford: Stanford University Press, 1975.

———. *The Return of Martin Guerre.* Cambridge, MA: Harvard University Press, 1983.

de Bary, William T. "Individualism and Humanitarianism." In *Self and Society in Ming Thought*, edited by William T. de Bary, 145–248. New York: Columbia University Press, 1970.

———. *Learning for One's Self: Essays on the Individual in Neo-Confucian Thought.* New York: Columbia University Press, 1991.

de Certeau, Michel. *The Practice of Everyday Life*, translated by Steven Rendall. Berkeley: University of California Press, 1984.

de Gournay, Marie. *Oeuvres completes.* 2 vols. Édition critique par Jean-Claude Arnould et al. Paris: Honoré Champion, 2002.

Delègue, Yves. *Montaigne et la mauvaise foi: L'écriture de la verité.* Paris: Honoré Champion, 1998.

d'Elia, Pasquale M, ed. *Fonti Ricciane: Documenti originali concernenti Matteo Ricci e la storia delle prime relazione tra l'Europa e la Cina, 1579–1615.* 3 vols. Rome: Libreria dello Stato, 1942–1949.

DellaNeva, Joann, ed. *Ciceronian Controversies*, translated by Brian Duvick. Cambridge, MA: Harvard University Press, 2007.

Dennis, Joseph. *Writing, Publishing, and Reading Local Gazetteers in Imperial China, 1100–1700*. Cambridge, MA: Harvard University Asia Center, 2015.

Derrida, Jacques. "White Mythology: Metaphor in the Text of Philosophy." In *Margins of Philosophy*, translated by Alan Bass, 202–272. Chicago: University of Chicago Press, 1982.

Desan, Philippe. *Les Commerces de Montaigne: Discourse économique des Essais*. Paris: Nizet, 1992.

———. *L'Imaginaire économique de la renaissance*. Paris: Schena, 2002.

———. *Montaigne dans tous ses états*. Fasano, Italy: Schena, 2001.

———. *Montaigne in Print: The Presentation of a Renaissance Text*. Chicago: University of Chicago Press, 1995.

de Santa María, Juan. *Policie Unveiled: Wherein may be learned the order of true policie in kingdoms, and commonwealths: the matters of justice, and government, the addresses, maxims, and reasons of state: the science of governing well a people, and where the subject may learne true obedience unto their kings, princes, and soveriegnes. Written in Spanish and translated into English by I. M. of Magdalen Hall in Oxford*. London: Printed by Thomas Harper for Richard Collins, 1632.

———. *República y policía christiana*. Barcelona: por Geronymo Margarit y asu costa, 1617.

De Smet, Rudolf, ed. *Les Humanistes et leur bibliothèque: Actes du Colloque international. Bruxelles, 26–28 Août 1999*. Leuven: University of Brussels, 2002.

Ding Naifei 丁乃非. *Obscene Things: Sexual Politics in Jin Ping Mei*. Durham, NC: Duke University Press, 2002.

Dong Gu 董穀. *Bili zacun* 碧裡雜存. Beijing: Zhonghua shuju, 1985.

Doty, Richard G. "Money: How Do I Know It's OK?" In *Money: Lure, Lore and Literature*, edited by John Louis DiGaetani, 41–48. Westport, CT: Greenwood Press, 1994.

Du Bellay, Joachim. *La Défense et illustration de la langue française*. Paris: Nelson, 1936.

Eco, Umberto. *The Search for the Perfect Language*, translated by James Fentress. Oxford: Blackwell, 1995.

Egan, Ronald. "On the Circulation of Books During the Eleventh and Twelfth Centuries." *Chinese Literature: Essays, Articles, Reviews* 30 (Dec. 2008): 9–17.

Eisenstein, Elizabeth. *The Printing Press as an Agent of Change: The Printing Revolution in Early Modern Europe. A History of Reading in the*

West. *The Cultural Uses of Print in Early Modern Europe.* 2nd edition. Cambridge, UK: Cambridge University Press, 2005.

Elman, Benjamin. *A Cultural History of Civil Examinations in Late Imperial China.* Berkeley: University of California Press, 2000.

Eoyang, Eugene Chen. "Polar Paradigms in Poetics: Chinese and Western Literary Premises." In *The Transparent Eye: Reflections on Translation, Chinese Literature, and Comparative Poetics,* 238–269. Honolulu: University of Hawaii Press, 1993.

Epstein, Maram. *Competing Discourses: Orthodoxy, Authenticity, and Engendered Meaning in Late Imperial Chinese Fiction.* Cambridge, MA: Harvard University Asia Center, 2001.

———. "Li Zhi's Self-Fashioning as a Filial Son." In *The Objectionable Li Zhi: Fiction, Syncretism, and Dissent in Late Ming China,* edited by Pauline C. Lee, Rivi Handler-Spitz, and Haun Saussy. Manuscript in progress.

Erasmus, Desiderius. *The Adages of Erasmus.* Selected by William Barker. Toronto: University of Toronto Press, 2001.

———. *The Ciceronian: A Dialogue in the Ideal Latin Style,* translated by Betty I. Knott. In *The Collected Works of Erasmus: Literary and Educational Writings,* edited by A. H. T. Levi. Vol. 28 Toronto: University of Toronto Press, 1986.

Fang Yizhi 方以智. *Dongxijun* 東西均. Beijing: Zhonghua shuju, 1962.

Febvre, Lucien Paul Victor. *L'Apparition du livre.* Paris: Éditions A. Michel, 1958.

Feng Menglong 馮夢龍. *Stories to Awaken the World,* translated by Shuhui Yang and Yunqin Yang. Seattle: University of Washington Press, 2009.

———. *Stories to Caution the World,* translated by Shuhui Yang and Yunqin Yang. Seattle: University of Washington Press, 2009.

———. *Yushi mingyan. Jingshi tongyan. Xingshi hengyan zuben* 喻世明言, 警世通言, 醒世恒言足本. Changsha: Yuelu shushe, 1992.

Fiero, David. "When the Coin Is Madness: The Ambiguous Numismatic Metaphor in *Don Quijote.*" *SELECTA* 18 (1997): 95–100.

Fischer, Sandra K. *Econolingua: A Glossary of Coins and Economic Language in Renaissance Drama.* Newark: University of Delaware Press, 1985.

Fish, Stanley. "Literature in the Reader: Affective Stylistics." In *Reader-Response Criticism: From Formalism to Post-Structuralism,* edited by Jane P. Tompkins, 70–100. Baltimore: Johns Hopkins University Press, 1980.

Fisher, Douglas. "The Price Revolution: A Monetary Interpretation." *Journal of Economic History* 49.4 (1989): 883–902.

Fletcher, Joseph. "Integrative History: Parallels and Interconnections in the

Early Modern Period, 1500–1800." *Journal of Turkish Studies* 9 (1985): 37–57.

Flynn, Dennis O., and Arturo Giráldez. "Born with a 'Silver Spoon': The Origin of World Trade in 1571." *Journal of World History* 6.2 (1995): 201–219.

Fong, Wen. "The Problem of Forgeries in Chinese Painting, Part One." *Artibus Asiae* 25.2–3 (1962): 95–140.

Forke, Alfred, trans. *Lun-Hêng, Part I: Philosophical Essays of Wang Ch'ung [Wang Chong]*. Leipzig: Otto Harrassowitz, 1907.

———. *Lun-Hêng, Part II: Miscellaneous Essays of Wang Ch'ung [Wang Chong]*. Supplementary volume to Mittilungen des seminars fur orientalische sprachen, Jahrgang XIV. 2nd edition. New York: Paragon, 1962.

Forman, Valerie. "Material Dispossession and Counterfeit Investments: The Economics of *Twelfth Night*." In *Money and the Age of Shakespeare: Essays in New Economic Criticism*, edited by Linda Woodbridge, 113–128. New York: Palgrave, 2003.

Foucault, Michel. *Les Mots et les choses: Une archéologie des sciences humaines*. Paris: Éditions Gallimard, 1966.

———. *The Order of Things: An Archaeology of the Human Sciences*. No translator listed. New York: Vintage Books, 1994.

Foulk, T. Griffith. "The Form and Function of Koan Literature: A Historical Overview." In *The Kōan: Texts and Contexts in Zen Buddhism*, edited by Steven Heine and Dale S. Wright, 15–45. Oxford: Oxford University Press, 2000.

Frame, Donald. "Review of Barbara Bowen's *The Age of Bluff: Paradox and Ambiguity in Rabelais and Montaigne*." *Renaissance Quarterly* 25.3 (1972): 342–343.

Frank, André Gunder. *ReOrient: Global Economy in the Asian Age*. Berkeley: University of California Press, 1998.

Fuchs, Ronald W., II, and David S. Howard. *Made in China: Export Porcelain from the Leo and Doris Hodroff Collection at Winterthur*. Lebanon, NH: University Press of New England, 2005.

Garber, Marjorie. *Vested Interests: Cross-Dressing and Cultural Anxiety*. New York: Routledge, 1992.

Gardner, Daniel K. *Learning to Be a Sage: Selections from the Conversations of Master Chu, Arranged Topically*. Berkeley: University of California Press, 1990.

———. "Transmitting the Way: Chu Hsi and His Program of Learning" *Harvard Journal of Asiatic Studies* 49.1 (1989): 141–172.

Ge Liangyan. "Authorial Intention: Jin Shengtan as Creative Critic." *Chinese Literature: Essays, Articles, Reviews* 25 (Dec. 2005): 1–24.

Geiss, J. P. "Peking under the Ming, 1368–1644." PhD diss., Princeton University, 1979.

Geng Dingxiang 耿定向. *Geng Tiantai xiansheng wenji* 耿天臺先生文集, edited by Shen Yunlong 沈雲龍. 4 vols. Yonghe: Wenhai chubanshe, 1970.

Gerritsen, Anne, and Stephen McDowall. "Global China: Material Culture and Connections in World History." *Journal of World History* 23.1 (2012): 3–8.

Glassman, Debra, and Angela Redish. "Currency Depreciation in Early Modern England and France." *Explorations in Economic History* 25: 75–97.

Glidden, Hope. "Recouping the Text: The Theory and Practice of Reading." In *Montaigne: A Collection of Essays. A Five-Volume Anthology of Scholarly Articles*, edited by Dikka Berven. Vol. 5: *Reading Montaigne*, 145–156. New York: Garland, 1995.

Godley, Michael. "The End of the Queue: Hair as Symbol in Chinese History." *East Asian History* 8 (Dec. 1994): 53–72.

Goldstone, Jack. "Divergence in Cultural Trajectories: The Power of the Traditional within the Early Modern." In *Comparative Early Modernities 1100–1800*, edited by David Porter, 165–192. New York: Palgrave, 2012.

Gong Duqing 龔篤清. *Mingdai baguwen shitan* 明代八股文史探. Changsha: Huhan renmin chubanshe, 2006.

Goux, Jean-Joseph. *Freud, Marx, économie et symbolique*. Paris: Éditions du Seuil, 1973.

Grafton, Anthony. *Forgers and Critics: Creativity and Duplicity in Western Scholarship*. Princeton, NJ: Princeton University Press, 1990.

———. "The Humanist as Reader." In *A History of Reading in the West*, edited by Guglielmo Cavallo and Roger Chartier and translated by Lydia G. Cochrane, 179–212. Amherst: University of Massachusetts Press, 1999.

———. "John Dee Reads Books of Magic." In *The Reader Revealed*, compiled and edited by Sabrina Alcorn Baron with Elizabeth Walsh and Susan Scola, 31–38. Washington, DC: Folger Shakespeare Library and University of Washington Press, 2001.

Gray, Floyd. "Ambiguity and Point of View in the Prologue to *Gargantua*." *Romanic Review* 56 (1965):12–21.

Gray, Richard T. "Buying into Signs: Money and Semiosis in Eighteenth Century German Language Theory." In *The New Economic Criticism: Studies at the Intersection of Literature and Economics*, edited by Martha Woodmansee and Mark Osteen, 95–113. New York: Routledge, 1999.

Greenbaum, Jamie. *Chen Jiru (1558–1639): The Background to, Development and Subsequent Uses of Literary Personae*. Leiden: Brill, 2007.

Grendler, Paul F. "Printing and Censorship." In *The Cambridge History of*

Renaissance Philosophy, edited by C.B. Schmitt, Quentin Skinner, Eckhard Kessler, and Jill Kraye, 25–53. Cambridge, UK: Cambridge University Press, 1984.

Groebner, Valentin. "Describing the Person, Reading the Signs in Late Medieval and Renaissance Europe: Identity Paper, Vested Figures, and the Limits of Identification, 1400–1600." In *Documenting Individual Identity: The Development of State Practices in the Modern World*, edited by Jane Caplan and John Torpey, 15–27. Princeton, NJ: Princeton University Press, 2001.

Gu Xiancheng 顧憲成. *Gu Duanwen gong yishu* 顧端文公遺書. [Qing Kangxi imprint]. In *Xuxiu siku quanshu* 續修四庫全書. Accessed on April 28, 2016. *Diaolong Full Text Database of Chinese and Japanese Ancient Books.*

Gu Yanwu 顧炎武. *Gu Yanwu shiwen xuanyi* 顧炎武詩文選譯, edited and translated by Li Yongyou 李永祐 and Guo Chengtao 郭成韜. Chengdu: Bashu shushe, 1991.

———. *Rizhilu jishi* 日知錄集釋, edited by Huang Rucheng 黃汝成. 3 vols. Shanghai: Shanghai guji chubanshe, 2006.

———. *Tianxia junguo libing shu* 天下郡國利病書. 6 vols. Kunshan Gu Yanwu yanjiu huibian 昆山顧炎武研究彙編. Shanghai: Shanghai kexue jishu wenxian chubanshe, 2002.

Guo Lixuan 郭立暄. "Lun Liu Yingxi kanben 'Li Zhuowu xiansheng piping *Xixiangji*'" 論劉應襲刊本'李卓吾先生批評西廂記. *Tushuguan zazhi* 圖書館雜誌 25.5 (2005): 74–78.

Guo Shaoyu 郭紹虞. *Zhongguo lidai wenlun xuan* 中國歷代文論選. 3 vols. Jiulong: Zhonghua shuju, 1979.

Hamilton, Earle J. "American Treasure and Andalusian Prices, 1503–1660." *Journal of Economic and Business History* 1 (Nov. 1928): 1–35.

Han Feizi xinyi 韓非子新譯, edited by Lai Yanyuan 賴炎元 and Fu Wuguang 傅武光. Taipei: Sanmin shuju, 2003.

Hanan, Patrick. *The Chinese Vernacular Story*. Cambridge, MA: Harvard University Press, 1981.

Handler-Spitz, Rivi. "Provocative Texts: Li Zhi, Montaigne, and the Promotion of Critical Judgment in Early Modern Readers." *Chinese Literature: Essays, Articles, Reviews* 35 (Dec. 2013): 123–153.

Handler-Spitz, Rivi, Pauline C. Lee, and Haun Saussy, eds. and trans. *A Book to Burn and a Book to Keep (Hidden): Selected Writings*. New York: Columbia University Press, 2016.

Hawkes, David (1923–2009), trans. *Ch'u Tz'u: The Songs of the South, An Ancient Chinese Anthology*. Boston: Beacon Press, 1959.

Hawkes, David (b. 1964). "Exchange Value and Empiricism in the Poetry of

George Herbert." In *Money and the Age of Shakespeare: Essays in Economic Criticism*, edited by Linda Woodbridge, 79–96. New York: Palgrave, 2003.

He Jiaoyuan 何喬遠. *Min shu* 閩書. [Ming Chongzhen imprint]. Vol. 207 of *Siku quanshu cun mu congshu* 四庫全書存目叢書. Jinan: Qi Lu shushe chubanshe, 1996.

He Xinyin 何心隱. *He Xinyin ji* 何心隐集, edited by Rong Zhaozu 容肇祖. Beijing: Zhonghua shuju, 1960.

He Yuming. *Home and the World: Editing the "Glorious Ming" in Woodblock-Printed Books of the Sixteenth and Seventeenth Centuries*. Cambridge, MA: Harvard University Press, 2013.

Head, Richard. *The English Rogue Continued in the Life of Meriton Latroon, and Other Extravagants Comprehending the Most Eminent Cheats of Most Trades Professions. The Second Part*. London: Printed for Francis Kirkman, 1668.

Hegel, Robert. "Performing Li Zhi." In *The Objectionable Li Zhi: Fiction, Syncretism, and Dissent in Late Ming China*, edited by Pauline C. Lee, Rivi Handler-Spitz, and Haun Saussy. Forthcoming. Manuscript in progress.

Heinzelman, Kurt. *The Economics of the Imagination*. Amherst: University of Massachusetts Press, 1980.

Ho Ping-ti. *The Ladder of Success in Imperial China: Aspects of Social Mobility, 1368–1911*. New York: Columbia University Press, 1962.

Ho, Wai-kam. "Late Ming Literati: Their Social and Cultural Ambiance." In *The Chinese Scholar's Studio: Artistic Life in the Late Ming Period. An exhibition from the Shanghai Museum*, edited by Chu-tsing Li and James C. Y. Watt, 23–36. New York: Asia Society, 1987.

Hoey, Allen. "The Name on the Coin: Metaphor, Metonymy, and Money." *Diacritics* 18.2 (1988): 26–37.

Hoffmann, George. *Montaigne's Career*. Oxford: Clarendon Press, 1998.

Hollander, Anne. *Seeing through Clothes*. New York: Viking Press, 1978.

Hsiao Li-ling. *The Eternal Present of the Past: Illustration, Theatre and Reading in the Wanli Period, 1573–1619*. Leiden: Brill, 2007.

Hu Yinglin 胡應麟. *Shaoshi shanfang bicong* 少室山房筆叢. Shanghai: Shanghai shudian chubanshe, 2009.

Huang, Ellen C. "From the Imperial Court to the International Art Market: Jingdezhen Porcelain Production as Global Visual Culture." *Journal of World History* 23.1 (2012): 115–145.

Huang Lin 黃霖. "*Fenshu* yuanben de jige wenti" 焚書原本的幾個問題. *Wenxue yichan* 文學遺產 5 (2002): 89–95.

Huang, Martin W. "Author(ity) and Reader in Traditional Chinese Xiaoshuo

Commentary." *Chinese Literature: Essays, Articles, Reviews* 16 (Dec. 1994): 41–67.

———. *Desire and Fictional Narrative in Late Imperial China*. Cambridge, MA: Harvard University Asia Center, 2001.

———. "The Perils of Friendship: Li Zhi's Predicament." In *The Objectionable Li Zhi: Fiction, Syncretism, and Dissent in Late Ming China*, edited by Pauline C. Lee, Rivi Handler-Spitz, and Haun Saussy. Manuscript in progress.

———. *Snakes' Legs: Sequels, Continuations, Rewritings and Chinese Fiction*. Honolulu: University of Hawai'i Press, 2004.

Huang, Philip C. C. "Development or Involution in Eighteenth-Century Britain and China?" *Journal of Asian Studies* 61 (May 2002): 501–538.

Huang, Ray. *1587: A Year of No Significance. The Ming Dynasty in Decline*. New Haven, CT: Yale University Press, 1981.

———. *Taxation and Governmental Finance in Sixteenth-Century Ming China*. London: Cambridge University Press, 1974.

Huang Tsung-hsi 黃宗羲. *The Records of Ming Scholars*, edited and translated by Julia Ching. Honolulu: University of Hawai'i Press, 1987.

Huang Zongxi 黃宗羲. *Mingru xue'an* 明儒學案. 2 vols. Taipei: Mingwen shuju, 1991.

———. *Ming wen hai* 明文海. Beijing: Zhonghua shuju, 1987.

Hughes, Diane Owen. "Sumptuary Law and Social Relations in Renaissance Italy." In *Disputes and Settlements: Law and Human Relations in the West*, edited by John Bossy, 69–99. Cambridge, UK: Cambridge University Press, 1983.

Hung Mingshui. *The Romantic Vision of Yuan Hung-tao, Late Ming Poet and Critic*. Taipei: Bookman Books, 1997.

Hunt, Alan. *Governance of the Consuming Passions: A History of Sumptuary Law*. New York: St. Martin's Press, 1996.

Huppert, George. "Divinatio et Eruditio: Thoughts on Foucault." *History and Theory* 13.3 (1974): 191–207.

Irwin, Richard. *The Evolution of a Chinese Novel: Shui-hu-chuan*. Harvard-Yenching Institute Studies 10. Cambridge, MA: Harvard University Press, 1953.

Iser, Wolfgang. "The Reading Process: A Phenomenological Approach." In *Reader-Response Criticism: From Formalism to Post-Structuralism*, edited by Jane P. Tompkins, 50–69. Baltimore: Johns Hopkins University Press, 1980.

Jardine, Lisa. *Worldly Goods: A New History of the Renaissance*. London: Macmillan, 1996.

Jardine, Lisa, and Anthony Grafton. "'Studied for Action': How Gabriel Harvey Read His Livy." *Past and Present* 129 (1990): 30–78.

Jauss, Hans Robert. *Toward an Aesthetic of Reception*, translated by Timothy Bahti. Minneapolis: University of Minnesota Press, 1982.

Jia Yi 賈誼. *Xin shu* 新書, annotated by Fang Xiangdong 方向東. Beijing: Zhonghua shuju, 2012.

Jiang Yihua 蔣以化. *Xitai manji* 西臺漫記. Shanghai: Shanghai guji chubanshe, 1995–99.

Jiang Yingke 江盈科. *Jiang Yingke ji* 江盈科集, edited by Huang Rensheng 黃人生. Changsha: Yuelu shushe, 1997.

———. *Xuetao xiaoshu* 雪濤小書. Shanghai: Zhongyang shudian, 1948.

Jiang Yonglin, trans. *The Great Ming Code*. Seattle: University of Washington Press, 2005.

Jiao Hong 焦竑. *Danyuanji* 澹園集. 2 vols. Beijing: Zhonghua shuju, 1999.

———. *Jiao shi bisheng* 焦氏筆乘. 1606. In Vol. 107 of *Siku quanshu cun mu congshu* 四庫全書存目叢書. Jinan: Qi Lu shushe chubanshe, 1995.

Jifu tongzhi 畿輔通志, 300 juan. Guangxu 10 [1885] printed edition. Harvard Yenching call number 3128.2552.87.

Jin Jiang. "Heresy and Persecution in Late Ming Society—Reinterpreting the Case of Li Zhi." *Late Imperial China* 22.2 (2001): 1–34.

Jin Shengtan 金聖嘆. *Jin Shengtan quanji* 金聖嘆全集. 4 vols. Nanjing: Jiangsu guji chubanshe, 1985.

Johns, Adrian. *The Nature of the Book: Print and Knowledge in the Making*. Chicago: University of Chicago Press, 1998.

Jones, Anna Rosalind, and Peter Stallybrass. *Renaissance Clothing and the Materials of Memory*. Cambridge, UK: Cambridge University Press, 2000.

Jonson, Ben. *The Works of Ben Jonson*, edited by C. H. Herford Percy and Evelyn Simpson. 11 vols. Oxford: Clarendon Press, 1925–52.

Kafalas, Philip A. "Weighty Matters, Weightless Form: Politics and the Late Ming *Xiaopin* Writer." *Ming Studies* 39: 50–85.

Keffer, Ken. "La Textomachie: La protection des *Essais* de Montaigne." In *Marie de Gournay et l'édition de 1595 des Essais de Montaigne*, 135–143. Actes du colloque organisé par la Société Internationale des Amis de Montaigne les 9 et 10 juin 1995 en Sorbonne. Paris: Honoré Champion, 1996.

Kleutghen, Kristina. *Imperial Illusions: Crossing Pictorial Boundaries in Qing Palaces*. Seattle: University of Washington Press, 2015.

Knoblock, John. *Xunzi: A Translation and Study of the Complete Works*. 3 vols. Stanford: Stanford University Press, 1994.

Ko, Dorothy, "Bondage in Time: Footbinding and Fashion Theory." In *Modern Chinese Literary and Cultural Studies in the Age of Theory*, edited by Rey Chow, 199–226. Durham, NC: Duke University Press, 2000.

Kwa, Shiamin. *Strange Eventful Histories: Identity, Performance, and Xu Wei's Four Cries of a Gibbon*. Cambridge, MA: Harvard University Press, 2012.

Kwa, Shiamin, and Wilt L. Idema, eds. and trans. *Mulan: Five Versions of a Classic Chinese Legend with Related Texts*. Indianapolis: Hackett, 2010.

Lach, Donald. *Asia in the Making of Europe*. 3 vols. Chicago: University of Chicago Press, 1965.

La Croix du Maine, François Grudé de. *Les Bibliothèques Françoises de la Croix du Maine et de Du Verdier, Sieur de Vauprivas. Nouvelle Édition dédiée au roi*, edited by M. Rigoley De Juvigny, conseilleur honoraire au parlement de Metz. 6 vols. Paris: Saillant & Nyon, 1772.

Laing, Ellen Johnston. "*Suzhou Pian* and Other Dubious Paintings in the Received *Oeuvre* of Qiu Ying." *Artibus Asiae* 59: 3–4 (2000): 265–295.

Lang Ying 郎瑛. *Qixiu leigao* 七修類稿. Shanghai: Zhonghua shuju, 1961.

Lanling Xiaoxiaosheng 蘭陵笑笑生. *Jin Ping Mei cihua* 金瓶梅詞話, edited by Tao Muning 陶慕寧. 2 vols. Beijing: Renmin wenxue chubanshe, 2000.

Lau, D. C., trans. *The Analects*. London: Penguin, 1979.

Lee, Pauline C. *Li Zhi, Confucianism, and the Virtue of Desire*. Albany: State University of New York Press, 2012.

Legge, James, trans. *The Lî Kî*. Vols. 27 and 28 of *The Sacred Books of the East: The Texts of Confucianism*, edited by F. Max Müller. Oxford: Clarendon Pres, 1885.

Lejeune, Philippe. *Le pacte autobiographique*. Paris: Éditions du Seuil, 1975.

Levasseur, Émile. *Histoire du commerce de la France, première partie: Avant 1789*. Paris: Arthur Rousseau Éditeur, 1911.

Li Defeng 李德鋒. "Li Zhi *Cang shu* yu Tang Shunzhi *Zuo bian* zhi guanxi kaoshu" 李贄'藏書'與唐順之'左編'之關係考述. *Shixueshi yanjiu* 史學史研究 141 (2011): 42–50.

Li Le 李樂. *Jianwen zaji* 見聞雜記. 2 vols. Taipei: Weiwen tushu banshe, 1977.

Li Wai-yee. "The Collector, the Connoisseur, and Late-Ming Sensibility." *T'oung Pao* 81.4–5 (1995): 269–302.

———. "The Problem of Genuineness in Li Zhi." In *The Objectionable Li Zhi: Fiction, Syncretism, and Dissent in Late Ming China*, edited by Pauline C. Lee, Rivi Handler-Spitz, and Haun Saussy. Manuscript in progress.

———. "The Rhetoric of Spontaneity in Late-Ming Literature." *Ming Studies* 35 (Aug. 1995): 32–52.

Li Yu. *Li Yu xiqu ji* 李玉戲曲集, edited and annotated by Cheng Guyu 陳古

虞, Chen Duo 陳多, and Ma Shenggui 馬聖貴. Shanghai: Shanghai guji chubanshe, 2004.

Li Zhi 李贄. *Cangshu* 藏書 in *LZQJZ*, vols. 4–8.

———. *Chutanji* 初潭集 in *LZQJZ*, vols. 12–13.

———. *Fenshu* 焚書, edited by Guan Yulin 管玉林. Beijing: Zhonghua shuju, 1961.

———. *Li Wenling ji* 李溫陵集. [Ming imprint]. In vol. 126 of *Siku quanshu cun mu congshu* 四庫全書存目叢書. Jinan: Qi Lu shushe chubanshe, 1997.

———. *Li Zhi wenji* 李贄文集, edited by Zhang Jianye 張建業. 7 vols. Beijing: Shehui kexue wenxian chubanshe, 2000.

———. *Xu Fenshu*. 續焚書. Vol. 3 of *LZQJZ*.

Lieberman, Victor. *Strange Parallels: Southeast Asia in Global Context c. 800–1830*. 2 vols. Cambridge, UK: Cambridge University Press, 2003.

Liezi 列子. Shanghai: Shanghai guji chubanshe, 1995.

Liji jin zhu jin yi 禮記今註今譯, annotated by Wang Meng'ou 王夢鷗. 2 vols. Tianjin guji chubanshe, 1987.

Lin Haiquan 林海權. *Li Zhi nianpu kaolüe* 李贄年譜考略. Fuzhou: Fujian renmin chubanshe, 1992.

Lin Liyue 林麗月. "Mingdai jinsheling chutan" 明代禁奢令初探. *Guoli Taiwan shifan daxue lishi xuebao* 國立台灣師範大學歷史學報 22 (June 1994): 57–84.

Lin Qixian 林其賢. *Li Zhuowu de Foxue yu shixue* 李卓吾的佛學與世學. Taipei: Wenjin chubanshe, 1992.

Lin Yaling 林雅玲. "Ye Zhou xiaoshuo pingdian xilun: Yi 'Li Zhuowu xiansheng piping *Zhongyi Shuihuzhuan*,' 'Li Zhuowu xiansheng piping *Sanguozhi*,' 'Li Zhuowu xiansheng piping *Xiyouji*' wei yanjiu zhongxin" 葉晝小說評點析論：以《李卓吾先生批評忠義水滸傳》、《李卓吾先生批評三國志》、《李卓吾先生批評西遊記》為研究中心. In *Chuanbo, jiaoliu yu ronghe—Mingdai wenxue, sixiang yu zongjiao guoji xueshu yantaohui lunwenji*. 傳播交流與融合—明代文學思想與宗教國際學術研討會論文集, 101-122. Nanhua daxue wenxuexi. Taipei: Xinwenfeng, 2005.

Liszka, James. *A General Introduction to the Semeiotic of Charles Sanders Peirce*. Bloomington: University of Indiana Press, 1996.

Liu, James J. Y. *Chinese Theories of Literature*. Chicago: University of Chicago Press, 1975.

Liu Tong 劉侗 and Yu Yizheng 于奕正. *Dijing jingwulue* 帝京景物略, edited by Luan Baoqun 欒保群. Beijing: Beijing guji chubanshe, 1980.

Liu Xiaoyi. "Clothing, Food, and Travel: Ming Material Culture as Reflected in *Xingshi yinyuan zhuan*." PhD diss., University of Arizona, 2010.

Liu Xie 劉勰. *Wenxin diaolong* 文心雕龍. Shanghai: Shanghai guji chubanshe, 1984.

Lowry, Kathryn A. *The Tapestry of Popular Songs in 16th- and 17th-Century China: Reading: Imitation, and Desire*. Leiden: Brill, 2005.

Lu Jiye 盧冀野, ed. *Ming zaju xuan* 明雜劇選. Shanghai: Shangwu yinshuguan, 1940.

Lu Mingjun. "Natural Inspiration of Poetic Creation: The Non-Mimetic Tradition in Plato and Zhong Rong's Poetics." Paper presented at the American Comparative Literature Association conference, Harvard University, March 19, 2016.

Lu, Tina. *Persons, Roles, and Minds: Identity in Peony Pavilion and Peach Blossom Fan*. Stanford: Stanford University Press, 2001.

Lunyu 論語. In *Xinyi sishu duben* 新譯四書讀本, edited by Xie Bingying 謝冰瑩. Taipei: Sanmin chubanshe, 2002.

Luo Xiaoxiang. "From Imperial City to Cosmopolitan Metropolis: Culture, Politics, and State in Late Ming Nanjing." PhD diss., Duke University, 2006.

Lurie, Alison. *The Language of Clothes*. New York: Random House, 1981.

Ma Jinglun 馬經綸. *Li Wenling waiji* 李溫陵外紀, edited by Pan Zenghong 潘曾紘. Taipei: Weiwen tushu chubanshe, 1977.

Ma Ning. *The Age of Silver: The Rise of the Novel East and West 1500–1800*. Oxford: Oxford University Press, 2016.

Ma Tiji 馬蹄疾, ed. *Shuihu ziliao huibian* 水滸資料彙編. Beijing: Zhonghua shuju, 1980.

Mair, Victor, ed. *The Columbia History of Chinese Literature*. New York: Columbia University Press, 2001.

Makeham, John. *Name and Actuality in Early Chinese Thought*. Albany: State University of New York Press, 1994.

Mao Heng 毛亨. *Maoshi zhengyi* (shang) 毛詩正義(上), annotated by Zheng Xuan 鄭玄 and edited by Kong Yingda 孔穎達. In *Shisanjing zhu shu* (3) 十三經注疏 (3). Beijing: Beijing daxue chubanshe, 1999.

Martin, Henri-Jean. *The French Book: Religion, Absolutism, and Readership, 1585–1715*. Translated by Paul Saenger and Nadine Saenger. Baltimore: Johns Hopkins University Press, 1996.

———. *Livre, pouvoirs et société à Paris au 17 siècle (1598–1701)*. Geneva: Librairie Droz, 1969.

Marx, Karl. *Capital: A Critique of Political Economy*, translated by Ben Fowkes. London: Penguin, 1976.

McDermott, Joseph Peter. *A Social History of the Chinese Book: Books in Late Imperial China*. Hong Kong: Hong Kong University Press, 2006.

———. *State and Court Ritual in China.* Cambridge, UK: Cambridge University Press, 1999.

McKeon, Richard, ed. *Introduction to Aristotle.* New York: Modern Library, 1947.

McLaren, "Constructing New Reading Publics in Late Ming China." In *Printing and Book Culture in Late Imperial China*, edited by Cynthia J. Brokaw and Kai-wing Chow, 152–183. Berkeley: University of California Press, 2005.

Mendoza, Juan González de. *The History of the Great and Mighty Kingdom of China and the Situation Thereof*, edited by Sir George T. Staunton. 2 vols. London: Hakluyt Society, 1853.

Meskill, John. *Ch'oe Pu's Diary: A Record of Drifting across the Sea.* Tucson: University of Arizona Press, 1965.

Miao Yonghe 繆詠禾. *Mingdai chubanshi* 明代出版史. Nanjing: Jiangsu renmin chubanshe, 2000.

Ming shilu 明實錄. 162 vols. Nangang: Zhongyang yanjiuyuan lishi yuyan yanjiusuo, 1966.

Mizoguchi Yūzō 溝口雄三. *Ri Takugo: Seidō o ayumu itan* 李卓吾: 正道を步む異端. Tokyo: Shūeisha, 1985.

Montaigne, Michel de. *The Complete Essays of Montaigne*, translated by Donald Frame. Stanford: Stanford University Press, 1958.

———. *Journal de Voyage*, edited by Fausta Garavini. Paris: Éditions Gallimard, 1983.

———. *Les Essays*, edited by Pierre Villey. Paris: Presses Universitaires de France, 1924.

Moraru, Christian. "The Worlding of Nations: Comparatism and the Ethics of Reading in the Wake of the Global Turn." *Yearbook of Comparative and General Literature* 52 (2005–2006): 187–198.

Moyer, Johanna B. "Sumptuary Laws in Ancien Régime France 1229–1806." PhD diss., Syracuse University, 1996.

Muecke, D. C. *Irony and the Ironic.* London: Methuen, 1982.

Munro, John H. "Money and Coinage in the Age of Erasmus: An Historical and Analytical Glossary with Particular Reference to France, the Low Countries, England, the Rhineland, and Italy." In *The Collected Works of Erasmus*, vol. 1: *Letters 1 to 141 1484–1500*, translated by R. A. B. Mynors and D. F. S. Thomson, 311–347. Toronto: University of Toronto Press, 1974.

Nakam, Géralde. *Les Essais de Montaigne, miroir et procès de leur temps: Témoignage historique et création litéraire.* Paris: Librairie A.-G. Nizet, 1984.

Needham, Joseph. *Science and Civilisation in China*. Vol. 1: *Introductory Orientations*. Cambridge, UK: Cambridge University Press, 1954.

Ng, On-cho. "The Epochal Concept of Early Modernity and the Intellectual History of Late Imperial China." *Journal of World History* 14.1 (2003): 37–61.

Niu Jianqiang 牛建強. *Mingdai houqi shehui bianqian yanjiu* 明代後期社會變遷研究. Taipei: Wenjin chubanshe, 1997.

North, Michael, ed. *Artistic and Cultural Exchanges between Europe and Asia 1400–1900*. Burlington, VT: Ashgate, 2010.

Nugent, Teresa Lanpher. "Usury and Counterfeiting in Wilson's *The Three Ladies of London* and *Three Lords and Three Ladies of London*, and in Shakespeare's *Measure for Measure*." In *Money and the Age of Shakespeare: Essays in New Economic Criticism*, edited by Linda Woodbridge, 201–218. New York: Palgrave, 2003.

Obeyesekere, Gananath. *Medusa's Hair: An Essay on Personal Symbols and Religious Experience*. Chicago: University of Chicago Press, 1981.

Odell, Dawn. "Porcelain, Print Culture and Mercantile Aesthetics." In *The Cultural Aesthetics of Eighteenth-Century Porcelain*, edited by Alden Cavanagh and Michael Elia Yonan, 141–158. Burlington, VT: Ashgate, 2010.

Olin, John, C., ed. and trans. *Christian Humanism and the Reformation: Desiderius Erasmus, Selected Writings*. New York: Harper and Row, 1965.

Olivelle, Patrick. "Hair." In *The Encyclopedia of Buddhism*, edited by Robert E. Buswell, 313. Farmington Hills, MI: Thomson/Gale, 2004.

Owen, Stephen. *Readings in Chinese Literary Thought*. Cambridge, MA: Harvard University Press, 1992.

Pallier, Denis. *Recherches sur l'imprimerie à Paris pendant la Ligue (1585–1594)*. Geneva: Librairie Droz, 1976.

Palumbo-Liu, David. "The Utopias of Discourse: On the Impossibility of Chinese Comparative Literature." In *China in a Polycentric World: Essays in Chinese Comparative Literature*, edited by Zhang Yingjin, 36–49. Stanford: Stanford University Press, 1998.

Park, J. P. *Art by the Book: Painting Manuals and the Leisure Life in Late Ming China*. Seattle: University of Washington Press, 2012.

Peirce, Charles Sanders. "Prolegomena to an Apology for Pragmaticism." In *Peirce on Signs: Writings on Semiotic by Charles Sanders Peirce*, edited by James Hoopes, 249. Chapel Hill: University of North Carolina Press, 1991.

Peng Shaosheng 彭紹升. *Jushi zhuan* 居士傳, edited by Zhi Guizi 知歸子. 2 vols. Taipei: Liuli jingfang, 1995–1999.

Peng Xinwei 彭信威. *Zhongguo huobishi* 中國貨幣史. Shanghai: Shanghai renmin chubanshe, 1958.

Peraita, Carmen. "Marginalizing Quevedo: Reading Notes and the Humanistic Persona." In *Reading Notes*, edited by Dirk Van Hulle and Wim Van Mierlo, 37–60. Amsterdam: Rodopi, 2004.

Peterson, Willard J. *The Bitter Gourd: Fang I-chih and the Impetus for Intellectual Change*. New Haven, CT: Yale University Press, 1979.

———. "What to Wear? Observation and Participation by Jesuit Missionaries in Late Ming Society." In *Implicit Understandings: Observing, Reporting, and Reflecting on the Encounters between Europeans and Other Peoples in the Early Modern Era*, edited by Stuart B. Schwartz, 403–421. Cambridge, UK: Cambridge University Press, 1994.

Plaks, Andrew H. "The Aesthetics of Irony in Late Ming Literature and Painting." In *Words and Images: Chinese Poetry, Calligraphy, and Painting*, edited by Alfreda Murck and Wen C. Fong, 487–500. Princeton NJ: Princeton University Press, 1991.

———. *Four Masterworks of the Ming Novel*. Princeton, NJ: Princeton University Press, 1987.

———. "Full-Length *Hsiao-shuo* and the Western Novel: A Generic Reappraisal." *New Asia Academic Bulletin* 1 (1978): 163–176.

———. "The Prose of Our Time." In *The Power of Culture: Studies in Chinese Cultural History*, edited by Willard J. Peterson, 206–217. Hong Kong: Chinese University Press, 1994.

Plato. *Cratylus*, translated by C. D. C. Reeve. Indianapolis: Hackett, 1998.

Pomel, Fabienne. "La Fonction critique de l'ironie dans *l'Apologie de Raimond Sebond*." *Bulletin de la Société des Amis de Montaigne* 35–36 (Jan.–June 1994): 79–89.

Pomeranz, Kenneth. *The Great Divergence: China, Europe, and the Making of the Modern World Economy*. Princeton, NJ: Princeton University Press, 2000.

Poon, Mingsun. "Books and Printing in Sung China (960–1279)." PhD diss., University of Chicago, 1979.

Porter, David. *Comparative Early Modernities, 1100–1800*. New York: Palgrave, 2012.

———. "Global Satire." Paper presented at the American Comparative Literature Association, Providence, RI, March 30, 2012.

———. *Ideographia: The Chinese Cipher in Early Modern Europe*. Stanford: Stanford University Press, 2001.

———. "Sinicizing Early Modernity: The Imperatives of Historical Cosmopolitanism." *Eighteenth-Century Studies* 43.3 (2010): 299–306.

Potter, Clifton W., Jr. "Images of Majesty: Money as Propaganda in

Elizabethan England." In *Money: Lure, Lore, and Literature*, edited by John Louis DiGaetani, 69–76. Westport, CT: Greenwood Press, 1994.

Qian Jibo 錢基博. *Mingdai wenxue* 明代文學. Hong Kong: Shangwu yinshuguan, 1965.

Qian Maowei 錢茂偉. *Mingdai shixue de licheng* 明代史學的歷程. Beijing: Shehui kexue wenxian chubanshe, 2003.

Qian Qianyi 錢謙益. *Muzhai youxueji* 牧齋有學集, edited by Qian Zhonglian 錢仲聯. 3 vols. Shanghai: Shanghai guji chubanshe, 1996.

Qian Xiyan 錢希言. *Xi xia* 戲瑕. [Ming imprint]. In vol. 97 of *Siku quanshu cun mu congshu* 四庫全書存目叢書. Jinan: Jinan shushe chuban faxing, 1995.

Quanzhoufu zhi 泉州府志, edited by Huang Ren 黃任 and Guo Gengwu 郭賡武. 4 vols. Tainan: Zhangquanfu zhi bianji weiyuanhui, 1964.

Queen, Sarah A., and John S. Major, trans. *Luxuriant Gems of the Spring and Autumn*. Authorship attributed to Dong Zhongshu. New York: Columbia University Press, 2016.

Rabelais, François. *Gargantua and Pantagruel*, translated by Burton Raffel. New York: Norton, 1990.

———. *Oeuvres complètes*. Édition établie, annotée et preface par Guy Demerson. Paris: Éditions du Seuil, 1973.

Rawski, Evelyn S. "Economic and Social Foundations of Late Imperial China." In *Popular Culture in Late Imperial China*, edited by David Johnson, Andrew J. Nathan, and Evelyn Rawski, 3–33. Berkeley: University of California Press, 1985.

Rendall, Steven. "*Mus in Pice*: Montaigne and Interpretation." In *Montaigne: A Collection of Essays. A Five-Volume Anthology of Scholarly Articles*, edited by Dikka Berven. Vol. 5: *Reading Montaigne*, 62–78. New York: Garland, 1995.

Ricci, Matteo. *China in the Sixteenth Century: The Journals of Matteo Ricci: 1583–1610*, translated by Louis J. Gallagher. New York: Random House, 1953.

———. *On Friendship: One Hundred Maxims for a Chinese Prince*, translated by Timothy Billings. New York: Columbia University Press, 2009.

Rickett, W. Allyn, trans. *Guanzi: Political, Economic, and Philosophical Essays from Early China. A Study and Translation*. Princeton, NJ: Princeton University Press, 1985.

Rigolot, François. "The Renaissance Fascination with Error: Mannerism and Early Modern Poetry." *Renaissance Quarterly* 57.4 (2004): 1219–1234.

———. "Review of Barbara Bowen's *The Age of Bluff: Paradox and Ambiguity in Rabelais and Montaigne*." *Bibliothèque d'Humanisme et Renaissance* 32.2 (1972): 363–365.

Robinson, Ken. "The Book of Nature." In *Into Another Mould: Change and Continuity in English Culture, 1625–1700*, edited by T. G. S. Cain and Ken Robinson, 86–106. London: Routledge, 1992.

Rolston, David L., ed. *How to Read the Chinese Novel*. Princeton, NJ: Princeton University Press, 1990.

———. *Traditional Chinese Fiction and Fiction Commentary: Reading and Writing between the Lines*. Stanford: Stanford University Press, 1997.

Rosenthal, Margaret F., and Ann Rosalind Jones. *The Clothing of the Renaissance World: Europe, Asia, Africa, and the Americas. Cesare Vecellio's Habiti Antichi et Moderni*. London: Thames and Hudson, 2008.

Rowe, William T. *Crimson Rain: Seven Centuries of Violence in a Chinese Community*. Stanford: Stanford University Press, 2007.

Roy, David T., trans. *The Plum in the Golden Vase, or Chin P'ing Mei*. 5 vols. Princeton, NJ: Princeton University Press, 1993.

Ruan Yuan 阮元, ed. *Shisanjing zhu shu* 十三經注疏. 1816. Taipei: Dahua, 1987.

Rusk, Bruce. "Artifacts of Authentication: People Making Texts Making Things in Late Imperial China." In *Antiquarianism and Intellectual Life in Europe and China, 1500–1800*, edited by François Louis and Peter Miller, 180–204. Ann Arbor: University of Michigan Press, 2012.

———"Old Scripts, New Actors: European Encounters with Chinese Writing, 1550–1700." *EASTM* 26 (2007): 68–116.

———. "The Rogue Classicist: Feng Fang (1493–1566) and His Forgeries." PhD diss., University of California, Los Angeles, 2004.

———. "Silver, Liquid and Solid: The Matter of Money in the Ming-Qing Marketplace." Paper presented at the conference Coin of the Realm: Money and Meaning in Late Imperial China, Harvard University, April 18, 2014.

Sargent, Thomas J., and François R. Velde. *The Big Problem of Small Change*. Princeton, NJ: Princeton University Press, 2002.

Scholes, Robert. *Protocols of Reading*. New Haven, CT: Yale University Press, 1989.

Shakespeare, William. *As You Like It*, edited by S. C. Burchell. Yale Shakespeare. New Haven, CT: Yale University Press, 1917.

———. *The Life of King Henry the Eighth*, edited by John M. Burdan and Tucker Brooke. Yale Shakespeare. New Haven, CT: Yale University Press, 1925.

———. *The Merchant of Venice*, edited by Wilbur L. Cross and Tucker Brooke. Yale Shakespeare. New Haven, CT: Yale University Press, 1917.

———. *The Tragedy of Romeo and Juliet*, edited by Richard Hosley. Yale Shakespeare. New Haven, CT: Yale University Press, 1917.

Shang Wei. "*Jin Ping Mei* and Late Ming Print Culture." In *Writing and Materiality in China: Essays in Honor of Patrick Hanan*, edited by Judith T. Zeitlin and Lydia H. Liu, with Ellen Widmer, 187–238. Cambridge, MA: Harvard University Press, 2003.

———. "The Making of the Everyday World: *Jin Ping Mei cihua* and Encyclopedias for Daily Use." In *Dynastic Crisis and Cultural Innovation: From the Late Ming to the Late Qing and Beyond*, edited by David Der-wei Wang and Shang Wei, 63–92. Cambridge, MA: Harvard University Asia Center, 2005.

Sharpe, Kevin. "Uncommonplaces? Sir William Drake's Reading Notes." In *The Reader Revealed*, compiled and edited by Sabrina Alcorn Baron with Elizabeth Walsh and Susan Scola, 59–65. Washington, DC: Folger Shakespeare Library and University of Washington Press, 2001.

Shell, Marc. *The Economy of Literature*. Baltimore: Johns Hopkins University Press, 1978.

Shen Defu 沈德符. *Wanli yehuo bian* 萬曆野獲編. 3 vols. Beijing: Zhonghua shuju, 1959.

Shen Zijin 沈自晉. *Shen Zijin ji* 沈自晉集, edited by Zhang Shuying 張樹英. Beijing: Zhonghua shuju, 2004.

Shih, Vincent Yu-Chung, trans. *The Literary Mind and the Carving of Dragons: A Study of Thought and Pattern in Chinese Literature*. New York: Columbia University Press, 1959.

Sima Qian 司馬遷. *Shiji* 史記. 10 vols. Beijing: Zhonghua shuju, 1962.

Simpson, Evelyn M. *A Study of the Prose Works of John Donne*. Oxford: Oxford University Press, 1924.

Son, Suyoung. "Between Writing and Publishing Letters: Publishing a Letter about Book Proprietorship." In *A History of Chinese Letters and Epistolary Culture*, edited by Antje Richter, 878–899. Leiden: Brill, 2015.

———. "Writing for Print: Zhang Chao and Literati-Publishing in Seventeenth-Century China." PhD diss., University of Chicago, 2010.

Song Kefu 宋克夫 and Han Xiao 韓曉. *Xinxue yu wenxue lungao* 心學與文學論稿. Beijing: Zhongguo shehui kexue chubanshe, 2002.

Steinberg, Leo. "Velazquez' *Las Meninas*." *October* 19 (Winter 1981): 45–54.

Sternlicht, Sanford. "Shakespeare and Renaissance Coinage." *Renaissance Papers* 1972: 59–63.

Stubbes, Philip. *The Anatomie of Abuses*, edited by Margaret Jane Kidnie. Tempe: Arizona State University Press, 2002.

Su Lanfeng 蘇蘭風. "Chanxue yu Li Zhi zhexue" 禪學與李贄哲學. In *Li Zhi yanjiu* 李贄研究, edited by Xu Zaiquan 許在全 et al., 91–98. Beijing: Guangmin bao chubanshe, 1989.

Suzuki Torao 鈴木虎雄. "Ri Takugo nenpu, jō" 李卓吾年譜上. *Shinagaku* 支那學 7.2 (1934): 1–59.

Struve, Lynn. *The Qing Formation in World-Historical Time*. Cambridge, MA: Harvard University Asia Center, 2004.

Tang Xianzu 湯顯祖. *Mudan ting* 牡丹亭. Shanghai: Shangwu yinshuguan, 1934.

———. *The Peony Pavilion*, translated by Cyril Birch. Boston: Cheng and Tsui, 1980.

———. *Tang Xianzu ji* 湯顯祖集. 4 vols. Shanghai: Shanghai renmin chubanshe, 1973.

Tollemer, Alexandre. *Analyse par l'abbé Tollemer du Journal Manuscrit d'un Sire de Gouberville, Gentilhomme compagnard: Précédée d'une introduction par Emmanuelle Le Roy Ladurie*. Bricqueboscq, France: Éditions des champs, 1993.

The Torah: A Modern Commentary, edited by Gunther W. Plaut. New York: Union of American Hebrew Congregations, 1974.

Tory, Geofroy. *Champ Fleury*, translated by George B. Ives. New York: Grolier Club, 1927.

Vernus, Michel. *Histoire d'une pratique ordinaire: La lecture en France*. Saint-Cyr-sur-Loire, France: Alan Sutton, 2002.

Vilar, Pierre. "The Age of Don Quixote," translated by Richard Morris. In *Essays in European Economic History 1500–1800*, edited by Peter Earle, 100–112. Oxford: Clarendon Press, 1974.

Vinograd, Richard. *Boundaries of the Self: Chinese Portraits 1600–1900*. Cambridge, UK: Cambridge University Press, 1992.

———. "Cultural Spaces and the Problem of a Visual Modernity in the Cities of Late Ming Chiang-nan." In *Economic History, Urban Culture and Material Culture: Papers from the Third International Conference on Sinology, History Section*, 327–360. Taipei: Institute of History and Philology, Academia Sinica, 2002.

———. "Hiding in Plane Sight: Accommodating Incompatibilities in Early Modern Visual Culture." In *Comparative Early Modernities, 1100–1800*, edited by David Porter, 125–164. New York: Palgrave, 2012.

Vollmer, John E. *Silks for Thrones and Altars: Chinese Costumes and Textiles from the Liao through the Qing Dynasty*. Paris: Myrna Myers, 2003.

Volpp, Sophie. "The Gift of a Python Robe: The Circulation of Objects in *Jin Ping Mei*." *Harvard Journal of Asiatic Studies* 65.1 (2005), 133–158.

———. *The Worldly Stage: Theatricality in Seventeenth-Century China*. Cambridge, MA: Harvard University Press, 2011.

Von Glahn, Richard. *Fountain of Fortune: Money and Monetary Policy in China, 1000–1700*. Berkeley: University of California Press, 1996.

Wagner, Rudolf G. "Twice Removed from the Truth: Fragment Collection in 18th and 19th Century China." In *Collecting Fragments/Fragmente sammeln*, edited by Glenn W. Most, 34–52. Göttingen: Vandenhoeck und Ruprecht, 1997.

Waldenfels, Bernhard. "Response to the Other." In *Encountering the Other(s): Studies in Literature, History, and Culture*, edited by Gisela Brinker-Gabler, 35–44. Albany: State University of New York Press, 1995.

Wang Bu 王逋. *Yin'an suoyu* 蚓庵瑣語. Tainan: Zhuangyan, 1995.

Wang Chong 王充. *Lunheng jiaojian* 論衡校箋, edited by Yang Baozhong 楊寶忠. 2 vols. Shijiazhuang: Hebei jiaoyu chubanshe, 1999.

Wang Fansen 王汎森. "Mingdai houqi de weizao yu sixiang zhenglun" 明代後期的偽造與思想爭論. In *Wanming Qingchu sixiang* 晚明清初思想, 29–50. Shanghai: Fudan daxue chubanshe, 2004.

Wang Fuzhi 王夫之. *Chuanshan yishu quanji* 船山遺書全集. 22 vols. Taipei: Zhongguo chuanshan xuhui, 1972.

Wang Hongzhuan 王宏撰. *Shan zhi* 山誌. Shanghai: Shanghai guji chubanshe, 1995–1999.

Wang Ji 王畿. *Longxi Wang xiansheng quanji* 龍溪王先生全集. [Ming Wanli 15 imprint]. In vol. 98 of *Siku quanshu cun mu congshu* 四庫全書存目叢書. Jinan: Qi Lu shushe chubanshe, 1997.

Wang Shizhen 王世貞. *Yiyuan zhiyan jiaozhu* 藝苑卮言校注, edited by Lu Jiedong 陸潔棟 and Zhou Mingchu 周明初. Nanjing: Fenghuang chubanshe, 2009.

Wang Yu 王煜. "Li Zhuowu zarou Ru, Dao, Fa, Fuo si jia sixiang" 李卓吾雜揉儒、道、法、佛四家思想. In *Ming Qing sixiangjia lunji* 明清思想家論集, 1–60. Taipei: Lianjing chuban shiye gongsi, 1981.

Wenzel, Regina. *Changing Notions of Money and Language in German Literature from 1509–1956*. Lewiston, NY: Edwin Mellen Press, 2003.

White, Peter. "Bookshops in the Literary Culture of Rome." In *Ancient Literacies: The Culture of Reading in Greece and Rome*, edited by William A. Johnson and Holt N. Parker, 268–287. Oxford: Oxford University Press, 2009.

Wilhelm, Richard, trans. *The I Ching or Book of Changes*, rendered into English by Cary F. Baynes. New York: Pantheon Books, 1962.

Wilson, Bronwen. *The World in Venice: Print, the City, and Early Modern History*. Toronto: University of Toronto Press, 2005.

Wittgenstein, Ludwig. *Philosophical Investigations*, translated by G. E. M. Anscombe. New York: Macmillan, 1958.

Wong, R. Bin. *China Transformed: Historical Change and the Limits of European Experience*. Ithaca, NY: Cornell University Press, 1997.

Wong, R. Bin, and Jean-Laurent Rosenthal. *Before and beyond Divergence:*

The Politics of Economic Change in China and Europe. Cambridge, MA: Harvard University Press, 2011.

Woodbridge, Linda, ed. *Money and the Age of Shakespeare: Essays in Economic Criticism.* New York: Palgrave, 2003.

Woodmansee, Martha, and Mark Osteen, eds. *The New Economic Criticism: Studies at the Intersection of Literature and Economics.* London: Routledge, 1999.

Wright, Dale S. "The Significance of Paradoxical Language in Hua-yen Buddhism." *Philosophy East and West* 32. 3 (1982): 325–338.

Wu Cheng'en 吳承恩. *Xiyouji* 西遊記. Beijing: Zhonghua shuju, 1991.

Wu Cuncun 吳存存. *Ming Qing shehui xing'ai fengqi* 明清社會性愛風氣. Renmin wenxue chubanshe, 2000.

Wu Congxian 吳從先. *Xiao chuang zi ji* 小窗自紀. [Ming Wanli imprint]. In vol. 252 of *Siku quanshu cun mu congshu* 四庫全書存目叢書. Jinan: Jinan shushe chuban faxing, 1995.

Wu Guoping 鄔國平. "Ye tan *Fenshu* yuanben de wenti" 也談焚書原本的問題. *Qinghua daxue xuebao, zhexue shehui kexue ban* 清華大學學報, 哲學社會科學版 2. 19 (2004): 45–50.

Wu Han 吳晗. *Jiang Zhe cangshujia shilue* 江浙藏書家史略. Beijing: Zhonghua shuju, 1981.

Wu Hung 巫鴻. *The Double Screen: Medium and Representation in Chinese Painting.* Chicago: University of Chicago Press, 1996.

Wu Jiang. *Enlightenment in Dispute: The Reinvention of Chan Buddhism in Seventeenth-Century China.* Oxford: Oxford University Press, 2008.

Wu, K. T. "Ming Printing and Printers." *Harvard Journal of Asiatic Studies* 7.3 (1943): 203–260.

Wu Renshu 巫仁恕. "Mingdai pingmin fushi de liuxing fengshang yu shidafu de fanying" 明代平民服飾的流行風尚與士大夫的反應. *Xin shixue* 新史學 10.3 (1999): 55–109.

———. *Pinwei shehua: Wanming de xiaofei shehui yu shidafu* 品味奢華: 晚明的消費社會與士大夫. Taipei: Academia Sinica: Lianjing chubanshe, 2007.

Wu Rujun 吳汝鈞, ed. *Fojiao da cidian* 佛教大辭典. Beijing: Shangwu shuju, 1995.

Wu Yinghui. "Books in Pairs: Commentary, Illustration, and Creative Publishing of Drama in Seventeenth-Century China." Manuscript in progress.

Wu Yu 吳虞. *Wu Yu wenlu* 吳虞文錄. Shanghai: Yadong tushuguan, 1921.

Wu Yuancui 伍袁萃. *Lin ju manlu* 林居漫錄. [Ming Wanli imprint]. In *Xuxiu siku quanshu* 續修四庫全書. Diaolong Full Text Database of Chinese and Japanese Ancient Books. Accessed on April 28, 2016.

Bibliography

Xiamen daxue lishi xi 廈門大學歷史系. *Li Zhi yanjiu cankao ziliao* 李贄研究參考資料. 2 vols. Xiamen: Fujian renmin chubanshe, 1975.

Xiang Yannan 向燕南. *Zhongguo shixue sixiang tongshi: Mingdai juan* 中國史學思想通史. 明代卷. Hefei: Huangshan shushe, 2002.

Xiao jing yi zhu 孝經譯注, edited by Wang Shoukuan 汪受寬. Shanghai: Shanghai guji chubanshe, 2004.

Xiao Qing 蕭清. *Gudai huobi sixiang shi* 古代貨幣思想史. Beijing: Xinhua yinshua, 1987.

Xie Guozhen 謝國楨, ed. *Mingdai shehui jingji shiliao xuanbian* 明代社會經濟史料選編. 3 vols. Fuzhou: Fujian renmin chubanshe, 2004.

Xie Zhaozhe 謝肇淛. *Wuzazu* 五雜組. 2 vols. Beijing: Zhonghua shuju, 1959.

Xingshi yinyuan zhuan 醒世姻緣傳, edited by Zhu Dizhuo 朱迪卓. 3 vols. Beijing: Renmin zhongguo chubanshe, 1993.

Xiong Lihui 熊禮匯. *Ming Qing sanwen liupai lun* 明清散文流派論. Wuhan: Wuhan daxue chubanshe, 2003.

Xu Jianping 許建平. "'Kuangguai' he 'yu shi wu zheng'—Lun Li Zhi de shuangchong wenhua renge" 狂怪和與世無爭—論李贄的雙重文化人格. *Wenxue pinglun* 文學評論 6 (2005): 23–34.

———. *Li Zhi sixiang yanbian shi* 李贄思想演變史. Beijing: Renmin chubanshe, 2005.

Xu Wei 徐渭. *Xu Wei ji* 徐渭集. 4 vols. Beijing: Zhonghua shuju, 1983.

Xunzi 荀子. *Hsün Tzu: Basic Writings*, translated by Burton Watson. New York: Columbia University Press, 1963.

———. *Xunzi jicheng* 荀子集成, edited by Yan Lingfeng 嚴靈峯. Taipei: Chengwen chubanshe, 1977.

Yang Chenbin 楊臣彬. "Tan Mingdai shuhua zuowei" 談明代書畫作偽. *Wenwu* 文物 8 (1990): 72–87.

Yang Xin 楊新. "Shangpin jingji, shifeng yu shuhua zuowei" 商品經濟、世風與書畫作偽. In *Zhongguo lidai shuhua jianbie wenji* 中國歷代書畫鑒別文集, edited by Yang Xin 楊新, 1–9. Beijing: Zijincheng chubanshe, 1998.

Yang Yucheng 楊玉成. "Qimeng yu baoli" 啟蒙與暴力. In *Taiwan xueshu xin shiye* 臺灣學術新視野 *Zhongguo wenxue zhi bu (er)* 中國文學之部(二), edited by Lin Mingde 林明德 and Huang Wenji 黃文吉, 901–986. Taipei: Wunan tushu chuban gufen youxian gongsi, 2007.

Ye Sheng 葉盛. *Shuidong riji* 水東日記. Taipei: Taiwan shangwu yinshuguan, 1983.

Ye Yang. *Vignettes from the Late Ming: A Hsiao-p'in Anthology*. Seattle: University of Washington Press, 1999.

Yong Rong 永瑢, ed. *Siku quanshu zong mu* 四庫全書總目. 2 vols. Beijing: Zhonghua shuju, 1965.

Yu, Anthony C. "Cratylus and Xunzi on Names." In *Early China/Ancient Greece: Thinking through Comparisons*, edited by S. Shankman and S. W. Durrant, 235–250. Albany: State University of New York Press, 2002.

Yu Li. "A History of Reading in Late Imperial China, 1000–1800." PhD diss., Ohio State University, 2003.

Yu, Pauline. "Alienation Effects: Comparative Literature and the Chinese Tradition." In *The Comparative Perspective on Literature: Approaches to Theory and Practice*, edited by Clayton Koelb and Susan Noakes, 162–175. Ithaca, NY: Cornell University Press, 1988.

Yuan Hongdao 袁宏道. *Yuan Hongdao ji jianjiao* 袁宏道集箋校, edited by Qian Bocheng 錢伯城. 2 vols. Shanghai: Shanghai guji chubanshe, 1981.

Yuan Zhongdao 袁中道. *Kexuezhai ji* 珂雪齋集, edited by Qian Bocheng 錢伯城. 3 vols. Shanghai: Shanghai guji chubanshe, 2007.

Yuan Zongdao 袁宗道. *Bai Suzhai leiji* 白蘇齋類集. Shanghai: Shanghai guji chubanshe, 2007.

Yuan Zujie. "Dressing for Power: Rite, Costume, and State Authority in Ming Dynasty China." *Frontiers of History in China* 2.2 (2007): 181–212.

———. "Dressing the State, Dressing the Society: Ritual, Morality, and Conspicuous Consumption in Ming Dynasty China." PhD diss., University of Minnesota, 2002.

Zeitlin, Judith T. "Between Performance, Manuscript, and Print: Imagining the Musical Text in Seventeenth Century Plays and Songbooks." In *Text Performance and Gender in Chinese Literature and Music: Essays in Honor of Wilt Idema*, edited by Maghiel van Crevel, Tian Yuan Tan, and Michael Hockx, 263–292. Leiden: Brill, 2009.

Zhang Dafu 張大復. *Meihua caotang ji* 梅花草堂集. [Ming Chongzhen edition, with emendations from the Qing Shunzhi reign]. In vol. 104 of *Siku quanshu cunmu congshu* 四庫全書存目叢書. Jinan: Qi Lu shushe chubanshe, 1997.

Zhang Dai 張岱. *Zhang Dai shiwen ji* 張岱詩文集, edited by Xia Xianchun 夏咸淳. Shanghai: Shanghai guji chubanshe, 1991.

Zhang Han 張瀚. *Songchuang mengyu* 松窗夢語. In Ming Qing biji congshu 明清筆記叢書. Shanghai: Shanghai guji chubanshe, 1986.

Zhang Longxi. "The Challenge of East-West Comparative Literature." In *China in a Polycentric World: Essays in Chinese Comparative Literature*, edited by Zhang Yingjin, 21–35. Stanford: Stanford University Press, 1998.

———. *Mighty Opposites: From Dichotomies to Difference in the Comparative Study of China*. Stanford: Stanford University Press, 1998.

———. *Unexpected Affinities: Reading across Cultures*. Toronto: University of Toronto Press, 2007.

Zhang Shaokang 張少康, ed. *Zhongguo wenxue lilun pipingshi* 中國文學理論批評史. 2 vols. Beijing: Beijing daxue chubanshe, 2005.

Zhang Shiyi 張師繹. *Yuelutang ji* 月鹿堂集. In *Siku weishoushu jikan* 四庫未收書輯刊. Sixth series, vol. 30. Beijing: Beijing chubanshe, 1997.

Zhang Yanyuan 張彥遠. *Lidai minghua ji* 歷代名畫記, edited by Qin Zhongwen 秦仲文 and Huang Miaozi 黃苗子. Beijing: Renmin meishu chubanshe, 1963.

Zhang Ying. "Li Zhi's Image Trouble." In *The Objectionable Li Zhi: Fiction, Syncretism, and Dissent in Late Ming China*, edited by Pauline C. Lee, Rivi Handler-Spitz, and Haun Saussy. Manuscript in progress.

Zhouyi dazhuan jinzhu 周易大傳今注, edited by Gao Heng 高亨. Jinan: Jilu shushe, 1979.

Zhu Weizhi 朱維之. *Li Zhuowu lun* 李卓吾論. Fuzhou: Fujian xiehe daxue chubanshe, 1935.

Zhuangzi 莊子. *The Complete Works of Chuang Tzu*, translated by Burton Watson. New York, Columbia University Press, 1968.

——. *Zhuangzi duben* 莊子讀本. Taipei: Sanmin shuju, 1974.

Zito, Angela. "Skin and Silk: Significant Boundaries." In *Body, Subject, and Power in China*, edited by Angela Zito and Tani E. Barlow, 103–130. Chicago: University of Chicago Press, 1994.

Zuo Dongling 左東嶺. *Li Zhi yu wanming wenxue sixiang* 李贄與晚明文學思想. Tianjin: Tianjin renmin chubanshe, 1997.

Zuozhuan 左傳, edited by Li Mengsheng 李夢生. 2 vols. Shanghai: Shanghai guji chubanshe, 1998.

Zwicker, Steven N. "The Reader Revealed." In *The Reader Revealed*, compiled and edited by Sabrina Alcorn Baron with Elizabeth Walsh and Susan Scola, 11–18. Washington, DC: Folger Shakespeare Library and University of Washington Press, 2001.

——. "'What Every Literate Man Once Knew': Tracing Readers in Early Modern England." In *Owners, Annotators, and the Signs of Reading*, edited by Robin Myers, Michael Harris, and Giles Mandelbrote, 75–90. London: Oak Knoll Press and the British Library, 2005.

INDEX

"Adorned with Every Mark of Dignity" (Wu suo bu pei) (Li), 73–74
ambiguity/indeterminacy, 44–45, 68, 165n22; in communication, 18–19, 35, 40, 48, 130; social consequences of, 37–38
Analects, 140, 142; 6.24, 162n78; 8.13, 181n61; 9.4, 192n55; 12.11, 35; 13.23, 166n33; 13.3, 161n75; 14.38, 155n42
Another Book to Burn (*Xu Fenshu*), 15, 32, 144; posthumous prefaces, 109, 115–116, 122–126, 128
Another Book to Keep (Hidden) (*Xu Cangshu*), 16, 144
appearance vs. reality, 5–6, 74, 87, 108, 129, 152
"Appraisal of Liu Xie" (Zan Liu Xie) (Li), 75–78, 156n1, 171n29
Aristotle, 49–50
Art of War (Sunzi), 131
authenticity, 19, 22; as basis of economic value, 89; in *Don Quixote*, 58–59; emotional basis of, in literature, 28–32, 64; and falsity, as intellectual concern, 5–7, 68; produced by paradox, 48, 60. *See also* books
"Author's Preface" (Zi xu) (Li), 167n60, 167n64, 168n66–67

Bacon, Francis, 16, 20; *Advancement of Learning*, 42; *Essays*, 112
bagu wen. *See* examination essays
Bembo, Pietro, 23
Bentley, Tamara Heimarck, 57, 166n46
Bible, 20; Genesis and origins of language in, 39
Bibliander, Theodor, 42
"Biography of Li Wenling" (Li Wenling zhuan) (Yuan), 84

bluff, 21, 44, 50–51, 126; defined, 48–49, 165n22. *See under* Li Zhi
Bo Yi and Shu Qi, 52–54
Bodin, Jean, 16, 112
Book to Burn, A (*Fenshu*), 81, 83, 113, 144, *151*; as assemblage of genres, 14–15; commentary on, 150–151; date of publication, 156n52; preface to, 63–64
Book of Changes/Classic of Changes (*Yijing*), 33, 117, 131, 169n9: "Appended Sayings" (Xi ci zhuan), 133
Book to Keep (Hidden), A (*Cangshu*), 15–16, 60, 64, 141, 144; "Biographies of Confucian Historians: Sima Tan and Sima Qian," 159n38; "Famous Ministers who Enriched the Country," 95; "Famous Ministers who Enriched the Country," preface to, 179n37; preface (Li), 61–63, 65, 132, 136; preface (Liu), 61; preface (Mei), 61–62; preface (Zhu), 195n83
Book of Rites (*Liji*), 71, 75, 81
books: authenticity of, as concern, 118–119; burning, 4, 193n66; early modern book culture, 6, 107, 110; forgery/piracy of, 108, 115–117, 121; multiplicity of editions, 113; unauthorized editions, 113–114. *See under* censorship; connoisseurship; printing
Bowen, Barbara, 44, 48–49
Bo Yi and Shu Qi, 52–54
Brook, Timothy, 9, 185n54
Browne, Sir Thomas, 39
Buddhism, 146; eyes, different types of, 167n59; head shaving and, 79–80; Pure Land, 82. *See also* Chan
Burton, Robert, 112

233

Calcagnini, Celio, 28
calligraphy, 117
Cang Jie, 33
Cangshu. See Another Book to Burn
Cangshu shiji liezhuan zongmu qianlun. *See* "Preface to the Combined 'Dynastic Records' and 'Biographies' of *A Book to Keep (Hidden)*"
censorship: in China, 112–113; in Europe, 112
Cervantes, Miguel de, 89; *Don Quixote*, 58–60, 140
Chan, 51, 82. *See also* paradox
Chen Hongshou, 117; "Venerating Antiquity" playing cards, 56–57
Chen Jiru, 116
childlike mind (*tongxin*), 26, 30
Chinese language: European views of, 42; origins of, 20; origins of written language, 32–33; transparency (purity) of, 19–21, 32–38; vernacular, 24; *wen* and, 74
Chow Kai-wing, 143, 158n19, 159n34, 188n4
Chutanji. See Upon Arrival at the Lake
Ciceronianism, 21. *See also* Erasmus; Pietro Bembo
Classic of Poetry (Shijing), 50, 117, 143; "Great Preface" to, 30, 32
Cloister (Temple) of the Flourishing Buddha, 51, 69, 82, 102, 118, 130
clothing, 171n27; python robes, 170n21; as reflecting personal character, 75; social order and, 70–71; sumptuary laws and, 72–73, 76–77, 170n17; *wen* and, 74
Clunas, Craig, 117, 170n17, 171n30, 185n53
commentary, 25, 128, 130, 150–151, 160n58, 188n4; adversarial commentary, 15, 149. *See under* Li Zhi
Commentary on the Four Books (Si shu ping) (Li), 131, 141, 192n54
Confucianism, Confucius, 33; cultural continuity and, 24–25; hair, consideration of, 79–80; Neo-Confucianism, 136; poetry and/poetics of, 10, 29; five relationships in, 47; Six Classics, 143. *See also Analects*; examination system; rectification of names
connoisseurship: book and painting collecting/collectors, 117–122; in Europe, 118–120
contradiction, 48–49

corruption, 4, 102; of language, 28, 40, 78
Croix du Maine, François Grudé de la: *Bibliothèque françoise*, 119–120
Cruz, Gaspar da, 42
counterfeiting: of coins, 6, 89, 98–99; of coins, punishment for, 180n51; of identity, 75–76, 100–103; of virtue, 89, 103

Dao gu lu. See Record of the Antiquity of the Dao
demonetization, 89, 96
Deng Huoqu, 169n3
Deng Lincai (Shiyang), 31
Deng Yingqi (Dingshi), 81, 85
disease, as metaphor for social ills, 10–11
Disputing A Book to Burn (Fenshu bian), 156n52
dizi (disciple), 33–34
Don Quixote (Cervantes), 58–60; preface to, 140
Donne, John, 51, 89, 165n24, 177n12
doubt, 7, 45, 48, 50, 60, 65, 71, 116, 171n23
Dragon Lake, 4, 69
drama, 24, 56, 92, 131, 140, 143; commentaries on, 31, 128, 139, 149. *See under* Li Zhi
Du Bellay, Joachim: *Défense et illustration de la langue française*, 24
Du shu le. See "On the Joy of Reading"
Dürer, Albrecht, 107; "Satirical subject; study of three laborers," 109

early modernities, 7–10: common formal elements, 9–10; "horizontal continuities" in, 6
economy, of China, 91, 106; world economy, 9
editing, 15–16, 111–113, 119, 122–126
emotion, in literature: 22; as source of authenticity, 28–30
Erasmus, 16, 21, 107, 110, 112, 114; *The Ciceronian*, 23–24, 26–27
Essays (Montaigne), 67, 109, 112, 114, 122, 126; "De l'amitié" (On Friendship), 125; "Apologie de Raimond Sebond" (Apology for Raymond Sebond), 166n36; "Divers evenements de mesme conseil" (Various Outcomes of the Same Plan), 191n44; "De l'experience" (On Experience), 162–163n91; "De la gloire" (Of Glory), 162n90;

Index

"De l'institution des enfans" (Of the Education of Children), 191n45, 192n50; "Au lecteur" (To the Reader), 67, 168n78; "Des Menteurs" (Of Liars), 165n22; prefaces (Gournay), 109, 122, 125–126; "De la vanité" (Of Vanity), 183n23

ethics, 19; literary imitation and, 21–23. *See also* virtue

examination system: bypassing of, 6, 27; examination essays (*bagu wen*), 24–26; Li's books and, 63; study guides, 25

expression: involuntary, 30–32

eyes, 33; "of flesh," 63-64, 167n59; as organs of interpretation, 4, 123-125, 132–135

falsity/falsification. *See* authenticity

Feng Menglong, 116, 183n18

Fenshu. *See* A Book to Burn

forgery, 107–108, 115–117, 119, 121–123, 184n36, 184–185n45–46

Foucault, Michel, 38–39

friend (*pengyou*)/friendship, 34, 96; falsity of, 100; judgment of true/false, 105; soul mate (*zhiyin*), 124

Fugu pai. *See* Return to Antiquity Movement

Gankai pingsheng. *See* "Reflections on my Life"

Geng Dingli, 31, 47, 62

Geng Dingxiang, 46–47, 62, 81, 136, 175n82

Gesner, Konrad, 42; *Bibliotheca Universalis*, 119, 121

Gong'an School (Gong'an pai), 156n2

Gournay, Marie de, 109, 122, 125–126

Grafton, Anthony, 119, 138

Gu Yanwu, 179n39: *Records of Daily Knowledge* (Rizhi lu), 92

Guanzi, 72, 93

Guazzo, Stefano, 76–77

Han Feizi, 29, 49

He Jiaoyuan, 79

He Jingming, 35

He Xinyin, 14, 142, 156n1.

He Yuming, 14, 140

head shaving, 47, 79–90

heretic (*yiduan*), 45–47

Historical Records (Shiji) (Sima), 29, 64

history, writing of, 12–13

Hu Yinglin, 118, 121

Huang, Martin, 128

Huang Zongxi, 159n34

hypocrisy, 3, 5, 20, 55, 100; verbal, 75

identity: and clothing, 76–78; doubled/mistaken, 56; imposture/counterfeit identity, 75–76, 100–103

imitation: of the classics in China, 19–20; of clothing; in literature, 21–28; critique of, in China, 23; critique of, in Europe, 23–24; poetry and, in Europe, 30

indeterminacy. *See* ambiguity

inflation: paper currency and, in China, 90, of money, in Europe, 92; of prices, 94–95

"An Inscription for the Image of Confucius in the Cloister of the Flourishing Buddha" (Ti Kongzi xiang yu Zhifo Yuan") (Yi), 154n10, 190n23

interpretation, concerns regarding, 11–14; of Li's physical appearance 82; of monetary value 93–94. *See also* judgment

irony, 10, 44–45, 50–51, 165n22

Jia Yi: "Discourse on Dress" (Fuyi), 71–72

Jiang Yihua, 130–131, 147

Jiang Yingke, 23, 32

Jiao Hong (Moling, Rihuo, Yiyuan), 22–23, 28, 46, 62, 97, 113, 120, 146; preface to *Another Book to Burn*, 122–125; preface to *A Book to Keep* (Hidden), 148–149, 192n53

Jin ping mei. *See* Plum in the Golden Vase

Jin Shengtan, 31, 35, 128, 139–140, 192n58

Johns, Adrian, 126, 188n92

Jonson, Ben, 78

Journey to the West (Xiyou ji), 55–56

judgment: of book editions as legitimate/forged, 107–108, 123; failure of, 105; of meaning, 97

Lang Ying, 115

language: crisis of meaning, 19, 97; as mirror of society, 78; theorizing of, in Europe, 38–43; vernacular, in Europe, 24; vernacular fiction, in China, 110; word inflation/deflation, 89, 96. *See also* Chinese language; literacy

Left Scribe's Record, The (Lidai shi zuobian) (Tang), 64, 167n63

letters (Li), 3, 8, 15, 45, 65; to Deng Lincai: 31; "Reply to Deng Shiyang [Deng Lincai]" (LZQJZ 1.26), 164n6; "Reply to Deng Shiyang" (LZQJZ 1.8), 160n54; to Geng Dinglih, 62; to Geng Dingxiang: 47, 136; "Reply to Censor Geng," 179n41; "Reply to Justice Minister Geng," 162n81, 173n59; "Sent in Reply to Senior Censor Geng, 190n29; to Jiao Hong: 62, 97, 113; "Another letter to Jiao Moling [Jiao Hong]," 156n57; "Another letter to Jiao Ruohou [Jiao Hong]" (Fu Jiao Ruohou), 158n32; "Another letter to Jiao Ruohou [Jiao Hong]" (You yu Jiao Ruohou), 101–102, 180n59, 181n64; "To Jiao Ruohou [Jiao Hong]," 179n42, 180n56, (Xu fenshu) 189n6, 190n21; "To Jiao Yiyuan [Jiao Hong]," 167n56; "Reply to Jiao Yiyuan [Jiao Hong]," 164n5, 183n30; to Liu Dongxing: "A Letter in Reply to Provincial Officer Liu," 96, 179n40; "A Reply to District Chief Liu," 161n63, 165n26, 175n80; "Reply to a friend's letter," 102, 181n67; "Reply to Zhou Erlu," 173n57, 175–176n82; "A Response to Zhou Liutang," 159n34, 187n80; "To Zeng Jiquan," 46, 85; to Zhou Sijing [Zhou Youshan], 83; "Another Letter to Zhou Youshan," 161n65; "To Zhou Youshan" (Fenshu), 175n72–73, 194n73; "To Zhou Youshan" (Xu Fenshu), 194n76

Liji. See Book of Rites

Li Le, 76

Li Mengyang, 22

"Li sao." See "Encountering Sorrow"

literacy, 110

Literary Mind and the Carving of Dragons (Wenxin diaolong) (Liu), 124

Literature: imitation in, 21–28; popular genres in China, 14, 140, 143; relation with society, 10. See also poetry; prefaces

Li sheng shi jiao wen. See "On Mr. Li's Ten Kinds of Association"

Li Wai-yee, 54–55

Li Zhi: appearance, 79–87; appearance as bluff, 69–70; authenticity, concern with, 28–30, 105; biographical details, 4–5; bluff in work of, 5, 44–45, 52–68, 51, 90, 97; Buddhism and, 80, 82; on clothing, 73–74; commentaries by, 128, 131, 141–142; commentaries by, faked, 116; as Confucian scholar, 4, 8, 10, 34, 53, 69–70, 79, 82, 86, 98; destruction of work, 65; drama, writing on, 3, 8, 116, 131, 143; on economic matters, 95–96; genre variety and, 8; head shaving by, 79–86, 168n1; as/as not heretic, 45–48; historical analysis, 144–145; hypocrisy, critique of, 100–103; imitation, critique of, 19–21, 25–26; letters of, 46; literary style of, 5; misattribution of works to/forgery, 108, 115–116, 121; popular literature, views on, 143–144; poverty of, 88; publication history, 15–16, 156n52; publication process, 15, 113; puncturing/piercing as metaphor, use of, 50; reactions to work of, 145–151; as reader, 127–138; social intercourse, relation to, 104–105; transparency of language as concern of, 32–33, 41, 46–48; virtue as concern of, 6, 27–28; as Zhuowu, 97–98. See also letters (Li); individual works

Liu Dongxing, 61, 96, 130, 137: prefaces to works by Li, 179n40

Liu Jincheng (Chenglao), 166n35

Liu Tong: Survey of Scenery and Mountains in the Capital (Dijing jingwulue) (w/ Yu), 84

Liu Xie (ca. 465–ca. 522), 133; Literary Mind and the Carving of Dragons (Wenxin diaolong), 124

Liu Xie (fl. 1570), 75–78

"Liu Yan, Extraordinary Individual" (Liu Yan, miao ren) (Li), 179n3

Longhu. See Dragon Lake

Ma Jinglun, 114

Macheng, 5, 69, 75, 85, 100

maodun (contradiction), 49–50

Marriage Destinies to Awaken the World (Xingshi yinyuan zhuan), 76

meaning: of texts, 127–128; words' loss of, 7

Mei Guozhen, 61: preface to A Book to Keep (Hidden), 144

Mencius, 53, 100, 133, 135, 138

Mendoza, Juan González de: Historia de las cosas mas notables, ritas y costumbres del gran reyno de la China, 42

Index

Mengzi. See Mencius
Min Qiji: illustrations for *The Romance of the Western Chamber* (Xixiang Ji), 57, 59, 139
Ming state: counterfeiting and, 99; paper currency and, 90; printing by, 113; regulation of coin value, 94. See also sumptuary laws
misprints. See under printing
misreading. See under reading
"Mr. Five Willows" (Wu liu xiansheng zhuan) (Tao), 141–142
money: coins, 91; coins, weight of, 90, 92; copper vs. silver, 91; copper used as, 90–92, 99; counterfeiting of, 6, 89, 98–99; counterfeiting, punishment for, 180n51; different forms of, 88; forms, in Europe, 90–91; Gresham's law, 103; instability of value of, 93–94; paper currency, 90; Spanish coins, 92. See also inflation; demonetization
Montaigne, Michel de, 3, 16, 40, 53, 76, 89, 114, 165n22; *Journal de Voyage*, 172n36; on reading, 139–140. See also *Essays*.

nature: as source of language, 33; as source of literary inspiration, 30

"On the Childlike Mind" (Tongxin shuo) (Li), 26, 135–137, 150, 156n1, 158n25, 190n26, 190n31, 193n59, 195n90
"On Five Types of Death" (Wu si pian), 105
"On Friendship" (Pengyou pian) (Li), 34, 180n54, 180n57
"On the Joy of Reading" (Du shu le) (Li), 175n74, 189n6–7, 11, 16: preface, 130, 132–133
"On Loftiness and Cleanliness" (Gao jie shuo) (Li), 103
"On Miscellaneous Matters" (Za shuo) (Li), 159n37, 159n45, 160n52
"On Mr. Li's Ten Kinds of Association" (Li sheng shi jiao wen) (Li), 178–179n35, 181n72, 181n75
Outlaws of the Marsh (Shuihu zhuan), 29, 116, 131, 143. See also "Preface to The Loyal and Righteous Outlaws of the Marsh"
Outline of History with Critical Comments (Shigang pingyao) (Li), 141, 144, 149
Owen, Stephen, 30

painting: forgery of, 117, 184n36; of Xu Wei, 30–31
paradox, 10, 44–45, 53, 67; Chan paradox, 51, 165n25
perspective (in visual art), 9, 57
Pico della Mirandola, Gianfrancesco, 21, 23
plagiarism, 23, 26
Plum in the Golden Vase, The (Jin ping mei), 50, 140–141, 161n64, 170n21
poetry: as outlet for emotion, 29–30
Porter, David, 8, 42
Postel, Guillaume, 42
"Preface to the Combined 'Dynastic Records' and 'Biographies' Sections of *A Book to Keep (Hidden)*" (Cangshu shiji liezhuan zongmu qianlun) (Li), 167n52, 189n15, 190n27, 190n32, 191n36
"Preface to *The Loyal and Righteous Outlaws of the Marsh*" (Zhongyi Shuihuzhuan xu) (Li), 159n39, 167n62, 172n33, 193n61
prefaces: to *Gargantua and Pantagruel* (Rabelais), 66; by Ming writers, 66. See also *Book to Burn, A*; *Book to Keep (Hidden), A*; *Don Quixote*; *Essays*; *Record of Acting First*; *Upon Arrival at the Lake*
prices, variance in, 85; Price Revolution, 94. See also inflation
printing: errors/misprints, 111–112; reprinting, 112; text alteration/piracy by printers, in China and Europe, 115
publication: as ongoing process, 16–17, 112

Qian Xiyan: *Playing with Flaws* (Xi xia), 121
Qin Shihuang, 66, 193n66
Qu Yuan, 64
Quanzhou (Fujian), 84, 92, 95

Rabelais, François, 77, 89; *Gargantua and Pantagruel*, 66
reading: "centripetal reading," 129; hucksterish (baifan)/generative reading, 14, 140; misreading, 14, 142; oppositional reading (fandu), 131, 144; reader as friend, 124–125; as recovery of authorial intent, 133; subjective/activist reading, 129, 135–141
Record of the Antiquity of the Dao (Dao gu lu) (Li), 114, 179n40

Record of Causes and Effects (Yinguo lu) (Li), 131
"Record of Master Geng Chukong" (Geng Chukong xiansheng zhuan) (Li), 31
Records of Daily Knowledge (Rizhi lu) (Gu), 92, 194n75
rectification of names (*zhengming*), 20, 35–37; and European language theory, 38–43; rectification of language, 41, 43, 44, 90
"Reflections on my Life" (Gankai pingsheng) (Li), 84–85, 175n79–82
representation, 48: "second-order representations," 10
reputation, 27, 96
Return to Antiquity Movement (Fugu pai), 21–23
Ricci, Matteo, 6, 14, 72–73, 182n7; *Mnemonic Techniques of the West* (Xiguo jifa), 35, 161n68; *On Friendship* (Jiaoyou lun), 35
Rizhi lu. *See Records of Daily Knowledge*
Romance of the Western Chamber, The (Xixiang ji), 57, 59, 131, 139
Ronsard, Pierre de, 16, 112
"Rules Agreed Upon in Advance" (Yu yue) (Li), 153n8, 165n27; preface to 161n66
Rusk, Bruce, 34, 39

Sang Hongyang, 95–96, 193n66
School of the Mind (Xinxue pai), 21; Taizhou school (Taizhou pai), 26, 75, 169n3
"Self-Appraisal" (Zi zan) (Li), 52–60
self-contradiction, 10, 44–45, 67
self-presentation: ethics and, 70; social status and, 70–79
Shakespeare, William, 40, 89, 177n12: *As You Like It*, 56; *The Life of King Henry the Eighth*, 172n40; *The Merchant of Venice*, 166n43; *Romeo and Juliet*, 40, 162n89; *Twelfth Night*, 56
shanren (recluse, mountain man), 101–102
Shen Defu: *Unofficial Gleanings of the Wanli Era* (Wanli yehuo bian), 121
Shigang Pingyao. *See Outline of History with Critical Comments*
Shiji. *See Historical Records*
Shijing. *See Classic of Poetry*
Shu Jin Chuan Weng shoujuan hou. *See* "Written to Old Mr. Jin Chuan at the End of the Volume in Honor of His Birthday"

Shu Xiaoxiu shoujuan hou. *See* "Written at the End of Xiaoxiu's [Yuan Zhongdao's] Hand Scroll"
Shuihu zhuan. *See Outlaws of the Marsh*
Shuo shi xu. *See* "Preface on Poetry"
Shuowen jiezi, 33
sign-signifier relationship, 5, 21, 30; in Chinese, 32–34, 39; clothing and, 74; in early modern world, 68; in European languages, 38–40
silver, 91, 92, 178n25
Sima Qian, 15, 53, 65–66: *Historical Records* (Shiji), 29, 64
Si shu ping. *See Commentary on The Four Books*
"A Sketch of Zhuowu: Written in Yunnan" (Zhuowu lunlue Dianzhong zuo) (Li), 158n22, 176n3, 178n35
Struve, Lynn, 11
Stubbes, Philip, 77
Student Huang (Huang Kehui), 100–102
sumptuary laws, 27, 70: in Europe, 76–77, 170n17; regulation of clothing; 71–72; violations of, 73, 171–172n32

Taizhou School. *See under* School of the Mind
Tang Shunzhi, 15: *The Left Scribe's Record* (Lidai shi zuobian), 64, 167n63
Tang Xianzu, 31; *The Peony Pavilion* (Mudan ting), 56
Tao Qian, 57; "Mr. Five Willows" (Wu liu xiansheng zhuan), 141–142
"Three essays for two monks of Huang'an" (Wei Huang'an er shangren san shou) (Li), 158n33
"Ti Kongzi xiang yu Zhifo Yuan." *See* An inscription for the image of Confucius in the Cloister of the Flourishing Buddha
titles, sale of, 6, 28
tongxin. *See* childlike mind
Tongzhou, 4, 81
Tory, Geofroy: *Champ Fleury*, 40–41
trade, 6, 39, 73, 88, 90; foreign currency and, 92; lifting of ban on, in China, 91
truth. *See* authenticity

Unofficial Gleanings of the Wanli Era (Wanli yehuo bian) (Shen), 121
Upon Arrival at the Lake (Chutanji) (Li), 146; preface to, 158n23, 176n85, 179n43, 190n22

value, 89. *See also* money
Velázquez, Diego Rodriguez: *Las Meninas*, 57, 58
Vermeer, Johannes, 9: *Woman Holding a Balance*, 93
Vigenère, Blaise de, 20, 42
Vimalakīrti Monastery (Macheng), 69, 102
Vinograd, Richard, 57, 166n38
virtue, 6; clothing as expression of, 75; counterfeiting of, 89, 103
vision. *See* eyes

Wang Benke, 15, 32, 150; posthumous preface to *Another Book to Burn*, 122–125, 147–148
Wang Chong, 74, 160–161n62
Wang Gen, 75
Wang Hongzhuan, 150
Wang Ji, 158n26
Wang Keshou, 79–82
Wang Shizhen, 23, 117
Wang Yangming, 21–22, 26, 75, 136
Wanli yehuo bian. *See Unofficial Gleanings of the Wanli Era*
Webb, John, 20: *Historical Essay*, 42–43
Wei Huang'an er shangren san shou. *See* "Three essays for two monks of Huang'an"
wen (pattern/literature), 74
Wenxin diaolong. *See Literary Mind and the Carving of Dragons*
Wilson, Bronwen, 77–78
"Written in Commemoration of Past Events" (Yin ji wang shi) (Li), 171n24
"Written at the End of Xiaoxiu's Hand Scroll" (Shu Xiaoxiu shoujuan hou) (Li), 163n3, 174n67
"Written to Old Mr. Jin Chuan at the End of the Volume in Honor of His Birthday" (Shu Jin Chuan Weng shoujuan hou) (Li), 179n36
Wu Congxian: preface to *Outline of History with Critical Commentary*, 144, 149
Wu si pian. *See* "On Five Types of Death"
Wu suo bu pei. *See* "Adorned with Every Mark of Dignity"

Xie Zhaozhe, 111
xin (trust), 102
Xingshi yinyuan zhuan. *See Marriage Destinies to Awaken the World*
Xixiang ji. *See Romance of the Western Chamber*
Xiyou ji. *See Journey to the West*
Xu Cangshu. *See Another Book to Keep (Hidden)*
Xu Fenshu. *See Another Book to Burn*.
Xu Wei, 22, 30–31, 35, 55, 179n42; "Preface on Poetry" (Shuo shi xu), 139–140
Xunzi, 36, 71

Yan Hui, 33, 46
Yang Xiong (Ziyun), 63–65, 167n60
Yang Yucheng, 131
Ye Zhou, 121
Yijing. *See Book of Changes*
Yinguo lu. *See Record of Causes and Effects*
Yu Xiangdou, 116, 185n48
Yu Yizheng: *Survey of Scenery and Mountains in the Capital* (Dijing jingwulue) (w/ Liu), 84
Yu yue. *See* "Rules Agreed Upon in Advance"
Yu yue xiao yin. *See under* "Rules Agreed Upon in Advance"
Yuan Hongdao, 31, 83, 116, 121, 195n85
Yuan Zhongdao (Xiaoxiu), 31, 32, 115–116, 150; "Biography of Li Wenling" (Li Wenling zhuan), 84, 131, 137, 160n58, 172n47, 175n75
Yuan Zongdao, 22

Za shuo. *See* "On Miscellaneous Matters"
Zan Liu Xie. *See* "Appraisal of Liu Xie"
Zen Buddhism. *See* Chan
Zeng Jiquan, 46, 85
Zhang Chao, 114
Zhang Dai, 3
Zhang Longxi, 9, 13
Zhang Nai: posthumous preface to *Another Book to Burn*, 122–125
Zhang Wenda, 3, 64–65, 145–147, 149
zhengming. *See* rectification of names
zhi yin. *See* friend/friendship
Zhong Xing, 116
Zhongyi Shuihuzhuan xu. *See* "Preface to *The Loyal and Righteous Outlaws of the Marsh*"
Zhou Sijing (Youshan), 83
Zhou Sijiu, 81
Zhuowu. *See* Li Zhi
Zhuowu lunlue Dianzhong zuo. *See* "A Sketch of Zhuowu: Written in Yunnan"
Zhu Xi, 25, 189n20, 190n21, 191n40
Ziyun, 63–64

www.ingramcontent.com/pod-product-compliance
Lightning Source LLC
Chambersburg PA
CBHW030618230426
43661CB00053B/2045